READING EZEKIEL

Smyth & Helwys Publishing, Inc.
6316 Peake Road
Macon, Georgia 31210-3960
1-800-747-3016
© 2013 by Marvin A. Sweeney
All rights reserved.
Printed in the United States of America.

The paper used in this publication meets the minimum
requirements of American National Standard for Information
Sciences—Permanence of Paper for Printed Library Materials.
ANSI Z39.48–1984   (alk. paper)

Library of Congress Cataloging-in-Publication Data

Sweeney, Marvin A. (Marvin Alan), 1953-
  Reading Ezekiel : a literary and theological commentary / by Marvin A. Sweeney.
     pages cm
  Includes bibliographical references (pages   ) and indexes.
  ISBN 978-1-57312-658-8 (pbk. : alk. paper)
  1. Bible. O.T. Ezekiel--Commentaries. I. Title.
  BS1545.53.S94 2013
  224'.407--dc23
                          2012043338

Disclaimer of Liability: With respect to statements of opinion or fact available in this work of nonfiction, Smyth & Helwys Publishing Inc. nor any of its employees, makes any warranty, express or implied, or assumes any legal liability or responsibility for the accuracy or completeness of any information disclosed, or represents that its use would not infringe privately-owned rights.

Reading Ezekiel

A Literary and Theological Commentary

Marvin A. Sweeney

Also by Marvin A. Sweeney

*Tanak: A Theological and Critical Introduction
to the Jewish Bible*

*Reading the Hebrew Bible after the Shoah:
Engaging Holocaust Theology*

1 and 2 Kings: A Commentary (Old Testament Library)

The Prophetic Literature (Interpreting Biblical Texts)

Zephaniah (Hermeneia)

The Twelve Prophets (Berit Olam)

Isaiah 1-39, with an Introduction to Prophetic Literature
(Forms of the Old Testament Literature)

Dedicated to the memory of
William H. Brownlee and Moshe Greenberg

Acknowledgments

It is always a great pleasure to acknowledge those who have played important roles in bringing a volume to publication.

I would first like to thank Professor Mark Biddle, editor of the Smyth & Helwys *Reading the Old Testament* series, for his invitation to contribute a volume of my choosing for the new series and for his careful work in editing the manuscript. It is a rare honor to receive such an invitation, and I was delighted to choose Ezekiel. Ezekiel has always held a special fascination for me, most notably because of its role as the foundational text of the Jewish mystical tradition and for the prophet's role as a halakhic innovator on par with Moses. Dr. Biddle's invitation provided me with an opportunity to explore this strange and intriguing book and to bring its understanding of holiness and its engagement with G-d to light.

My own engagement with Ezekiel began as a child in religious school at Temple B'nai Abraham in Decatur, Illinois, and continued as an undergraduate student at the University of Illinois, as a graduate student at the Claremont Graduate School, and as a professor at the University of Miami, Claremont School of Theology, Claremont Graduate University, Claremont Lincoln University, Hebrew Union College–Jewish Institute of Religion in Los Angeles, and the Academy for Jewish Religion, California. The views expressed in this volume began to take shape in a lecture that was presented in three different versions during the year 2000, "Ezekiel: Zadokite Priest and Visionary Prophet of the Exile." The first version of the lecture was presented in April 2000 as the William H. Brownlee Memorial Lecture at the Institute of Antiquity and Christianity in Claremont. It was subsequently published as Number 41 of the IAC Occasional Papers. I am indebted to Professor Dennis MacDonald for the invitation to present this lecture. The second version of the lecture was presented before the Korea Old Testament Society at the Korea Bible Society Library in Seoul. The Methodist Theological Seminary, Seoul, subsequently published it in English and

Korean. I am indebted to Professor Tai-Il Wang of the Methodist Theological Seminary and Professor Young-Jin Min of the Korean Bible Society for the invitation to present the lecture and for its publication. The third version of the lecture was presented before the Theological Perspectives on the Book of Ezekiel Seminar of the Society of Biblical Literature meeting in Nashville, Tennessee. This version of the lecture appeared in the *Society of Biblical Literature Seminar Papers* (Atlanta: SBL, 2000, 728–51). I am indebted to the leadership of the Ezekiel seminar at that time, including Stephen L. Cook, Katheryn Pfisterer Darr, Margaret S. Odell, Corrine L. Patton, John T. Strong, and Steven S. Tuell. Other members of the SBL Ezekiel program unit have also played important roles as dialogue partners in Ezekiel, including Dexter Callendar, Julie Galambush, John Kutsko, Andrew Mein, Paul Joyce, Dalit Rom-Shiloni, Baruch Schwarz, and William Tooman. The definitive version of this essay now appears in my collected essays, *Form and Intertextuality in Prophetic and Apocalyptic Literature* (FAT 45; Tübingen Germany: Mohr Siebeck, 2005, 125–43).

I was able to carry out the research and writing for this volume with the support of two major institutions, the Claremont School of Theology and Yonsei University. Dean Philip Clayton of the Claremont School of Theology made it possible for me to have some release time in the spring 2011 semester, which enabled me to complete some key portions of the manuscript. My appointment as Underwood Professor of Divinity at Yonsei University, Seoul, Korea, for the fall 2011 semester made it possible for me to complete the work. I am indebted to Dean Suk-Hwan Jueng, Associate Dean Hyun-Shik Jun, Associate Dean Soo-Young Kwon, Assistant Professor Kyoung-Shik Min, Assistant Professor Hohyun "Harold" Sohn, and Dr. Woo Chul Shin, of the Yonsei University College of Theology and United Graduate School of Theology, for their collegiality and support. I am also indebted to Professor Yoonjong Yoo of the Korea Bible Society Library for his support. Portions of the introduction focused on the theology of the book of Ezekiel were presented in a workshop at Doshisha University, Kyoto, Japan, on December 9, 2011. I am indebted to Professor Ada Taggar Cohen, Professor Akira Echigoya, and Mr. Tetsu Kitamura for their hospitality and support during my visit to Doshisha University.

Very special thanks go to Mr. Hakseo Kim, my teaching assistant at Yonsei, for his incomparable efforts on my behalf. Very special thanks also go to my current and former Claremont students in Korea, including Dr. Koog-Pyeong Hong, Dr. Hye Kyung Park, Mr. Seong-eun Jeong, Ms. Jung-Hyung Yi, Professor Seokgyu Jung, Dr. Bumsik Kim, Dr. Jinseong Woo, and Dr. Sok-Chung Chang for their selfless support. Thanks are also due to

Professor Taek-Joo Woo, Professor Kyung Sook Lee, and Professor Kyung TaekHa, for their support.

I am also indebted to my Claremont research assistant, Ms. Soo Jung Kim, for her sharp eye. I would also like to thank Ms. Leslie Andres, Smyth & Helwys Publishers, for her careful attention in preparing the proofs. Any errors that remain are my own responsibility.

My wife, Muna, and our daughter, Leah, are the foundations of my life that make everything possible.

I would like to dedicate this volume to two of my former teachers, the late Professor William H. Brownlee of Claremont Graduate School and the late Professor Moshe Greenberg of the Hebrew University of Jerusalem. Professor Brownlee was one of my doctoral committee members at Claremont and taught my first PhD seminar on Ezekiel in the program in the fall 1976 semester. I still remember finding him on the floor of Harper Hall one afternoon experimenting with a metal wheel within a wheel contraption made by his machinist brother. As my own brother is also a machinist, I had a particular appreciation for his efforts! Professor Greenberg was my senior mentor during my year as Yad Hanadiv/Barecha Foundation Fellow in Jewish Studies at Hebrew University in 1989–1990. Although I did not study Ezekiel with him, I learned much from him on Targumic Aramaic, Jewish Bible exegesis, and philological method. The commentaries on Ezekiel by both of these scholars have been influential in my own thinking on the book.

San Dimas, California
3 Av 5772
22 July 2012

Contents

Introduction 1
    Orientation to the Book of Ezekiel 1
    Modern Interpretation of Ezekiel......................................3
    Literary Form of the Book of Ezekiel................................4
    Theology in the Book of Ezekiel 9
    Ezekiel in Later Jewish, Christian, and Muslim Traditions................19

Ezekiel's Oracles concerning His Inaugural Vision (Ezek 1:1–7:27)....23
    The Initial Oracular Account of Ezekiel's Inaugural Vision
    (1:1–3:15) 24
    The Second Oracular Account of Ezekiel's Inaugural Vision:
    Commission as Watchman and Symbolic Acts (3:16–5:17)..............35
    The Third Oracular Account of Ezekiel's Inaugural Vision:
    Commission concerning the Mountains of Israel (6:1-14)................42
    The Fourth Oracular Account of Ezekiel's Commission concerning
    Judgment against Israel on the Day of YHWH (7:1-27) 46

Presentation of Ezekiel's Oracles following His Vision of Jerusalem's Destruction/YHWH's Departure from Jerusalem (Ezek 8:1–19:14)....51
    Autobiographical Vision Account: Sixth Year (592/591 BCE), Sixth
    Month, Fifth Day (8:1–11:25) 52
        The Initial Date and Setting of Ezekiel's Oracles concerning the
        Destruction of Jerusalem: Ezekiel's House, the Elders, and the
        Angelic Guide (8:1-2) 54
        New Setting: North Gate of Jerusalem: Ezekiel's Vision of the
        Offensive Image (8:3-6) 55
        New Setting: North Gate of the Inner Court: Hole in the Wall
        (8:7-13) 56

New Setting: North Gate of the Temple: Women Wailing for
Tammuz (8:14-15) 57
New Setting: Entrance to the Temple Main Hall: Ezekiel's
Vision of the Destruction of Jerusalem and the Departure of
YHWH (8:16–10:22) 58
    Transport to the Temple Entrance (8:16aα$^{1-7}$) 58
    Vision Report of the Abomination in the Temple and its
    Consequences (8:16aα^{8}–10:22) 58
        First Episode: Twenty-Five Men Face East to
        Worship the Sun (8:16aα^{8}-b)...58
        Instruction Report: Rhetorical Question Employed
        to Assert a Provocation against YHWH (8:17-18) 59
        Second Episode: The Destruction of Jerusalem and the
        Departure of YHWH's Divine Presence (9:1–10:22) 59
            Ezekiel's Report of YHWH's Summons to
            the Officials Who Will Kill the People of
            Jerusalem (9:1) 60
            Ezekiel's Portrayal of the Killing of Jerusalem's
            Inhabitants (9:2-11) 60
            Ezekiel's Description of the Preparations to
            Destroy the City with Fire (10:1-8) 62
            Ezekiel's Description of YHWH's Departure
            from the City of Jerusalem (10:9-22) 64
New Setting: East Gate of the Temple Disputation Oracle
Sequence concerning the Purging of Jerusalem (11:1-23) 65
    Account of YHWH's First Oracle: The Premise to
    Be Refuted (11:1-4) 66
    Account of YHWH's Second Oracle: Affirmation of
    Punishment (11:5-12) 67
    Account of YHWH's Third Oracle: YHWH's Promise
    of Restoration following Punishment and Exile
    (11:13-21) 68
    Concluding Segment: YHWH's Departure from Jerusalem
    (11:22-23) 69
New Setting: Ezekiel's Return to Babylonian Exile
(11:24-25) 69
Oracular Account: Symbolic Action concerning the Exile as
Reversal of the Exodus (12:1-7)...69
Oracular Account: Ezekiel's Explanation of the
Symbolic Action (12:8-16) 71

Contents   xiii

    Oracular Account: Symbolic Action concerning
    Eating and Drinking (Exodus Reversal) (12:17-20) 72
    Oracular Account: Disputation concerning the Efficacy
    of the Vision (12:21-25) 72
    Oracular Account: Concerning the Imminent Fulfillment
    of YHWH's Oracles (12:26-28)...73
    Oracular Account: Concerning False Prophets (13:1-23).................73
    Oracular Account: Threats against False Prophets and
    Diviners (14:1-11)...78
    Oracular Account: Concerning Individual Righteousness
    and Guilt (14:12-23)...80
    Oracular Account: The Allegory of Jerusalem as a
    Useless Vine (15:1-8)...82
    Oracular Account: The Allegory of Jerusalem as YHWH's
    Adulterous Wife (16:1-63) 83
    Oracular Account: The Allegory of the Eagles, the Vine,
    and the Cedar (17:1-24) 88
    Oracular Account: Concerning the Responsibility of the
    Individual and the Demise of the Princes of Israel (18:1–19:14) 92

Ezekiel's Oracles concerning the Punishment of All Israel
(Ezek 20:1–23:49) 101
    Introduction (20:1) 102
    Oracular Account: Concerning Ezekiel's Assessment of Israel's
    Past and Future (20:2-44) 102
    Oracular Account: Condemnation of the Negev (21:1-5) 106
    Oracular Account: The First Oracle concerning YHWH's
    Sword (21:6-12) 108
    Oracular Account: YHWH's Second Oracle concerning the
    Sword (21:13-22) 109
    Oracular Account: The Third Oracle concerning YHWH's
    Sword (21:23-37) 110
    Oracular Account: Concerning Bloodshed in Jerusalem
    (22:1-16)...111
    Oracular Account: Concerning the Smelting of Jerusalem
    (22:17-22)...114
    Oracular Account: Condemnation of the Leadership and
    People of Jerusalem (22:23-31) 114
    Oracular Account: Concerning Oholah and Oholibah: Allegorical
    Portrayal of Judgment against Samaria and Jerusalem (23:1-49) 116

Ezekiel's Oracles concerning the Destruction of Jerusalem and the Condemnation of Neighboring Nations (Ezek 24:1–25:17) 121
    Oracular Account: The Allegory of the Pot (24:1-14) 122
    Oracular Account: The Death of Ezekiel's Wife (24:15-27) 124
    Oracular Account: Condemnation of Judah's Immediate Neighbors, Ammon, Moab, Edom, and Philistia (25:1-17) 125

Ezekiel's Oracles concerning Tyre and Sidon (Ezek 26:1–28:26) 131
    The First Oracular Account: Concerning Tyre (26:1-21) 132
    The Second Oracular Account: Concerning Tyre (27:1-36)............135
    Oracular Account: Concerning the Prince of Tyre (28:1-10) 138
    Oracular Account: Dirge for the King of Tyre (28:11-19) 140
    Oracular Account: Concerning Sidon and Israel (28:20-26) 141

The First Oracular Account: Concerning Egypt (Ezek 29:1-16) 143

The Second Oracular Account: Concerning Egypt (Ezek 29:17–30:19) 147

The First Oracular Account: Concerning Pharaoh (Ezek 30:20-26) 151

The Second Oracular Account: Concerning Pharaoh (Ezek 31:1-18) 153

The Third Oracular Account: Concerning Pharaoh and Egypt (Ezek 32:1-16) 157

Final Oracles concerning the Nations and Ezekiel's Role as Watchman (Ezek 32:17–33:20)..161
    Oracular Account concerning the Impending Downfall of Egypt (32:17-32)...162
    Oracular Account concerning Ezekiel's Role as Israel's Watchman (33:1-20)...163

Oracles concerning the Impending Restoration of Israel (Ezek 33:21–39:29) 167
    Introduction: Ezekiel Resumes Speaking following the Downfall of Jerusalem (33:21-22) 168

Oracular Account concerning Ezekiel's Role as a Prophet of
YHWH (33:23-33) 169
Oracular Account concerning Israel's Leaders (34:1-31) 170
Oracular Account concerning the Contrasting Fates of
Edom and Israel (35:1–36:15)...174
Oracular Account concerning the Purification of the
Land of Israel (36:16–37:14) 179
Oracular Account concerning the Restoration of the
People of Israel (37:15-28)...183
The Purification of the Land of Israel from the Army of Gog
from Magog (38:1–39:29) 186

Ezekiel's Vision of the New Temple (Ezek 40:1–48:35) 195
   Introduction: Chronological Setting (40:1) 197
   The First Vision Account: Tour of the New Temple
   (40:2–42:20) 198
      Vision Account Introduction (40:2) 198
      First Stage: Outer Walls and Gates (40:3-16) 198
      Second Stage: Outer Courts and Gates (40:17-27) 199
      Third Stage: Inner Court and South Gate (40:28-31) 200
      Fourth Stage: Inner Court and East Gate (40:32-34) 200
      Fifth Stage: Inner Court and North Gate (40:35-47) 200
      Sixth Stage: The Ulam (Portico) (40:48-49) 201
      Seventh Stage: Heikhal and Holy of Holies (41:1-26) 201
      Eighth Stage: The Chambers of the Outer Court (42:1-14) 204
      Summation: Measurements of the Entire Temple Complex
      (42:15-20) 206
   The Second Vision Account: Halakhot pertaining to the Temple
   (43:1–48:35) 206
      First Stage: East Gate, Entry of Divine Presence (43:1-4) 207
      The Second Stage: The Inner Court (43:5-27) 208
      The Third Stage: East Gate, Outer Court (44:1-3) 211
      The Fourth Stage: North Gate before the Temple:
      Halakhot/Laws concerning the Priests and Levites
      (44:4–46:18)...211
         Introduction: Guidance to the North Gate and Presence of
         YHWH (44:4) 211
         Account of YHWH's Instruction Speech (44:5–46:18).......212
      The Fifth Stage: Northern Chambers of the Priests:
      The Kitchens (46:19-20) 220

The Sixth Stage: The Outer Court: Corner Structures and
Kitchens for the Preparation of the People's Sacred Meals
(46:21-24) 220
The Seventh Stage: Return to the East Gate: Water Flowing
Eastward (47:1)..221
The Eighth Stage: Outer Eastern Gate (47:2-6a)......................221
The Ninth Stage: Return the Wadi Bank: Portrayal of New
Creation (47:6b–48:35) 222
    Ezekiel's Account of His Guide's Portrayal of the New
    Creation at the Dead Sea (47:6b-12) 222
    Ezekiel's Account of YHWH's Speech concerning
    the New Creation of Israel around the Temple
    (47:13–48:35) 223

Works Cited 229

Abbreviations 237

Introduction

Orientation to the Book of Ezekiel

The book of Ezekiel is one of the most interesting and compelling books of the Hebrew Bible, and it is simultaneously one of the Bible's most difficult and perplexing books. The book presents the visions and oracles of Ezekiel ben (son of) Buzi, who was a Judean priest and prophet exiled to Babylonia in 597 BCE together with King Jehoiachin ben Jehoiakim of Judah as part of the first exile by King Nebuchadnezzar of Babylon (see 2 Kings 24:8-17; 2 Chr 36:9-10). This first exile took place some ten years prior to 587/586 BCE, when Nebuchadnezzar invaded Judah a second time to destroy Jerusalem and the Temple of Solomon and to exile a major portion of the surviving Jerusalemite/Judean population to Babylonia. Ezekiel was a priest of the line of Zadok who was trained to serve at the altar of the Jerusalem Temple during the last years of the Judean monarchy. Once he was taken into captivity, he was settled at a city called Tel Aviv, which in Hebrew means "hill of spring," or *til abubi* in Akkadian, which can mean "hill of flood" (Kobayashi, 344). When Ezekiel reached his thirtieth birthday, the age at which he would have begun service in the Jerusalem Temple had he not been exiled to a foreign land, he saw visions of G-d, which marked the beginning of his new career as a visionary prophet of YHWH (n.b., in Judaism, one does not pronounce the holy name of G-d, and so I render it with the capitalized consonants of the name YHWH, but not the vowels. Likewise, I do not spell out terms such as G-d and L-rd).

Ezekiel's visions include a vision of YHWH's throne chariot in Ezekiel 1, which appears to him while he stands on the banks of the Chebar Canal in Babylonia; a vision in Ezekiel 8–11 of YHWH's decision to destroy the city of Jerusalem and to kill or exile its population; a vision of the new temple in Ezekiel 40–48, which portends not only a new temple structure in Jerusalem, but a renewed and reconstituted Twelve Tribes of Israel and even creation at large. Ezekiel's visions are characterized by bizarre imagery and concepts, such as the four cherubim who bear YHWH's throne chariot through the heavens, each of whom has a body of burnished bronze, the feet of cattle, three sets of wings, and four faces, which represent four aspects of the divine character. His vision of the restoration of the dry bones in Ezekiel 37 plays a major role in defining expectations concerning resurrection in both Judaism and Christianity. His vision of the restored temple in Ezekiel 40–48 differs markedly from what is known of the First Temple, built by King Solomon ben David, and the Second Temple, built at the beginning of the Persian period. His actions are also frequently bizarre, e.g., he cuts off his hair, divides it into three portions, and chops, burns, and scatters it to illustrate the fate of the people of Judah in Ezekiel 5; he refuses to mourn for his dead wife to emulate YHWH's response to Jerusalem's demise in Ezekiel 24; and he serves as watchman to warn his people concerning the approach of danger, including danger due to their own alleged wrongdoing in Ezekiel 3 and Ezekiel 33.

Ezekiel's attempts to describe the presence of YHWH and his differences with Mosaic Torah made him a controversial figure in rabbinic Judaism. The Babylonian Talmud reports that Rabbi Hanina ben Hezekiah burned 300 barrels of oil working nights to reconcile the differences between Ezekiel and the Torah so that the book of Ezekiel might be included among the prophets of the Bible (*b. Shabbat* 13b; *b. Hagigah* 13a; *b. Menahot* 45a). Only fragments of Rabbi Hanina's decisions are preserved in the Talmud, but his efforts were successful. Ezekiel now stands as the third book of the Latter Prophets following Isaiah and Jeremiah and preceding the book of the Twelve in the Tanak (the name for the Jewish version of the Bible; it is an acronym for the Tanak's three major sections: Torah, "Instruction"; Nevi'im, "Prophets"; Ketuvim, "Writings"), although some authorities place it second following Jeremiah and preceding Isaiah and the book of the Twelve (*b. Bava Batra* 14b). Ezekiel is considered as a halakhic (*halaka* is the Hebrew term for Jewish law) authority on par with Moses, and his vision of the temple in Ezekiel 40–48 is considered to be a vision of the Third Temple that will appear in the eschatological future according to Jewish tradition (see the Rabbinic historical work, *Seder Olam Rabbah* 26:51-52; commentaries on Ezekiel 40–48 by Rashi [Rabbi Solomon ben Isaac, 1040–1105 CE] and Radaq [Rabbi David Kimhi, 1160–1235 CE]). Ezekiel is considered the major founding figure in the Jewish mystical and Kabbalistic tradition. His visions of YHWH provided the impetus for the *Heikhalot* (palaces) or *Merkavah* (chariot) texts of the Talmudic period that portrayed the rabbinic ascent to heaven to appear before the throne of G-d (see Gruenwald; Halperin 1980; Elior 2005; Schäfer 2009). The *Heikhalot/Merkavah* tradition later developed into the Kabbalistic tradition that attempted to posit the experience of divine presence within the finite world of human reality. In Christianity, Ezekiel is especially influential in the conceptualization of the image of Christ in the book of Revelation, which itself is based in the early *Heikalot/Merkavah* tradition. In both Judaism and Christianity, Ezekiel 37 is a crucial text in defining views concerning the future resurrection of the righteous.

Modern Interpretation of Ezekiel

Ezekiel has not always fared particularly well among modern interpreters. Although late nineteenth-century critical scholarship considered the book of Ezekiel to be a unity (e.g., Smend's 1880 commentary), later critical scholars tore the book to shreds in an effort to prove that Ezekiel the prophet had been co-opted by efforts to portray him as a priest. Gustav Hölscher's 1924 study of Ezekiel argued that only about one-eighth of the book could be attributed to Ezekiel. Charles Cutler Torrey argued that the entire book was a third-century BCE Hellenistic forgery designed to portray Ezekiel as a prophet from the time of King Manasseh ben Hezekiah of Judah. William H. Brownlee argued that Ezekiel never went into exile in Babylonia, but remained in the land of Israel for his entire life. Because of his bizarre imagery and theological world view, many have argued that Ezekiel was mentally unbalanced or suffered from psychological problems (e.g., Halperin 1993). Others have argued that he was a misogynist who refused even to mourn the death of his wife (e.g., Galambush).

As scholarship has progressed over the course of the twentieth and twenty-first centuries, scholars have advanced their understandings of this very unusual prophetic book. Walther Eichrodt (1970) concentrated on separating presumed later additions to Ezekiel from the work of the original prophet. Georg Fohrer (1955) attempted to trace the traditions, such as the exodus, upon which Ezekiel relied as it grew over the course of time. Walther Zimmerli's detailed 1979–1983 commentary on Ezekiel made extensive use of tradition-historical, form-critical, and redaction-critical methodology (study of the editorial and compositional formation of a literary work) to posit that much of the material in Ezekiel went back to the prophet himself, and attempted to trace the development of Ezekiel's thought among his disciples following his death. John Wevers (1971) made great use of text-critical evidence in his efforts to interpret the book. Moshe Greenberg (1983, 1997) employed a holistic reading methodology in his regrettably unfinished commentary to posit that the book of Ezekiel must be read as a coherent whole. Ronald Hals (1989) presented a form-critical analysis of the book of Ezekiel in its entirety, although he largely followed Zimmerli in tradition-historical and redaction-critical matters. Leslie Allen (1990, 1994) combined form- and literary-critical analysis in an attempt to treat the book of Ezekiel as a whole. Karl-Friedrich Pohlmann (1996–2001) employed redaction-criticism in an attempt to argue that Ezekiel was edited from the late-monarchic period through the Second Temple period. Katheryn Pfisterer Darr (2001) employed a very sophisticated literary-reading strategy together with ancient Near Eastern evidence to highlight the literary and theological features of Ezekiel against its background in the ancient Near Eastern world. Daniel Block (1998) and Margaret D. Odell (2005) focused especially on ancient Near Eastern background. Steven Tuell (2009) made great use of redaction-criticism in attempting to posit later Zadokite (the Zadokite line of priests served in the Jerusalem Temple) influence in the formation of the book. Paul Joyce (2007) employed a largely holistic and theological reading of the text. Nancy Bowen (2010) read Ezekiel as a figure traumatized by the destruction and exile of his nation. The present commentary reads the book holistically as a synchronic or literary whole with only light redactional work. It especially emphasizes Ezekiel's identity as a Zadokite priest and his efforts to carry out his priestly role in the very changed circumstances of Babylonian exile.

Literary Form of the Book of Ezekiel

The book of Ezekiel presents the visions and oracles of Ezekiel ben Buzi, the Zadokite priest and prophet of the Babylonian exile. The book begins with Ezekiel's inaugural vision in Ezekiel 1, in which he sees a vision of YHWH's throne chariot while he is in exile in Babylonia, and it culminates in Ezekiel 40–48 with Ezekiel's vision of the new temple that will be built in Jerusalem to replace the destroyed Temple of Solomon. Although interpreters have attempted to define the genre of prophetic book by pointing to common patterns among the prophetic books, each book is unique. Fundamentally, the books of Isaiah, Jeremiah, Ezekiel, and the book of the Twelve Prophets each present the oracles and visions of their respective prophets and narratives about them. Each book likewise attempts to present an interpretation of Israel's or Judah's experience in the world. The book of Ezekiel attempts to interpret the destruction of the city of Jerusalem and the Jerusalem Temple, the Babylonian exile, and the future restoration of Israel, Jerusalem, and the temple as an act of YHWH. It asserts that YHWH's intention is to purge Jerusalem, the temple, Israel, and creation at large as a basis for restoring a new creation with Jerusalem, the temple, and Israel at its center.

The book of Ezekiel appears to have been written largely by Ezekiel himself, and it was completed at some point after 570 BCE, the twenty-seventh year of King Jehoiachin's exile, the last date given in the book (see Ezek 29:17). Whereas books such as Isaiah, Jeremiah, and many of the Twelve Prophets were heavily edited, Ezekiel shows evidence only of light editing. It is written primarily in first-person narrative form. A third person voice appears in Ezekiel 1:2-3, apparently to interpret the enigmatic statement concerning Ezekiel's inaugural vision in Ezekiel 1:1. The date formula in Ezekiel 29:17 also appears to have been edited, perhaps by Ezekiel himself, to account for the lengthy amount of time it took for King Nebuchadnezzar of Babylon to conclude the siege of Tyre. Many commentators argue that Ezekiel 38–39 and 40–48 are later, possibly apocalyptic, additions to the book. Ezekiel 38–39 matches the formal characteristics of the book and it fits well into Ezekiel's scheme to represent the purification of the land of Israel prior to the building of the new temple. Although Ezekiel's temple vision in Ezekiel 40–48 diverges from the formal characteristics of the rest of the book, its use of guidance formulas (e.g., and he brought me/led me) in place of prophetic word formulas (and the word of YHWH came to me) is appropriate to Ezekiel's tour of the new temple. Furthermore, the temple vision provides an appropriate and necessary culmination to the book that would otherwise make little sense without its climactic vision (cf. Levenson 1976, 7–19). When its bizarre imagery and priestly world view are properly understood, the book of Ezekiel emerges as a coherent literary and conceptual whole (Sweeney 2005d, 125–43; 2005f, 127–64).

Problems in the interpretation of the book of Ezekiel result largely from a failure to understand its priestly imagery and language. Such a conclusion applies to the textual versions as well. Many scholars claim that the Greek Septuagint version of the book (the Septuagint is the name given to the ancient Greek translation of the Hebrew Bible employed in early Christianity) represents an earlier version of Ezekiel. But the relative coherence and clarity of the Greek version of Ezekiel represents the efforts of its translators to interpret a difficult proto-Masoretic Hebrew text (the Masoretic text is the Hebrew text employed in the Jewish version of the Bible) for an educated Greek reading public that was accustomed to a coherent and aesthetically pleasing literary style. Unfortunately, no examples of Ezekiel appear among the Dead Sea Scrolls (ancient scrolls of the Bible and other works dating from the second century BCE through the first century CE that were discovered by the Dead Sea in Israel) apart from small fragments that do little to advance our understanding of the development of the Hebrew text.

Most modern interpreters hold that the book of Ezekiel is structured according to an alleged prophetic tri-partite pattern in the organization of prophetic books that includes oracles of judgment against Israel in Ezekiel 1–24, oracles concerning the nations in Ezekiel 25–32, and oracles of restoration for Israel and the nations of the world in Ezekiel 33–48 (e.g., Renz, 57–130). Such a pattern actually derives from the concerns of systematic Christian theology that posits that Israel and the nations must suffer judgment prior to eschatological salvation.

A closer reading of the prophetic books indicates that such a pattern does not fully explain the organization of the examples brought forward. Isaiah 1–39, which places the oracles concerning the nations in Isaiah 13–23, does not constitute a prophetic book, but is a component of the entire book of Isaiah. Indeed, the first part of Isaiah in Isaiah 1–12 anticipates restoration for Israel and the nations. The Septuagint form of Jeremiah, which places the oracles concerning the nations in its middle, constitutes only one form of the book, and the Masoretic Hebrew version of Jeremiah places the oracles concerning the nations near the end of the book. Even so, both LXX (LXX is the symbol used for the Septuagint) and MT (Masoretic Text) Jeremiah present limited material on the restoration of Israel or Judah. Although the Masoretic form of the book of the Twelve Prophets includes books concerned with foreign nations near its middle (such as Obadiah, Jonah, and Nahum), books concerned with the punishment of Israel (such as Hosea, Amos, Micah, and Habakkuk) also anticipate Israel's restoration, and books that anticipate Israel's restoration (such as Zephaniah, Haggai, and Zechariah) also point to punishment. Indeed, the two forms of the book of the Twelve in the LXX and MT are organized according to very different sets of principles, viz., the LXX version of the Twelve Prophets employs Israel's experience as a model for that of Judah, and the MT of the Twelve Prophets demonstrates its concern for the city of Jerusalem throughout (Sweeney 2000, xv–xxxix). In the case of Ezekiel, concern with restoration appears together with judgment against Israel in Ezekiel 1–24, and concern with judgment for Israel appears together with restoration in Ezekiel 33–48.

The book of Ezekiel is organized according to its introductory chronological formulas, which begin with the first example in Ezekiel 1:1-3 and continue throughout the book (Sweeney 2005d, 125–43; 2010, 555–74; cf. Mayfield 2010). Ezekiel 1:1-3 dates Ezekiel's inaugural vision to the fifth day of the fourth month of the thirtieth year. The significance of the thirtieth year is left unexplained, although v. 2 indicates that it is to be identified with the fifth year of the exile of King Jehoiachin of Judah, which would be ca. 592 BCE. Subsequent chronological introductions appear in Ezekiel 8:1,

20:1, 24:1, 26:1, 29:1, 29:17, 30:20, 31:1, 32:1, 32:17, 33:21, and 40:1. The sequence of dates given in these formulas indicates a twenty-year period for the presentation of Ezekiel's oracles from the fifth year of Jehoiachin's exile in 592 BCE according to Ezekiel 1:1-3 through the twenty-fifth year of his exile in 572 BCE according to Ezekiel 40:1. An exception to this sequence appears in Ezekiel 29:17, which refers to Nebuchadnezzar's siege of Tyre in the twenty-seventh year, i.e., in 570 BCE. Interpreters have pointed out, however, that Nebuchadnezzar's siege of Tyre lasted for an unanticipated lengthy period, but it actually began shortly after the fall of Jerusalem in 587/586 BCE, which would correspond to the tenth or the eleventh year of Jehoiachin's exile in keeping with the preceding formula in Ezekiel 29:1 and the following formula in Ezekiel 30:20. Interpreters posit that Ezekiel himself may have changed the date following the successful conclusion of Nebuchadnezzar's siege by 570 BCE.

The twenty-year chronology points to the significance of the reference to the thirtieth year in Ezekiel 1:1-3. Numbers 4:3, 23, and 30 specify that priests who are descended from Kohath, the ancestor of the high priest Aaron, are to serve in the Tent of Meeting, i.e., the holy of holies of the sanctuary, from the age of thirty until the age of fifty. Numbers 8:25 specifies that all other Levites who serve in support of the Tent of Meeting serve from the age of twenty-five until the age of fifty. Insofar as Ezekiel is a Zadokite priest, he was born and trained to serve in the temple itself, whereas the Levites would only serve in support roles and would not enter the most holy precincts of the temple. As a Zadokite priest, Ezekiel would be active from the age of thirty until retirement at the age of fifty, i.e., the span of years from his initial vision in the thirtieth year (his thirtieth birthday in the fifth year of King Jehoiachin's exile) until his fiftieth year, which would correspond to the twenty-fifth year of King Jehoiachin's exile. The chronological timespan of the book of Ezekiel from chapter 1 through chapters 40–48 corresponds to the years of active service that Ezekiel would expect as a Zadokite priest at the temple.

Other features of Ezekiel's experience support this contention. Ezekiel was reared for service in the Jerusalem Temple, but once he was exiled in 597 BCE at the age of twenty-five, he would never be able to do so. As a Zadokite priest, he would have been ordained for service in the temple in a special seven-day ritual that corresponded to the dedication of the temple altar. Exodus 29, Leviticus 8, and Numbers 8 describe the ceremony. The prospective priests are ordained over a course of seven days in which the appropriate offerings are made for them at the temple altar as they go through the transition from their former unconsecrated status to their new status as holy priests of the temple. At the conclusion of the seven-day period, the priests are then considered holy and are able to present offerings at the temple. We do not know all of the details of the consecration, but Samuel's consecration as a priest as presented in 1 Samuel 3 entails a visionary experience of YHWH in which the young Samuel heard YHWH calling him to divine service. Ezekiel's visionary experience on the banks of the Chebar Canal would qualify as such a visionary experience calling him to divine service, and its duration of seven days, in which he is silent, would correspond to the seven-day ordination period described in Exodus 29, Leviticus 8, and Numbers 8. Ezekiel could not serve as a holy priest of YHWH in a foreign land outside the Jerusalem Temple. Instead, he experiences a different sort of seven-day revelatory experience analogous to that of priestly ordination that enables him to serve as a visionary prophet of YHWH in Babylonia for the same thirty-year period that he would have served as a temple priest.

The sequence of chronological statements in Ezekiel identifies and introduces the units that constitute the formal literary structure of the book of Ezekiel from Ezekiel's thirtieth until his fiftieth year. Ironically, they present a sequence of events over his professional lifetime that would enable him to oversee the purging of the profaned Jerusalem Temple in Ezekiel 8–11 through the projected restoration of a new and purified holy temple that would take its place in Ezekiel 40–48. Instances of the prophetic word formula *wayehi debar yhwh 'el PN* [Proper Name] *l'emor*, "and the word of YHWH came to PN [Proper Name] saying . . . ," define the subunits within each unit defined by a chronological formula. By identifying the above-noted chronological statements in Ezekiel 1:1, 8:1, 20:1, 24:1, 26:1, 29:1, 29:17, 30:20, 31:1, 32:1, 32:17, 33:21, and 40:1 and their subunits introduced by the prophetic word formula as the structural markers of the book, the following thirteen-part formal structure for the book of Ezekiel results:

Ezekiel's visions concerning the purge of Jerusalem
    I. Ezekiel's oracles concerning his inaugural vision (Ezek 1–7)
    II. Ezekiel's oracles concerning his vision of YHWH's departure from the Jerusalem Temple and its significance (Ezek 8–19)
    III. Ezekiel's oracles concerning the punishment of all Israel (Ezek 20–23)
    IV. Symbolic actions concerning the destruction of Jerusalem and the punishment of neighboring nations (Ezek 24–25)
    V. Oracles concerning Tyre and its rulers (Ezek 26–28)
    VI. The first oracle concerning Egypt (Ezek 29:1–16)
    VII. The second block of oracles concerning Egypt (Ezek 29:17–30:19)

VIII. The first oracle concerning Pharaoh (Ezek 30:20-26)
IX. The second oracle concerning Pharaoh (Ezek 31)
X. The third oracle concerning Pharaoh and Egypt (Ezek 32:1-16)
XI. Final oracles concerning the nations and Ezekiel's role as watchman (Ezek 32:17–33:20)
XII. Oracles concerning the restoration of Israel (Ezek 33:21–39:29)
XIII. The vision of the restored temple (Ezek 40–48)

Theology in the Book of Ezekiel

The interest in presenting the Zadokite priest Ezekiel as a visionary prophet who oversees the purging of Jerusalem points to some important theological dimensions of the book of Ezekiel.

In ancient Judean thought, the Jerusalem Temple was the holy center of creation (Levenson 1984). Proper maintenance of the temple's sanctity aided in securing the welfare of Israel or Judah in particular and the world of creation at large. YHWH is the creator and the temple serves as a symbol for the sanctity and stability of creation. The morning service of the temple symbolizes creation itself. It takes place at the break of dawn when the sun shines over the Trans-Jordanian mountain ranges and illumines the interior of the temple, which faces east, to reveal the various features of its construction to emulate the role of light as the first element in the order of creation as portrayed in Genesis 1. The Genesis narrative makes it clear that YHWH will act against creation if the sanctity of creation is not maintained. YHWH unleashes a flood to destroy creation, because the shedding of blood has corrupted the sanctity of creation, and makes a covenant with humanity in the aftermath of the flood that specifies the means by which blood, considered holy because it is the source of life, may be shed (Gen 6–9). Consequently, the temple serves as a means to give expression to the sanctity of creation. Blood is shed there in the context of liturgical worship of YHWH when animal offerings are presented to honor YHWH and to provide meat for human beings to eat. The holy context in which such offerings are made is meant to limit human violence, i.e., by limiting the types of animals that may be offered and by circumscribing the circumstances in which such offerings are made. Special care is given to the treatment of blood, which conveys the life of the animal and is thereby considered holy. Bloodshed must be limited and blood must be returned to the ground, and the temple ritual is designed to ensure that blood—and therefore the holiness of life—is properly treated. The improper shedding of blood defiles the temple—and creation itself—and requires that the temple and creation be purged or resanctified in the aftermath of such defilement.

Other elements are also involved. The proper function of the temple liturgy is to symbolize and establish the holiness of the temple and to sanctify the relationship between Israel and YHWH—and thus of the world at large. Time is sacred in Judaism and the observance of sacred time, the Shabbat or Sabbath on every seventh day (Saturday) and the holidays, i.e., Rosh ha-Shanah (the New Year), Yom Kippur (the Day of Atonement), Sukkot (Booths or Tabernacles), Pesach (Passover), Shavuot (Weeks or Pentecost), and other observances, are key to acknowledging and preserving the sacred order of creation. But the sanctity of the temple and the creation that it represents is not only expressed in ritual terms; it is expressed in moral terms as well. Ancient Judean religion and modern Judaism require the observance of YHWH's moral laws as well as YHWH's ritual laws that appear throughout the Torah or Pentateuch. Leviticus 19 is exemplary in this regard because of the manner in which it combines ritual and moral requirements for human beings. Indeed, the entrance liturgies in Psalms 15 and 24 make the moral imperative clear by stating that those who would enter the temple precincts must be persons who have observed YHWH's commands—ritual and moral. In the view of the Zadokite priesthood—and Ezekiel—failure to observe YHWH's moral commands defiles the temple and creation just as much as the failure to observe the ritual commands. When the temple is defiled in ancient Judean thought, it must be purged or purified to restore its sanctity and the sanctity of creation. Examples of temple reform/purging by kings Asa (1 Kings 15:9-14; 2 Chr 14:1-6), Hezekiah (2 Kings 18:3-7; 2 Chr 29–31), Josiah (2 Kings 22:3–23:25; 2 Chr 34–35), and Judah the Maccabee (1 Macc 4:36-59) provide examples of such purges to reconstitute the sanctity of the temple.

YHWH addresses Ezekiel as Ben Adam, "son of Adam" throughout the book. As a Zadokite priest with access to the holy of holies of the Jerusalem Temple, Ezekiel represents humanity before YHWH. Only Zadokite priests had access to the temple structure, and the high priest would only enter the holy of holies where the Ark of the Covenant was kept on Yom Kippur, the Day of Atonement, to atone before YHWH on behalf of the nation Israel and the world of creation at large (Lev 16). The Jerusalem Temple was built to symbolize the Garden of Eden. Its interior walls were paneled with wood, which were carved and inlaid with figures of cherubs, animals, fruits, trees, etc., to symbolize the garden (Levenson 1984, 1985). Indeed, the cherub embroidered on the curtain that covered the entry into the holy of holies was meant to represent the cherub who guarded the Garden of Eden and its Tree of Life once Adam and Eve had been expelled (Gen 3:24). The high priest's entry into the holy of holies on Yom Kippur, where he would pronounce the name of YHWH as part of the atonement ceremony, symbolized humanity, i.e., the sons of Adam, attempting to reenter the Garden of Eden (Hayward, 88–93, 111–18). Modern readers will never know if Ezekiel would have become the high priest had he remained in Jerusalem, but he would likely have been a possibility. As a Zadokite priest qualified to appear before YHWH as the holy representative of Israel and humankind at large, he is entitled to be addressed as Ben Adam.

Most importantly, the book of Ezekiel presents the Babylonian destruction of Jerusalem and the temple as a process of purging in which YHWH determines that the Jerusalem Temple has become impure, thereby requiring its consecration. Such consecration of the temple was a common practice in the ancient Judean world as the coordination of the consecration of the priests with the consecration of the altar noted above in Exodus 29, Leviticus 8, and Numbers 8 demonstrates. But such an effort in the book of Ezekiel points to an effort to interpret the Babylonian destruction of Jerusalem in such a manner as to protect and assert the power, presence, holiness, and righteousness of YHWH as G-d of Israel/Judah. YHWH was not overwhelmed by Babylonian power or by Marduk, the god of Babylon. Rather, Ezekiel portrays YHWH as the holy sovereign of creation who deliberately purges the temple as part of an effort to purge and renew creation itself. The Jerusalem Temple served as the holy center of both Israel/Judah and all creation in ancient Judean thought (Levenson 1984), and the purge of the temple entails the purge of creation as well. Consequently, the restored Jerusalem Temple depicted in Ezekiel 40–48 portrays a restored twelve tribes of Israel and a Dead Sea that now serves as a source of fertility and life in the newly created world portrayed in these chapters (Levenson 1976, 7–53). The book of Ezekiel defends YHWH. Ezekiel asserts that YHWH did not abandon Jerusalem and Judah during the Babylonian destruction of the city. Rather, YHWH was the One who called for such destruction as part of an effort to purge the allegedly profaned temple and to renew creation by restoring the holy temple at its center (see Sweeney 2008, 128–46).

A further dimension of Ezekiel's interest in the purge and restoration of the Jerusalem Temple is Ezekiel's age and the context in which he was reared. If Ezekiel was thirty years old at the time of his inaugural vision of YHWH in 592 BCE, then he was born in 622 BCE. This date marked the eighteenth year of the reign of King Josiah ben Amon of Judah (2 Kings 22:3; 2 Chr 34:8), the year that Josiah's temple reforms and purging began. Ezekiel would have been born at the outset of Josiah's reform program. Josiah's reform called for both a restoration of the Jerusalem Temple and a restoration of a unified Israel under the rule of the Davidic monarch (Sweeney

2001, 3–20). As a prospective priest in the Jerusalem Temple, Ezekiel would have been reared and educated in the context of Josiah's program of religious reform and national restoration, which envisioned a unified Israel that looked to a restored Jerusalem Temple as its holy center.

Ezekiel would have been approximately thirteen years old when King Josiah was killed and his reform program brought to a halt, but this does not seem to have ended Ezekiel's interest in seeing to the realization of the goals that Josiah's reform had set out. We cannot know how Ezekiel's views developed during the years of Jehoiakim's reign (609–598 BCE). The death of Josiah and the reign of Jehoiakim must have prompted Ezekiel to rethink some aspects of the reform, but Ezekiel's mature vision of a restored twelve tribes of Israel and a restored temple in Ezekiel 40–48 appears to have developed from the goals and ideals of Josiah's reform. Just as Josiah purged the temple during his eighteenth year as a basis for his attempts to reform Judah and to regain control over the former northern kingdom of Israel, so Ezekiel envisions in Ezekiel 37:15-28 a reunification of Joseph or the house of Israel and the house of Judah under the rule of the Davidic king (Sweeney 2006, 239–53). Ezekiel rarely uses the Hebrew term *melek*, "king," for the Davidic monarch. Instead, he generally prefers the term *nasi'*, "prince," a term generally used for leaders in Israel. Ezekiel's use of such a term for the Davidic monarch would be appropriate during the period in which Judah had become a vassal to Babylonia, beginning with Babylon's subjugation of Judah in 605 BCE during the reign of Jehoiakim and continuing through the reign of Zedekiah, the uncle of the exiled king Jehoiachin, and throughout the Babylonian exile.

During the course of Ezekiel's lifetime, his views concerning the meaning, significance, and scope of Josiah's reform changed. With the death of Josiah in 609 BCE, the completion of the king's reform program must have come into question. With the exile of Ezekiel in 597 BCE, his own role in that reform would certainly have come to an end. Further, with the destruction of Jerusalem in 587/586 BCE, any realistic hope for completing the reform was dead. But Ezekiel's visions seem to have incorporated the recognition that the scope and parameters of Josiah's original reform program had to change. When Ezekiel reached the age of thirty, the year in which he would have been ordained for service in the Jerusalem Temple, he appears to have recognized that he could no longer serve in such a role and that another task in life was necessary, i.e., that of a visionary prophet. In this new role, Ezekiel could continue with his sacred vocation but in a very different form. He was no longer able to serve at the temple altar, but he adapted another role, that of the watchman (Heb., *tsofeh*), based on the role of the priestly gatekeepers who guarded the temple gates and helped to ensure the sanctity of the temple. First Chronicles 26 discusses the temple gatekeepers. Their task was to guard the gates of the temple complex to ensure that only those who were pure would enter. We can never know how exactly the temple gatekeepers carried out their tasks. It is difficult to imagine that they interrogated each person who sought to enter the temple complex to determine if they met the ritual and moral standards required of those who could enter the temple. But two entrance liturgies preserved in Psalms 15 and 24 suggest that their roles were largely symbolic. Both psalms define characteristics of those who would enter. Psalm 15 defines such a person as one who is blameless and does what is right, who speaks the truth in the heart, who does no harm to another or carries reproach for something done to another, who holds those who are abhorrent in contempt and honors those who revere YHWH, who keeps oaths, never lends money at interest, and never accepts a bribe. Psalm 24 has a shorter list of requirements that appear to represent general principles, viz., one who has clean hands and a pure heart, who has not taken a false oath or sworn deceitfully. By adopting the role of watchman for Israel (see Ezek 3; 33), Ezekiel takes on the role of the temple gatekeeper for the people of Israel as a whole to warn them of impending danger. Although some might assume that his role is to warn the people of impending exile, the exile had already begun; rather, Ezekiel's task was to warn them of wrongdoing and defilement, precisely the role that an Israelite or Judean priest was supposed to fill (see Lev 10:10-11). If he fails to warn the people, he is responsible. If he does in fact warn the people, they are responsible.

Ezekiel's understanding of wrongdoing and defilement appears throughout the discussion of guilt and innocence in Ezekiel 18. The purpose of this exercise is to challenge a popular proverb that posits that children suffer punishment for the sins of their elders. Ezekiel instead argues that each person suffers punishment or earns mercy based upon his or her own actions. He posits a number of cases, each one involving a person from a different generation, in which the guilt or innocence of the person must be forgiven. In the first instance, he describes a man who is righteous, i.e., he does not eat (impure meat slaughtered) on the mountains, worship idols, commit adultery, sleep with a menstruating woman, wrong anyone, keep a debtor's pledge, rob anyone, withhold bread and clothing from the needy, take interest in financial transactions, etc. Ezekiel cites a combination of ritual and moral actions, each of which is addressed in the Holiness Code of Leviticus 17–26 and elsewhere in the legal materials of the Pentateuch. A man who avoids such actions is considered righteous and is not subject to death. But if he has a son who does such things, the son will suffer punishment. As Ezekiel works through his examples, it becomes clear that only the person who engages in wrongdoing will suffer punishment. The righteousness of an ancestor will not save a wicked person from punishment, and the guilt of an ancestor will not result in punishment for a righteous person. Essentially, Ezekiel challenges the principles of the Deuteronomistic History (DtrH) that argue that the people of Israel suffer for the sins of their ancestors; i.e., that northern Israel was destroyed because its kings followed the example of the first northern Israelite king, Jeroboam ben Nebat, in worshipping the golden calf (see 2 Kings 17). Judah and Jerusalem were destroyed because of the sins of King Manasseh (2 Kings 21). Ezekiel's position is consistent with that of the Chronicler's History (ChrH), which rejects the view of the DtrH and holds that Jerusalem and the temple were destroyed because the people of the present generation had defiled the Jerusalem Temple (2 Chr 36:14). The provenance of the DtrH is uncertain, but it appears to be a Levitical history. The ChrH is a priestly or Zadokite history, and Ezekiel shares its perspective.

In Ezekiel's view, Jerusalem and the temple were destroyed because they had been defiled. Nevertheless, Ezekiel's view of human wrongdoing takes a long view. In the account of his symbolic actions in Ezekiel 5, Ezekiel constructs a model of the besieged city of Jerusalem and then lies before it on his right side for 390 days to account for the years of Israel's sins and for forty days on his left side to account for the years of Judah's sins. The years roughly correspond to the last forty years of Judean history from the time that Josiah turned to YHWH in the eighth year of his reign in ca. 632 BCE (2 Chr 34:3) until some point beyond Ezekiel's act. The 390 years of Israel's sins appear to account for the years from Jeroboam's reign beginning ca. 922 BCE until Josiah turned to YHWH. Ezekiel likewise accuses Israel and its ancestors in Ezekiel 20 (cf. Ezek 16) of having failed to observe YHWH's will for centuries. Nevertheless, these sins do not result in the destruction of the temple. Rather, the corruption of the temple is the cause, and in his vision of the corrupted temple in Ezekiel 8–11, Ezekiel identifies the "image of jealousy" (Heb., *semel haqqin'ah*) situated by the north gate of the altar as the fundamental cause of the temple's destruction (Sweeney 2005c, 144–55). This image appears to be a stele that would have been erected in the temple courtyard by King Nebuchadnezzar of Babylon to celebrate his subjugation of Jerusalem in 598 BCE at the time of Jehoiakim's failed revolt (2 Kings 24:1-4; 2 Chr 36:5-8). Babylonian steles typically included a text that announced the triumph of the king as well as pictorial depictions of the Babylonian gods who made the king's victory possible. Such a stele erected in the temple court would have constituted idolatry by depicting foreign gods in a holy place where foreigners were not to set foot. With the temple corrupted, other acts become idolatrous; i.e., women weep for the Babylonian god Tammuz, men worship the sun, the wall engravings of the temple appear to be ghastly idolatrous apparitions, etc. At this point, Ezekiel declares the temple corrupt and the vision of its destruction then proceeds.

Ezekiel's understanding of righteousness, repentance, and restoration is intimately linked to his understandings of wrongdoing, defilement, and punishment (Sweeney 2005b, 156–72). Just as human beings are capable of choosing to engage in wrongful and defiling behavior, so they are fully capable of choosing to engage in righteousness and holiness. As Ezekiel 18 makes clear, human beings are able to change their behavior, to repent before YHWH, and thereby to reform their lives and actions. Such a conceptualization lies at the basis of King Josiah's program of religious reform and political restoration that so influenced Ezekiel's own understandings of wrongdoing and defilement as well as repentance and restoration. But the book of Ezekiel does not posit a major human repentance that will lead to restoration; rather, YHWH chooses to bring about the restoration of Israel, Zion, and the temple for the sake of YHWH's holy name. Although the defilement of the temple marks the turning point in YHWH's decision to destroy Jerusalem and the temple in an effort to purge them of their defilement, Ezekiel's oracles concerning the history of Israelite and Judean wrongdoing make it clear that, in the view of YHWH and the prophet, Israel and Judah had committed trespasses and defiled themselves throughout their entire histories. As a result, YHWH does not wait for human repentance in the book of Ezekiel. Instead, the purge of the nation is designed to remove its allegedly impure elements and begin once again with a new basis that will lead to an ideally righteous and holy nation gathered around the new temple in Jerusalem at the center of a restored creation.

Two elements play key roles in Ezekiel's scenario of restoration: (1) the recognition of YHWH by Israel and Judah as well as by the nations of the world and (2) the sanctification of YHWH's holy name.

The recognition of YHWH permeates Ezekiel 1–39. Throughout these chapters, Ezekiel constantly employs the recognition formula "and they shall know that I am YHWH" to identify YHWH as the agent behind the momentous changes that are taking place in Israel and Judah as well as among the nations (Zimmerli 1982, 1–28). Such an agenda makes eminent sense in a world that sees the rise of the Babylonian empire and the destruction of Jerusalem, Judah, and the temple as the major events of Ezekiel's day. In such an environment, the general public would likely conclude that

Marduk, the city god of Babylon, was the preeminent deity of the time. Certainly, the *Enuma Elish*, the Babylonian creation epic, would support such a view insofar as it portrays Marduk's rise to power as the result of his efforts to defeat the forces of chaos in the world and to build a natural and political order that would place Marduk at the head of the gods and Babylon at the head of the nations (*ANET*, 60–72). As a result of Babylonia's conquests, which included the former Assyrian empire, Aram, and much of western Asia, Babylonia was rising to become the unchallenged power of the day. Following the conquest of western Asia, many in the world of the time expected that Babylon would take Egypt as well. But as a Zadokite priest of YHWH from the Jerusalem Temple, Ezekiel would hold no such views of Marduk's power and standing in the world. In Ezekiel's view, YHWH was the preeminent deity of the world of nature and human events, who formed creation in the first place, who raised Israel from a small line of wandering figures in Ur and Haran, who delivered Israel from Egyptian bondage, who revealed divine Torah to Israel at Mount Sinai, and who brought the tribes of Israel into the Promised Land. Consequently, Ezekiel's oracles constantly conclude with the recognition formula to demonstrate to his audience that YHWH is the true power in the world, who appears to him in Babylonia, who destroys the Jerusalem Temple, who brings the people of Judah into captivity, who brings down the mighty nations of the world, and who will restore the twelve tribes of Israel, the Jerusalem Temple, and creation at large. Ezekiel does not announce the downfall of Babylon. Like Isaiah who identifies YHWH successively with Assyria, Babylon, and Persia, Ezekiel identifies YHWH with Babylon. It is not Babylon or Marduk who destroys Jerusalem and exiles its people; it is YHWH. It is not Babylon who conquers Edom, Moab, Ammon, Phoenicia, and Egypt; it is YHWH. And it will not be Marduk who puts the world in order and subjugates it to Babylon; it is YHWH who puts the world in order and oversees it from Jerusalem.

The Jerusalem Temple is the holy center of Israel and creation at large. Although Jerusalem had been defiled and needed to be purged, Jerusalem also needed to be restored in order to reestablish a holy Israel and a holy creation. Ultimately, such restoration entails the holiness of YHWH's name. One of the major functions of the temple was to serve as the place where the holiness of the divine name—and thereby YHWH's presence—would be manifested in the world of creation. Insofar as YHWH's name and presence were manifested in creation, creation itself was sanctified and thereby functioned as it should, viz., as a potential Garden of Eden in which the ideals of creation could be realized on behalf of human beings and all that lived within. The temple—and its priesthood—thereby served as an intermediary between YHWH and creation. The temple provided the means to promote and maintain holiness among the people, and the people, through their holy and righteous action, strove to maintain the divine presence in the world of creation. For the people of Israel, this meant a special obligation to interrelate with YHWH and to observe YHWH's divine instruction or Torah (Heb., *torah*), thereby ensuring that creation provided the means to sustain life and security in the world. The temple liturgy, including the three major holidays of Pesach (Passover), Shavuot (Weeks, Pentecost), and Sukkot (Booths, Tabernacles), the Shabbat, the holidays of Rosh ha-Shanah (New Year, associated with Sukkot), Yom Kippur (Day of Atonement, associated with Sukkot), the offerings of animals and agricultural produce, and the observance of YHWH's instructions concerning morals and social justice, were intended as means for the people to honor and to interrelate with YHWH.

The priesthood would play a special role in this interrelationship with YHWH as its task was to represent the people before YHWH and to teach the people YHWH's expectations. The Zadokite priesthood, descended from Phineas ben Eleazar ben Aaron, had the obligation to serve at the altar before YHWH (Num 25) and the other priestly lines, including the descendants of Ithamar ben Aaron, and the Levites, in general, had the obligation to perform the tasks of the temple at large (Num 17–18). The high priest, chosen from among the Zadokites, had the obligation to appear before YHWH at Yom Kippur to atone for the people (Lev 16). His role was to offer the *hatta'at* or sin offering on behalf of the nation and to enter the holy of holies on Yom Kippur as part of the nation's effort to atone before YHWH. But with the temple defiled and destroyed, the means by which such atonement could be offered was unclear. With the Zadokite priesthood either dead or exiled away from Jerusalem and the site of the temple, such atonement was no longer possible. Consequently, YHWH would take action to see that the atonement would take place.

Ezekiel, a Zadokite priest in exile who might well have been the high priest one day, was designated to become YHWH's watchman or visionary prophet to communicate to the people YHWH's intentions and actions in the world (Ezek 1–3; 33). In addition to warning the people of wrongdoing and impending judgment, Ezekiel was to announce YHWH's intentions to act in the world to restore the holiness of the temple, Jerusalem, and all creation. Ezekiel 1–3 signals this intent when Ezekiel is commissioned as YHWH's prophet in his visionary experience of the divine throne chariot by the banks of the Chebar Canal and swallows the scroll offered to him by YHWH, thereby embodying YHWH's teaching that is to be passed on to the people of Israel. Ezekiel 3 makes Ezekiel's task especially clear when it designates him as YHWH's watchman to announce that YHWH will sanctify the divine name once again. In Zadokite thought, human profane conduct defiles YHWH's name or presence in the world and proper human action sanctifies it. Without a sanctified temple or priesthood to ensure the holiness of the divine name, YHWH acts alone to ensure the sanctification of the divine name, the restoration of Israel, the restoration of the temple, and the restoration of creation. At the conclusion of Ezekiel 8–11, in which YHWH departs from the defiled temple and commands its destruction, YHWH announces that YHWH will serve as a small sanctuary (*miqdash me'at*) that will represent YHWH's intention to gather the surviving people from exile, give them a new heart and new spirit that will ensure their observance of YHWH's instructions, and restore the relationship between YHWH and the people of Israel. Ezekiel 36:16-38 likewise expresses YHWH's intentions to purify the people of Israel, to restore them to the land of Israel, and to restore the land to an Eden-like state where the people can flourish and observe YHWH's instructions. Ezekiel 37:1-14 presents Ezekiel's vision of the dry bones in which the dead bones, presumably of the people of Israel, are brought back to life, thereby removing the impurity of death from the land and enabling its restoration. Ezekiel 37:16-28 foresees the restoration and reunification of the House of Joseph or Ephraim and the House of Judah, i.e., northern Israel and southern Judah, under the rule of a new Davidic king and gathered around YHWH's restored sanctuary. Ezekiel 38–39 envisions the purification of the land from the corpses of the army of Gog from Magog, the enemy of Israel whom YHWH defeated in the land. The purification of the land from the defilement of death thereby prepares the land for the restoration of the holy temple.

Ezekiel's vision of the new temple in Ezekiel 40–48 constitutes the culmination of the book. The passage is fraught with difficulties, most notably that Ezekiel's temple does not correspond to either Solomon's temple or to the Second Temple as described in any other source. Many modern scholars have attempted to argue that the temple vision is a late addition to the book of Ezekiel. Major considerations include the form of Ezekiel 40–48, which differs from that of Ezekiel 1–39. Ezekiel 40–48 no longer employs the proof saying or addresses Ezekiel as Ben Adam, and many claim that these chapters have an apocalyptic world view, which is based on temple imagery rather than upon presumed prophetic concerns. But Ezekiel's identity as both a Zadokite priest and as a visionary prophet of YHWH make the culminating vision of the book a necessity, particularly since the book of Ezekiel is organized around the notion of a purge of the Jerusalem Temple at the center of Jerusalem, Israel, and all creation, and their anticipated restoration. Indeed, the book of the priest and prophet Ezekiel makes little sense without the vision of the restored temple at the center of a restored Jerusalem, a restored Israel, and a restored creation (cf. Levenson 1976, 7–53). Insofar as the restored temple presumes that the people of Israel have recognized YHWH's actions in the world, the proof sayings are no longer necessary. Insofar as recognition has come about due to the efforts of Ezekiel, the Zadokite priest and visionary prophet of YHWH, there is no further need to address him as Ben Adam to establish his priestly identity. According to the chronological statement in Ezekiel 40:1, Ezekiel would have passed the age of fifty when a priest would normally retire, and he would therefore not serve as a priest in the temple described in the vision. With the vision of the new temple in Ezekiel 40–48, Ezekiel's role as Zadokite priest and visionary prophet of YHWH is completed.

Ezekiel in Later Jewish, Christian, and Muslim Traditions

Ezekiel represents a unique perspective among the Major Prophets. Isaiah is a royalist and the book is especially influenced by the Davidic/Zion tradition that posits eternal divine protection for the house of David and the city of Jerusalem. Jeremiah is a priest of the line of Ithamar, and the book is especially influenced by the view that YHWH requires observance of divine Torah from Israel. Ezekiel has similarities to both. His book is heavily influenced by the Zion tradition of divine protection for Jerusalem and the temple, and given Ezekiel's identity as a Zadokite priest, it affirms observance of divine Torah. But Ezekiel differs from his senior colleagues by virtue of his Zadokite world view, which sees the Jerusalem Temple as the holy center of creation and maintains that the holiness of the temple ensures the holiness and well-being of Israel and all creation. Isaiah is concerned with Jerusalem throughout the book, but has little to say about the temple. As a descendant of the priestly line of Ithamar through Eli, which served in the Shiloh Temple, Jeremiah does not share Ezekiel's view that the Jerusalem Temple is the center of creation. Neither Isaiah nor Jeremiah posits a future for the house of David. Although the first portion of Isaiah anticipates a future, righteous Davidic monarch in Isaiah 9:1-6, 11:1-16, and 32:1-8, Isaiah 44:28 and 45:1 make it clear that King Cyrus of Persia is YHWH's anointed, and Isaiah 55 makes it clear that the Davidic covenant is applied to Israel at large. In the end, Isaiah 66:1 posits that YHWH is the true king. Jeremiah 23:1-8 anticipates a future, righteous Davidic monarch, but MT Jer 31:14-26 makes it clear that the Davidic covenant is applied to the city of

Jerusalem instead. LXX Jeremiah 33 lacks vv. 14-26, and so LXX Jeremiah continues to anticipate a righteous Davidic monarch. Ezekiel, however, anticipates that a Davidic monarch will continue to be a part of Israel's future when Ephraim and Judah are reunited in Ezekiel 37:15-28, when Israel is restored in Ezekiel 34, and in the new temple in Ezekiel 40–48. Nevertheless, the restoration of the temple is the main event for Ezekiel, and the Davidic monarch, whom the prophet calls *nasi'*, "prince," will lead the people in worshipping YHWH at the new temple.

Ezekiel exerted a marked influence on other prophetic books as well. Ezekiel's vision of YHWH in Ezekiel 1 influences Daniel's throne vision of YHWH in Daniel 7 heavily. Indeed, Daniel 7:13 refers to the *bar 'enash*, Aramaic for "son of Human," to represent the priest's approach to the throne of G-d. The book of the prophet Zechariah, who was also a Zadokite priest, shares Ezekiel's views concerning the sanctity of the Jerusalem Temple at the center of Israel and creation.

The Christian New Testament knows Ezekiel as well. Paul quotes Ezekiel 36:22 in Romans 2:24 when he states that the name of G-d is blasphemed among the nations. He also relies on Ezekiel 20:11 in Romans 10:5 and Galations 3:12 when he states that a man who practices righteousness based on the "law" (Greek, *nomos*, "law," employed by Paul to translate Hebrew, *torah*, "instruction") shall live by that righteousness. The question in 2 Peter 3:4, "Where is the promise of his coming?" relies on Ezekiel 12:22. The answer is forever since the father fell asleep and all continues just as it was from the beginning of creation. The Gospel of Mark frequently employs the term "Son of Man" to refer to Christ as the apocalyptic messianic figure (e.g., Mark 13). Finally, Revelation 21–23 makes extensive use of Ezekiel's visions in Ezekiel 1–3 and 40–48 to portray Christ in the heavenly temple.

Islam also acknowledges Ezekiel as a prophet. The Qur'an does not mention him explicitly, but later authorities accept him as such. The Qur'an mentions the prophet Dhul-Kilf or Zul-Kifl together with Ismail and Idris (Enoch) in Sura 21 (Al-Anbiya) vv. 85-86 and with Ismail and Elisha in Sura 38 (Sad) v. 48. The tomb of Zul-Kifl in southeastern Iraq along the Euphrates River is identified as the tomb of Ezekiel, although contemporary renovation of the tomb has covered over the Hebrew inscriptions that identify Ezekiel as the prophet interred there.

As noted above, Ezekiel proved to be a very controversial figure in rabbinic Judaism, in large measure because his book appears to conflict with Mosaic Torah at various points. Talmudic tradition states that Rabbi Hanina ben Hezekiah burned 300 barrels of oil working nights to resolve the discrepancies between Ezekiel and the Torah (*b. Shabbat* 13b; *b. Hagigah*

13a; *b. Menahot* 45a). Unfortunately, much of R. Hanina's discussion was lost, but some elements have been preserved in the Babylonian Talmud (Sweeney 2011, 11–23). As a result of R. Hanina's efforts, the book of Ezekiel remains a part of the Tanak, the Jewish Bible, and Ezekiel himself is recognized as a halakhic authority on par with Moses.

Ezekiel also had a profound influence on the tradition of Second Temple-period Jewish apocalypticism and the development of Jewish mysticism from antiquity through the present. Apocalyptic books such as 1 Enoch, 2 Baruch, 4 Ezra, and others attempt to replicate Ezekiel's vision of the heavenly throne of G-d (see Collins). Indeed, 1 Enoch 14 presents Enoch's vision of the divine throne in terms that are quite dependent upon Ezekiel. The depiction of Christ in the heavenly temple in the book of Revelation derives from late Second Temple-period Jewish apocalyptic. The book of Ezekiel at Qumran is preserved only in fragmentary form, but its influence is pervasive. The vision of the temple in the *Temple Scroll* from Qumran is based in part on Ezekiel's vision, and the *Songs of the Sabbath Sacrifice* present the liturgy of the heavenly temple based in part on the inspiration of the book of Ezekiel (see Martinez, 419–31).

Perhaps the most important legacy of Ezekiel is the development of the *Heikhalot* or *Merkavah* literature of rabbinic Judaism and the subsequent development of Kabbalah and Hasidism (Schäfer 1992, 2009; Elior 2005, 2006). Works such as the *Heikhalot Rabbati*, the *Heikhalot Zutarti*, and *3 Enoch* relate the rabbinic ascent to heaven to appear before the throne of G-d (Schäfer 1981). The term *Heikhalot*, "Palaces," refers to the seven palaces or levels of heaven through which one must pass to arrive at the divine throne, and the term *Merkavah*, "Chariot," recalls YHWH's throne chariot that appears in Ezekiel 1–3. Many interpreters recognize that Muhammad's ascent to heaven from Jerusalem derives from the *Heikhalot* tradition as well. The later Kabbalistic works, such as the *Bahir* and the *Zohar*, Lurianic Kabbalah, and the Hasidic movement of Judaism attempt to internalize the encounter with G-d by positing the divine *sefirot* (lit., the emanation of G-d) or emanations of G-d manifested in all human beings and throughout all creation (Scholem). Christian mystics, such as Saint Theresa of Avila, were also heavily reliant on Kabbalistic notions in positing their own means to encounter G-d (Kavanaugh).

Indeed, the book of Ezekiel is a foundational text in attempts to apprehend G-d. Ultimately, it represents a profound attempt to encounter the holy in the profane world and, based on that encounter, to sanctify the world in which we live.

Ezekiel's Oracles concerning His Inaugural Vision

Ezekiel 1:1–7:27

The first major unit of the book of Ezekiel appears in Ezekiel 1:1–7:27, which introduces the book with a presentation of Ezekiel's inaugural vision and the early oracles that follow from that experience (Sweeney 2005d, 125–43). This unit constitutes the foundation for the book insofar as it describes Ezekiel's initial encounter with YHWH and his designation as YHWH's prophet while in Babylonian exile. The formal literary structure of this unit is defined by the introductory chronological statement in Ezekiel 1:1 (see also the explanatory statements in Ezek 1:2-3) and variations of the classical prophetic word formula *wayehi debar-yhwh 'el* . . . , "and the word of YHWH came to . . . ," in Ezekiel 1:3, 3:16, 6:1, and 7:1, each of which introduces the basic subunits that comprise this text. Thus, Ezekiel 1:1–7:27 includes four subunits: the initial oracular account of Ezekiel's inaugural vision in Ezekiel 1:1–3:15; the second oracular account of Ezekiel's commission as the watchman for the people and his symbolic actions in Ezekiel 3:16–5:17; the third oracular account concerning Ezekiel's preaching to the mountains of Israel in Ezekiel 6:1-14; and the fourth oracular account concerning the announcement of judgment and the Day of YHWH in Ezekiel 7:1-27. The formal structure of the unit may be diagrammed as follows:

I. Introduction: Ezekiel's oracles concerning his inaugural vision (Ezek 1:1–7:27)
   A. The initial oracular account of Ezekiel's inaugural vision (1:1–3:15)
   B. The second oracular account of Ezekiel's commission as the watchman for the people and his symbolic actions (3:16–5:17)
   C. The third oracular account concerning Ezekiel's preaching to the mountains of Israel (6:1-14)
   D. The fourth oracular account concerning the announcement of judgment and the Day of YHWH (7:1-27)

The Initial Oracular Account of Ezekiel's Inaugural Vision
(1:1–3:15)

Ezekiel 1:1–3:15 presents the initial account of Ezekiel's inaugural vision of YHWH's throne chariot and the four *Hayot*, "(heavenly) creatures," who carry it through the heavens. This text is an example of the ancient Judean (and Israelite) throne vision in which a visionary priest or prophet perceives YHWH seated on the divine throne surrounded by the heavenly court (Zimmerli 1979–1983, 95–100; cf. Sweeney 2010, 559–63). Examples in the Hebrew Bible include visions of YHWH by Moses, Aaron, and the seventy elders (Exod 24), Micaiah ben Imlah (1 Kings 22), Isaiah (Isa 6), and Daniel (Dan 7). Other examples, such as Samuel (1 Sam 3) and Elijah (1 Kings 19), appear to reflect visionary experience. Examples outside the Hebrew Bible include John (Rev 14), Enoch (1 Enoch 14), and Rabbi Nehunyah ben ha-Qanah (*Heikhalot Rabbati* 20–30).

The spatial setting for such a vision is generally the holy of holies of the temple, insofar as the holy of holies is conceived as the throne room of YHWH, which corresponds to the holy of holies in the heavenly temple. The temporal and liturgical setting of the vision may be identified with Yom Kippur or Sukkot, both of which are major festivals in the Judean/Israelite calendar. Yom Kippur is the Day of Atonement, a day of fasting and worship in which the nation atones at the temple for wrongs committed during the preceding year. Leviticus 16 states that Yom Kippur is the observance on which the priest is to enter the holy of holies where YHWH appears to atone for the people. As a Zadokite priest, Ezekiel would have been trained to assume such a function in the event that he might someday serve as high priest. Alternatively, Sukkot would be the occasion for the ordination of priests, who are isolated for seven days as part of the process by which they are sanctified for holy service at the temple altar (Exod 29; Lev 8; Num 8). Sukkot is the seven-day festival of Booths, which celebrates Israel's wandering in the wilderness as well as the conclusion of the agricultural year when the fruit harvest is brought in prior to the onset of the fall rains. Both the wilderness wanderings and the fruit harvest evoke images of temporary dwellings or booths (Heb., *sukkot*) as the people would live in such shelters in order to remain out in the fields during the final harvest period. Insofar as Sukkot marks the beginning of the new agricultural season, it marks the time when the temple altar and new priests are consecrated. We know little of what the soon-to-be ordained priests would do during their seven days of incubation, but a sense of encounter and relationship with YHWH would likely be a part of the experience. Ezekiel's visionary experience of YHWH, which includes both a commission to speak on behalf of YHWH and a seven-day period of silence (see Ezek 3:15, 16), would then replicate to some degree the experience of priestly ordination that would then commission the prospective priest to serve at the temple altar.

Ezekiel 1:1–3:15 is defined as a subunit by the introduction in Ezekiel 1:1-3, which includes the above-noted chronological statement in Ezekiel 1:1 and the prophetic word formula in Ezekiel 1:3, and by the accounts of three visions, each of which is introduced by the verb, *wa'era'*, "and I saw," including the approach of YHWH's throne chariot borne by the four *Hayot* (creatures) in Ezekiel 1:4-14, the description of YHWH's throne chariot in Ezekiel 1:15-26, and the vision of YHWH speaking in Ezekiel 1:27–3:15 in which Ezekiel is commissioned to serve as YHWH's prophet.

The introduction to the account in Ezekiel 1:1-3 presents information about the setting of Ezekiel's vision. The passage begins with Ezekiel's first-person statement in v. 1 that he saw visions of G-d in the thirtieth year, in the fourth month of the year, and on the fifth day of the month while he was among the exiles located by the Chebar River in Babylonia (Thompson, 893). The Chebar River, known in Akkadian sources as the Nar Kaberi, was a canal dug by the Babylonians for water distribution, flood control, and transportation. It began at the Euphrates River north of Babylon and continued south for some sixty miles, passing the city of Nippur and rejoining the Euphrates south of Warka (the biblical city of Erech). The month and day would refer to the fifth day of the month of Tammuz in both the Jewish and Babylonian calendars, which would occur in late June or early July. The reference to the thirtieth year, however, is not so clear. Consequently, the third-person editorial statements in vv. 2-3 attempt to explain the references provided in v. 1. Verse 2 again states that Ezekiel's vision took place on the fifth day of the month, but it specifies that the year was the fifth year of King Jehoiachin's exile. Insofar as Jehoiachin was exiled in 597 BCE, the date for Ezekiel's vision would be 592 BCE. Verse 3 goes on to explain that the first-person speaker of v. 1 is the priest, Ezekiel ben Buzi. Nothing is known about his father, but his designation as a priest (Heb., *kohen*) indicates that he was a descendant of the line of Aaron, which was designated for service at the temple altar (see Num 17–18; 25), whereas the other Levitical families performed other duties. The version of the prophetic word formula in v. 3 is emphatically stated, "The word of YHWH surely came (Heb., *hayoh hayah*)," to highlight its role as the first of many occurrences of the prophetic word formula that introduce the oracles of Ezekiel throughout the book. Verse 3 also notes that Ezekiel is located in the land of the Chaldeans, the term employed in the Bible to refer to the Neo-Babylonian empire founded by Nebopolassar (r. 627–605 BCE) and later ruled by his son Nebuchadnezzar (r. 605–562 BCE). The mention of "the hand of YHWH" that came upon Ezekiel is a typical means to refer to the ecstatic experience of ancient prophets, such as Elijah (1 Kings 18:46) and Elisha (2 Kings 3:15), which enables YHWH to speak and act through the prophet (see also Ezek 3:14, 22; 8:1; 33:22; 37:1; 40:1).

Although the date of Ezekiel's vision is specified as the fifth year of Jehoiachin's reign, the significance of the reference to the thirtieth year remains unclear. Various proposals have been given, viz., it might refer to the thirtieth year of the Jubilee cycle, the date of the book's composition, the year of King Jehoiachin's exile, the reform of King Josiah, or Ezekiel's age. Indeed, a combination of the last two proposals best explains the reference to the thirtieth year. As a Zadokite priest, Ezekiel would have been ordained for service at the altar of the Jerusalem Temple when he was thirty years old (see Num 4:3); Numbers 8:23-25 states that the age of ordination is twenty-five, but this refers to the Levites who do not serve at the temple altar; (Sweeney 2005d, 125–43), and he would have continued to serve as a priest until the age of fifty. Because he had been exiled from the Jerusalem Temple to Babylonia, Ezekiel could not be ordained as a priest for service at the temple altar. Instead, his vision of YHWH's throne chariot inaugurates his career as a prophet in exile from the land of Israel. Because Ezekiel 1:2 specifies that the thirtieth year refers to the fifth year of Jehoiachin's exile, i.e., 592 BCE, Ezekiel would have been born in 622 BCE, the eighteenth year of Josiah's reign, when Josiah commenced his program of religious reform and national restoration (2 Kings 22:3; 2 Chr 34:8). Ezekiel's career as a prophet in exile culminates with his vision of the restored temple in Ezekiel 40–48, which takes place in the twenty-fifth year of the exile when Ezekiel would have turned fifty.

Ezekiel 1:4-14, introduced by Ezekiel's statement "and I saw," constitutes the first visionary event of Ezekiel's inaugural vision, which describes the approach of YHWH's throne chariot. The imagery of this vision is based in large measure on the imagery of the Ark of the Covenant, which was housed in the holy of holies or the inner chamber of the Jerusalem Temple until the Babylonian destruction of the temple in 587 BCE. Exodus 25:10-22 and 37:1-9 describe the Ark of the Covenant in detail as a chest of acacia wood overlaid with gold that contains the tablets of the Ten Commandments. Four cherubim or composite animal figures protect it; two are built on top of the cover of the ark and two more are placed in the holy of holies of the Jerusalem Temple (1 Kings 6:23-28; 1 Chr 3:10-14). Ancient Near Eastern art and architecture typically portray cherubim as guardians of royal thrones, temples, and city gates, and the Ark of the Covenant is likewise understood in Judah and Israel to function as YHWH's royal throne, insofar as YHWH is described as "YHWH who is enthroned over the cherubim" (see 1 Sam 4:4; 2 Sam 6:2; 1 Chr 13:6).

The ark normally resided in the Jerusalem Temple from the reign of Solomon on, but the fate of the Ark of the Covenant at the time of the Babylonian destruction of Jerusalem remains unknown. Ezekiel's vision portrays the ark as YHWH's throne chariot that conveys YHWH through the heavens so that YHWH might be revealed to Ezekiel in Babylonia and commissioned as YHWH's prophet. The imagery of the throne chariot is based in part on the imagery of the ark conveyed to Jerusalem on a wheeled cart during the reign of David (2 Sam 6; cf. 2 Chr 28:15, which describes the ark as a chariot), the use of chariot and cherubim imagery to portray YHWH traveling across the heavens (Hab 3; Ps 18; 68), and the Mesopotamian practice of employing a winged disk to portray their own gods traveling through the heavens. As an exile in Babylonia, Ezekiel would no doubt have encountered such imagery.

The vision begins in vv. 4-5a with Ezekiel's view of the approaching apparition. The first image is a whirlwind with thick cloud, flashing fire, and a brilliant radiance within. Such imagery is typical of theophanies (descriptions of the revelation of YHWH's presence) in the Hebrew Bible (Exod 19; 1 Kings 19; see Hiebert), and it recalls the imagery of the Jerusalem Temple during times of worship when the temple was filled with incense smoke and the menorahs or lamp stands were burning to symbolize YHWH's presence. As a priest, Ezekiel is very careful to employ the language of simile when describing aspects of the divine presence so as not to portray YHWH in tangible terms. Thus, he describes YHWH's presence at the center of the throne chariot as "like amber (Heb., *hashmal*) in the midst of fire." The precise meaning of *hashmal* is uncertain, although it appears to refer to a precious yellowish stone such as amber. In modern Hebrew, *hashmal* means "electricity." Ezekiel likewise employs the language of simile to describe the "likeness" (Heb., *demut*) of the four creatures that accompany YHWH's throne chariot.

Ezekiel then turns to a detailed description of the four creatures or cherubim in vv. 5b-14. Like typical ancient Near Eastern cherubim figures, Ezekiel's creatures are composite figures that combine various animal and human features (*ANEP*, 644–68). Each has four wings, each has a single leg with feet like a calf's hoof, each is portrayed as sparkling like polished bronze, each has human hands below their wings, and each has four faces. Although the English translations of the Bible portray the creatures as moving in the direction of "any" of their faces, the Hebrew indicates that they move in the direction of "all" of their faces at once. The vision after all attempts to employ finite human language to convey the infinite possibilities of divine movement and presence, viz., the creatures move in all directions at once.

Each of the creatures has four faces. The number four in this passage derives from the four horns of the temple altar that symbolize the four winds or four directions that encompass the entire world (Exod 27:2; 38:2; Zech 2:1-4). Each face represents a different divine quality. The first is the face of the human being, which conveys divine intelligence or the knowledge of good and evil gained by Eve in the Garden of Eden (Gen 3). The second is the face of the lion, which represents divine sovereignty, insofar as the lion symbolizes the royal tribe of Judah and the house of David. The face of the bull symbolizes divine strength, and the face of the eagle symbolizes divine mobility throughout the entire world.

Verses 13-14 return to the imagery of burning coals and sparkling fire to portray the dynamism, power, and utter holiness of the divine presence before Ezekiel.

Ezekiel 1:15-26, again introduced by the introductory statement *wa'era'*, "and I saw," presents the second visionary event in which Ezekiel describes YHWH's throne chariot. Ezekiel begins by focusing on the wheels of the chariot, which again presupposes the imagery of the Ark of the Covenant. In this case, the wheels would presuppose the wheels of the cart that conveyed the Ark of the Covenant from Kiriath Jearim to Jerusalem in 2 Samuel 6 or the rings built into the side of the ark so that the Levites can carry it with poles (Exod 25:12-15). The wheels gleam like beryl (Heb., *tarshish*), apparently presupposing the construction of the ark in which gold and later burnished bronze overlaid the acacia wood. A peculiar aspect of the wheels' construction is that one wheel is placed within the midst of the other. Some have argued that such a construction represents a hub, but the following statement in v. 17 indicates that the purpose of the wheels was to enable the throne chariot to move in all directions. Although it might be difficult for human beings to duplicate such a construction, readers must remember that Ezekiel's vision attempts to employ finite human language to portray a divine apparition that moves in all directions at once.

Ezekiel describes the rims of the wheel as filled with eyes. Again, a great deal of ink has been spilt to explain this phenomenon, but interpreters must recall that the throne chariot/Ark of the Covenant is overlaid with polished bronze or gold. When viewed in relation to the holy of holies of the temple, the many lights of the temple menorahs would reflect from the polished bronze/gold surface to give the impression of eyes looking out from the wheels/rings of the ark. The vision emphasizes that all four of the wheels move in unison with the rest of the throne chariot in accordance with the divine spirit that guides the chariot in Ezekiel's vision.

The vision turns to the broad expanse above the heads of the four creatures in v. 22. The Hebrew term for the expanse is *raqi'a*, the same term employed in Genesis 1:6-8 to describe the expanse of the heavens that were separated from the waters on the second day of creation. Insofar as the heavens are blue, the expanse is described as awe-inspiring crystal, although the Hebrew word *qerah* actually refers to ice. This feature appears to presuppose the sapphire pavement that appears below YHWH's feet in Exodus 24:10. Such a feature also calls to mind the golden cover of the ark described in Exodus 2:17-22 upon which the cherubim are placed. The ice-like expanse of the heavens would then appear above the creatures/cherubim where YHWH is enthroned.

Verses 23-25 describe the wings of the creatures. Two wings covered the bodies of the creatures and two more wings extended toward those of the others to surround the throne chariot as it moved through the heavens. The imagery of the vision turns to the audial qualities as well insofar as the wings of the creatures created a great noise described like mighty waters, the sound of Shaddai (a name for YHWH; see Exod 6:3 where YHWH is identified as El Shaddai, often translated as G-d Almighty), and the sound of a mighty army. Such audial features appear to presuppose the sounds of wind moving through the upper windows of the temple during temple worship to stir the incense smoke rising from the ten incense burners located inside the temple structure.

Finally, v. 26 concludes this segment of Ezekiel's vision of the throne chariot with a statement concerning his vision of YHWH. Because Ezekiel describes the presence of YHWH, he is very careful to employ simile so as not to assert that YHWH appears in tangible form. He begins with a reference to the expanse above the throne chariot, which he describes as "like the appearance (Heb., *kemar'eh*) of sapphire stone" to evoke the blue color of the heavens. Sapphire is often blue in color, but the refraction of light in the stone suggests streaks of red or other colors that hint at a reality behind the surface of the stone that evokes divine presence. Ezekiel continues with the statement that a semblance (Heb., *demut*) of a throne appeared above the heads of the four creatures, which refers to the role of the Ark of the Covenant as the throne of YHWH. He concludes with a reference to YHWH per se, whom he describes as "a semblance like the appearance of a human being (Heb., *'adam*)." Again, the use of similes points to the image of a human as a metaphorical means to describe the presence of YHWH, given the limits of human language to describe to the reality of divine presence. Of course, such a metaphor relates to Genesis 1:26, which states that human beings are created in the image (Heb., *tselem*) and likeness (Heb., *demut*) of YHWH—and not vice versa.

Ezekiel 1:27–3:15 presents YHWH's speech to Ezekiel as the third visionary event of Ezekiel's inaugural vision. Once again, the verb *wa'era'*, "and I saw," introduces the subunit. It begins with a brief account in Ezekiel 1:27-28a of what Ezekiel saw, and then it continues in Ezekiel 1:28b–3:15 with an account of Ezekiel's reaction to what he saw, viz., he falls upon his face and hears YHWH speaking to him. Of course, the primary content of YHWH's speech is to commission Ezekiel to serve as YHWH's "watchman" or prophet.

The account of what Ezekiel saw in Ezekiel 1:27-28a continues to employ simile and metaphor to describe the apparition of YHWH's holy presence. Once again, Ezekiel describes YHWH's presence as "like the appearance of amber (Heb., *ke'en hashmal*)" in an effort to employ the radiance and color of the precious stone as a metaphor for YHWH's appearance. He builds on this image by shifting to fire, viz., "like the appearance of fire (Heb., *kemar'eh 'esh*) encasing it." The metaphorical use of fire provides a combination of light and heat in intangible and yet visible and tactile form that attempts to present YHWH's intangible presence. Again, Ezekiel shifts to human metaphor by describing the appearance of YHWH's loins (Heb., *matenayv*, lit., "his loins"), but the term evokes the mid-point of YHWH's presence seated upon the throne; Ezekiel quickly returns to the imagery of fire and brilliance as a means to contextualize the use of metaphor to describe the divine presence. Ezekiel then shifts to the imagery of the bow in the clouds on a day of rain to portray YHWH's presence. The use of the metaphors is multidimensional. It refers to the rainbow that appears in the clouds at the end of a rain shower, thereby evoking images of YHWH as the bringer of rain (see Deut 11:13-15) and of YHWH's promise never again to destroy creation by flood (Gen 9:1-17). At the same time, the imagery points to Ezekiel's familiarity with Mesopotamian imagery, which so frequently portrays gods such as Assur, the chief god of Assyria, as flying in the heavens before his armies in a winged disk with his bow drawn. By employing such imagery, Ezekiel demonstrates an interest in portraying YHWH as a figure who both takes on the roles of Mesopotamian deities and surpasses them.

Ezekiel reacts in Ezekiel 1:28b–3:15 by falling on his face before YHWH and hearing the voice of YHWH speaking. His action is typical of worship, insofar as ancient Judean worshippers typically prostrated themselves before YHWH in the temple. It also evokes the imagery of ecstatic prophecy or trance position in which the deity speaks through the visionary (cf. Num 24:3-4, 15-16).

The account of YHWH's speech to Ezekiel appears in Ezekiel 2:1–3:11. It is an example of a prophetic commissioning speech in which YHWH commissions a prophet to speak on YHWH's behalf, although readers should note that such commissions frequently appear in the context of throne visions (e.g., Exod 3; 1 Sam 3; Isa 6; Jer 1:4-10; cf. Hals, 17–20). The account involves five occurrences of the speech formula *wayyo'mer 'elay*, "and he said to me," which mark the five basic segments of YHWH's commissioning speech to Ezekiel. They include Ezekiel 2:1-2 in which YHWH commands Ezekiel to stand, Ezekiel 2:3-10 in which YHWH sends Ezekiel to a rebellious Israel, Ezekiel 3:1-3 in which YHWH commands Ezekiel to eat the scroll, Ezekiel 3:4-9 in which YHWH commands Ezekiel to speak to Israel, and Ezekiel 3:10-11 in which YHWH commands Ezekiel to go to his people.

YHWH commands Ezekiel to stand in the first segment of YHWH's speech in Ezekiel 2:1-2. YHWH addresses Ezekiel as *ben-'adam*, lit., "son of Adam" or "son of a human." The idiom "son of" typically designates a party as a member of a particular class, e.g., "son of a prophet" in Amos 7:14. In such a case, the term would indicate that YHWH addresses Ezekiel as a human being or a mortal. But the term signifies much more in the case of Ezekiel. As a Zadokite priest who serves in the temple, Ezekiel—and all Zadokites for that matter—represents humanity at large as, quite literally, a "son of Adam" (cf. Hayward, 88–93, 111–18). Insofar as Judean thought conceives the holy of holies of the temple as the Garden of Eden, the priest's entry into the holy of holies, guarded by a cherub, at Yom Kippur signifies an attempt to reenter the Garden of Eden from which Adam and Eve were expelled (see Gen 3) and thereby to reestablish the once ideal relationship between human beings and YHWH. Ezekiel describes a "spirit" that enters into him, which must be identified as a means to describe the sense of trance possession in which the divine presence of YHWH will speak through Ezekiel as YHWH's prophet.

In Ezekiel 2:3-10, YHWH states to Ezekiel that he will be sent to the rebellious house of Israel. This is the first component of YHWH's commission to the prophet. Throughout the book, YHWH characterizes Israel as rebellious, corrupt, sinful, etc., characterizations that must be understood in context. Like all of the prophetic books, Ezekiel is a work of theodicy designed to explain why disaster has come upon the people of Israel and Judah, and how YHWH plans to overcome that disaster in the future. The theological problem of the book of Ezekiel is the question of YHWH's power, presence, and righteousness in the face of the Babylonian exile and the destruction of the Jerusalem Temple. YHWH was understood to be in eternal covenant with Israel to grant the people the land of Israel, to support their life in the land, and to defend them against threat. Indeed, the Jerusalem Temple was a tangible symbol of YHWH's presence among the people and fidelity to the covenant. But with the Babylonian exile and the destruction of the temple, YHWH's power, presence, and righteousness came into question. Rather than argue that YHWH had failed the people, the book of Ezekiel is designed to argue that the people had failed YHWH by corrupting the land and the temple by acts that contradicted YHWH's instructions for a holy and righteous life. Consequently, the Babylonian exile and the destruction of Jerusalem are conceived as necessary acts by YHWH to purge the people of Israel, the city of Jerusalem, and the temple itself in order to lay the foundation for a new creation by the end of the book. Such a conceptualization of the exile and destruction then asserts YHWH's power, presence, and righteousness by laying the blame on the people. It also functions as a means to instill in readers of the book the willingness to examine their own fidelity to YHWH and to make greater efforts to observe YHWH's expectations.

YHWH states that Ezekiel will go to the rebellious house of Israel to speak to them as a prophet, employing the formula *koh 'amar 'adonay yhwh*, "thus says my lord, YHWH," typically rendered as "thus says my L-rd, G-d." This is the classical prophetic messenger formula which conceives the prophet as a messenger or envoy sent by YHWH to convey YHWH's message to the people word for word. YHWH's commission betrays pessimism insofar as YHWH commands Ezekiel to speak whether the people listen or not. But the command also serves a revelatory function insofar as the YHWH revelation formula "and they will know that a prophet was in their midst" indicates that the purpose of YHWH's commission to Ezekiel is to reveal YHWH's presence through Ezekiel whether the people listen or not.

YHWH reassures Ezekiel that he should not fear the words of opposition anticipated from the people nor the thistles, thorns, and scorpions that might afflict him. Both of these statements presuppose Mesopotamian prophetic and incantational practice. The command "do not fear" is the well-known reassurance formula from Judean prophecy (e.g., Gen 15:1; Deut 3:2; 2 Kings 6:16; Isa 7:4; 35:4; 37:6; 40:9; 41:10; Job 5:21-22; Conrad), but it originates in Mesopotamian prophecy, where it likewise functions as a means to reassure the audience of a prophet that the gods will act on their behalf (e.g., Nissinen et al., 168, 173). The reference to thistles, thorns, and scorpions employs language that appears in Babylonian incantations indicating protection from the threats of others (see, e.g., *Maqlu* 3:153-4: "I am the spike of a thorn bush; you cannot step on me! I am the stinger of a scorpion; you cannot touch me!"; Odell, 42).

YHWH concludes this segment of the commissioning speech by calling on Ezekiel not to be rebellious and to eat the scroll that YHWH now offers him. Ezekiel notes that the scroll is inscribed on both sides with lamentations, dirges, and woes, which signal a message of judgment for the people.

YHWH commands Ezekiel to eat the scroll in Ezekiel 3:1-2 so that the prophet might go to the house of Israel and speak YHWH's message to them. The command constitutes a metaphorical symbolic act for Ezekiel's internalization of YHWH's message to the people of Israel to represent the fact that YHWH speaks through him. We do not know if he actually ate a scroll in public, but interpreters have noted that the book of Ezekiel is designed to be read as a literary work by the prophet's audience. When read as literature that presents Ezekiel's visionary experience, the act of eating the scroll then functions at face value to symbolize the prophet's full identification with YHWH as the spokesperson who conveys YHWH's message. Upon swallowing the scroll, Ezekiel states that it tasted like honey as a means to convey the sweetness and goodness of YHWH's word. Jeremiah also employs the metaphor of eating YHWH's scroll to symbolize his own internalization of YHWH's message. In Jer 15:16, the prophet states, "Your words were found, and I ate them, and your word became a delight and a joy for my heart, because your name, YHWH, G-d of Hosts, is called upon me."

Ezekiel 3:4-9 then presents YHWH's formal commission to Ezekiel to act as YHWH's prophet to Israel. The basic commission is presented simply as a command to go to the house of Israel and speak YHWH's words to them. The commission highlights the conceptualization of the prophet as a mere mouthpiece for YHWH who does not speak anything to the people but YHWH's word, much as the Aramean prophet, Balaam ben Beor, could not speak a word other than what YHWH commanded him to speak (see Num 22–24). The commission anticipates resistance to YHWH's message through Ezekiel insofar as it highlights the refusal of the people of Israel to listen to the prophet by contrasting them with foreigners who speak a foreign language who would readily listen to YHWH. Such a statement gives expression to the rhetorical and theological viewpoints of the book. The book charges that even the Babylonian invaders, who speak a foreign and unintelligible language, would more readily listen to YHWH than Israel. The book of Ezekiel is designed in part to vindicate YHWH from any charge of wrongdoing, negligence, or powerlessness in relation to the destruction of Jerusalem in 587 BCE. The book throughout charges Israel with wrongdoing that corrupted the temple, Jerusalem, and the land of Israel in an effort to argue that Jerusalem was destroyed as part of YHWH's efforts to purge the city of its impurity. In such a context, the people of Israel become responsible for the destruction of Jerusalem, not YHWH, who is portrayed as acting to correct the results of the abuses of which the people were accused. In such a scenario, YHWH emerges as a righteous, powerful, and holy G-d, whereas the people appear as problematic and responsible themselves for the destruction of Jerusalem and the Babylonian exile.

Ezekiel 3:10-11 presents YHWH's final statements of commission to Ezekiel. This segment of text basically sums up YHWH's commission to Ezekiel that he receive YHWH's words so that he might go and speak to the people as a spokesperson for YHWH whether they like it or not.

Ezekiel 3:12-15 concludes the initial oracular account of Ezekiel's inaugural vision with the prophet's description of his departure from the presence of YHWH to return to the exiles at Tel Aviv by the Chebar Canal. Again, Ezekiel employs the metaphor of the spirit of YHWH, which lifts him up to transport him to Tel Aviv. He describes the sounds of wind rushing as a means to portray the sound of the wings of the cherubim and the wheels as the divine chariot goes into motion. The blessing "Blessed is the Glory of YHWH from its Place" in v. 12 signals the liturgical character of YHWH's movement. The cherubim presumably sing this blessing as they lift the throne chariot into the heavens to convey the holy character of their divine charge. Priestly literature frequently employs the term "glory," Hebrew, *kavod*, as a metaphor for the divine presence. Ezekiel is taken to the town of Tel Aviv by the Chebar Canal. Tel Aviv, identified with the long-abandoned Babylonian site of *Til Abubi*, "hill of the flood," was believed by Babylonians to have been destroyed by the primeval flood (Kobayashi, *ABD* 6, 344). The name of the modern city of Tel Aviv, founded by Jews living in the land of Israel in 1909, is derived from this text in an effort to symbolize the rebirth of Jewish life in the land of Israel represented by the book of Ezekiel. Upon his return to Tel Aviv, Ezekiel sits in stunned silence for seven days, emulating the seven-day period of incubation required for the ordination of priests to serve at the Jerusalem Temple. At the end of the seven-day period, Ezekiel is ready to speak.

Ezekiel 1:1–7:27

The Second Oracular Account of Ezekiel's Inaugural Vision: Commission as Watchman and Symbolic Acts (3:16–5:17)

Ezekiel 3:16–5:17 constitutes the second oracular account of the introduction to the book of Ezekiel with its account of YHWH's commission of the prophet as watchman over his people and his symbolic actions which convey the message of judgment that Ezekiel must deliver (Sweeney 2005d, 129–34). The unit is demarcated at the outset by the introductory prophetic word formula in Ezekiel 3:16, which stipulates that YHWH spoke again to Ezekiel after a period of seven days. The next occurrence of the prophetic word formula in Ezekiel 6:1 signals that the present subunit concludes with Ezekiel 5:17. Within Ezekiel 3:16–5:17, third-person accounts attributed to Ezekiel portray the action of the narrative, thereby framing the speeches by YHWH to Ezekiel and Ezekiel's responses to YHWH. The prophetic word formula in Ezekiel 3:16 introduces the account of YHWH's first speech to the prophet in Ezekiel 3:16-21 in which YHWH commissions Ezekiel to serve as watchman. The narrative reference to the hand of YHWH in Ezekiel 3:22 introduces YHWH's second major speech to Ezekiel in Ezekiel 3:22–5:17 in which YHWH specifies Ezekiel's role as watchman. The account of YHWH's second speech to Ezekiel includes two segments, each defined by a narrative reference to YHWH's speech in Ezekiel 3:22 and 3:24. In each instance, Ezekiel recounts his response to YHWH's speech. The two segments include (1) an account of YHWH's initial command to Ezekiel to stand in the valley together with Ezekiel's compliance in Ezekiel 3:22-23 and (2) an account of YHWH's instructions to Ezekiel in Ezekiel 3:24–5:17 in which YHWH informs Ezekiel that he will speak only when authorized by YHWH (Ezek 3:24-27) and communicate the divine message by means of symbolic actions (Ezek 4:1–5:17).

The account of YHWH's first speech to Ezekiel in Ezekiel 3:16-21 conveys YHWH's commission of Ezekiel as watchman. The initial version of the YHWH word formula in Ezekiel 3:16 begins with a reference to the seven days that passed from the time of the initial oracular event related in Ezekiel 1:1–3:15. Insofar as Ezekiel's commission as a prophet occurs on his thirtieth birthday, the time when a Zadokite priest would be ordained for service at the temple altar, this reference to the passage of the seven days recalls the seven-day ordination period that a prospective priest would undergo prior to assuming his duties at the holy altar. Insofar as Ezekiel is among the exiles in Babylon, he is unable to serve as a priest at the altar of the Jerusalem Temple. His inaugural vision, therefore, conceives his status and duties differently, viz., he will instead serve as YHWH's prophet in exile.

Thus, the seven-day ordination period marks the period of his ordination as a prophet rather than as a priest. Throughout the book, Ezekiel nevertheless retains his priestly identity, practice, and perspectives.

YHWH once again addresses Ezekiel as Ben-Adam, "son of Adam," in recognition of his status as a priest who would approach YHWH in the holy of holies of the temple on Yom Kippur to atone for the nation. But YHWH's instructions to Ezekiel envision a different role in that he will serve as YHWH's watchman (Heb., *tsofeh*). The role of watchman derives from Ezekiel's priestly identity. All priests are enjoined to teach YHWH's Torah or instruction to the people so that they might understand what is sacred and profane and what is pure and impure (Lev 10:10-11; Deut 33:10; Ezek 44:23; Hag 2:20-23; 2 Chr 15:3; cf. Exod 24:12; 2 Kings 12:3). As part of the process by which the temple priests would ensure the purity of the temple and those who would enter, priestly sentinels or gatekeepers were posted at all entrances to the temple (1 Chr 9:17-27; 26:1-19). Interpreters lack a precise understanding of the procedures employed by the temple gatekeepers, i.e., it is not clear that their role is to check people's credentials to stop the impure from entering the temple. Rather, the two entrance liturgy psalms in Psalm 15 and Psalm 24 suggest that their role was to instruct people concerning their obligations to purify themselves both ritually and ethically before entering the temple precincts. The question of whether an individual was pure or not would then be left for YHWH to determine.

Although Ezekiel 33:1-20 defines Ezekiel's role as watchman more fully, the present instruction lays out the parameters of the prophet's role. Ezekiel is to communicate YHWH's judgment to persons in question, just as a priest would normally be expected to render judgments of guilt or innocence and purity or impurity when representing YHWH to the people. YHWH employs a technique also known from Ezekiel 18:1-32 to specify each case in which the prophet is responsible for communicating YHWH's will to human beings. In each case, YHWH is concerned with defining Ezekiel's responsibilities by asserting that he must warn those who are judged to be unrighteous so that they might have the opportunity to repent and thereby save their own lives. If Ezekiel does not fulfill his responsibilities as watchman, i.e., if he fails to warn a wicked man of his wickedness or a righteous man who has committed a moral or ritual trespass, Ezekiel is culpable and subject to death. In both cases, the guilty man is subject to death. A particularly controversial aspect of this discourse is YHWH's claim to place an obstacle before the guilty party to ensure his death, but such a statement ultimately recognizes the priestly (and nonpriestly) view that YHWH determines the fate of all persons. If Ezekiel warns a man of his wrongdoing and he corrects himself, then the man in question and Ezekiel will live. Insofar as the priests bear the sin of the people and the sanctuary (see Ezek 4:5; Num 18:1), Ezekiel continues to function in this respect much as a priest would in Jerusalem.

The account of YHWH's second speech in Ezekiel 3:22–5:17 then further specifies aspects of Ezekiel's role as watchman. The first segment of the speech appears in Ezekiel 3:22-23. The account begins in v. 22 with a statement that the hand of YHWH came upon Ezekiel as YHWH began to speak with him. YHWH's initial statement is to command Ezekiel to go to the valley so that they might speak. The identity of the valley is not clear, although it appears to be the same valley mentioned in the dry bones vision of Ezekiel 37:1-14. Ezekiel employs first-person language to state his compliance with YHWH's command, and upon seeing the presence of YHWH before him, he prostrates himself before YHWH, just as he would in the temple.

The second segment of the speech appears in Ezekiel 3:24–5:17. A spirit enters Ezekiel and stands him on his feet as YHWH begins the next segment of the speech in v. 24. YHWH's speech to Ezekiel begins in Ezekiel 3:24b-27 with a statement that Ezekiel will remain shut up in his house and speechless apart from times when YHWH authorizes him to speak a prophetic message. The imagery employed here is that Ezekiel will be bound with cords so that he is unable to leave his house and his tongue will cleave to the roof of his mouth so that he is unable to speak. Such an injunction is particularly important because it denies to Ezekiel an important aspect of his priestly role, viz., his ability to intercede on behalf of the people before YHWH. Both Moses and Aaron repeatedly interceded on behalf of the people throughout the period of wilderness wandering (e.g., Num 13–14; 16); indeed, Numbers 17–18 specifies that the priests are to bear the sin of the sanctuary, and Leviticus 16 specifies that the priest will lead the people in their atonement before YHWH on Yom Kippur. But whereas Ezekiel 3:16-20 indicates that Ezekiel will serve as YHWH's representative in judging the people, Ezekiel 3:24b-27 denies him the opportunity to represent the people before YHWH, apparently because YHWH has determined to render judgment against them. Like Balaam (Num 22–24), Ezekiel can only speak what YHWH commands him to speak, and he will speak only a prophetic message introduced by the classical prophetic messenger formula "thus says YHWH." Such an understanding of Ezekiel's and YHWH's roles appears to be an attempt to come to terms with the destruction of Jerusalem and the temple and the exile of the people. As sovereign of creation, YHWH must ultimately be responsible. Because YHWH is sovereign, the people must ultimately be guilty of polluting the temple. Consequently, the time for atonement is past as the judgment will now take place. When read in the aftermath of the Shoah or Holocaust, such a theological conceptualization is questionable insofar as it becomes a means to blame the victims for their own suffering. Nevertheless, such a strategy is an example of theodicy designed to defend the presence, integrity, and righteousness of YHWH by assigning blame to the victims instead.

YHWH's speech to Ezekiel continues in Ezekiel 4:1-8 with an instruction that the prophet engage in a symbolic action that will convey YHWH's intentions to lay siege to Jerusalem (Stacey, 180–86). This segment of the speech begins with an address form, "and you, Ben-Adam" (see also Ezek 4:9; 5:1 below), and instructs the prophet to set up a model of Jerusalem under siege. The model is constructed from a brick inscribed with some representation of Jerusalem, siege towers, siege mounds, battering rams, and an iron plate to represent the siege. The inscription on the brick is not clear; it could be the name Jerusalem written out or a portrayal of the walled city. The siege equipment would presumably be small objects and dirt piled up. The iron plate would be a common flat cooking griddle. Altogether the model is to be a sign (Heb., *'ot*) to represent YHWH's intentions concerning Jerusalem. Key to the symbolic act is the instruction that Ezekiel will lie on his right side for 390 days to represent the judgment against Israel and on his left side for forty days to represent the judgment against Judah. The significance of these numbers is often debated without success. It is noteworthy, however, that Ezekiel's own birth date coincides with the inauguration of Josiah's reform in the eighteenth year of his reign, i.e., 622 BCE (see 2 Kings 22:3; 2 Chr 34:8). This date marks Josiah's attempts to purify the temple, which provides the means for the nation to atone for its sins before YHWH. Josiah's program was designed to reunite the former northern kingdom of Israel with the southern kingdom of Judah under Davidic rule and the auspices of the Jerusalem Temple (cf. Ezek 37:15-28). Josiah's reform would then have marked an attempt to atone for the sins of Israel from its foundation under Saul until Josiah's reform, i.e., 1012–622 BCE, for a total of 390 years. The additional forty years would have constituted an attempt to account for Judah alone from 622 BCE until 582 BCE, some ten years beyond the date of Ezekiel's inaugural vision. Insofar as Josiah's reform had failed and Ezekiel anticipated the destruction of Jerusalem, the symbolic action would have accounted for both Israel as a whole and Judah alone. The use of the bared arm would then have symbolized YHWH's arm stretched out against Jerusalem, a metaphor of judgment commonly applied in the book of Isaiah (see Isa 5:25; 9:11; 9:17; 9:20; 10:4; cf. Exod 7:19; 8:1; 8:12; 14:26; 18:8-13).

YHWH's speech to Ezekiel continues in Ezekiel 4:9-17, again introduced by "and you" (cf. Ezek 4:1; 5:1), with instructions to engage in a symbolic action concerning the eating of bread and the drinking of water while Ezekiel lies on his side before his model of besieged Jerusalem (Stacey, 186–89). The initial instruction is that Ezekiel will make bread from a mixture of grains. Some maintain that the mixture of grains signifies impurity, but the laws pertaining to the mixture of seeds are designed to ensure the integrity of the crop (cf. Lev 19:19; Deut 22:9); nothing prevents these grains from being eaten together. Rather the issue is the shortage of food under siege (cf. 2 Kings 6:24-30) so that people make food from whatever they might find. A key point here is that Ezekiel's ration of bread is limited to twenty shekels, about 225 grams or ten ounces, and his ration of water is limited to a sixth of a hin, about six-tenths of a liter or two-thirds of a quart. These are siege or starvation rations. The issue of purity comes up when YHWH commands Ezekiel to cook his barley bread on a fire made with human excrement to symbolize the lack of fuel as well as the lack of food in the besieged city. Ezekiel protests to YHWH, citing his priestly status and the fact that he had never been defiled from his youth. YHWH relents and allows him to use cattle dung instead. This segment of the speech concludes with YHWH's statement summing up the exercise as one symbolizing YHWH's intentions to break the staff of bread and water in Jerusalem (cf. Isa 3:1) to depict the suffering of the people under siege.

YHWH's speech to Ezekiel continues in Ezekiel 5:1-17 with a prophetic oracle of judgment against Jerusalem that condemns the city to punishment and exile as a result of YHWH's charges that the people have rebelled against YHWH's laws and expectations and thereby defiled the holy temple in Jerusalem. This segment again begins with the address form "and you, O Ben-Adam," directed to Ezekiel, and it constitutes the culmination of YHWH's second speech in Ezekiel 3:24–5:17.

YHWH's oracle of judgment against Jerusalem appears in the context of instructions to Ezekiel to perform another symbolic action to illustrate YHWH's intentions to destroy Jerusalem and to exile the surviving population. The instructions appear in Ezekiel 5:1-4, in which YHWH commands Ezekiel to shave his head and beard, and divide the hair into three portions (Stacey, 189–92). At the conclusion of the siege of Jerusalem, Ezekiel is to burn one third of the hair in the city, chop up another third around the city, and scatter the last third to the wind while unsheathing a sword to pursue the scattered remnants of hair. Finally, he is to gather the last remnants of hair, tie them up in his clothing, and burn them in the fire to symbolize the fire that will pursue all Israel. Some have argued that the import of Ezekiel's act is to signify the loss of his status as a priest insofar as baldness is a sign of mourning and priests are forbidden to mourn. Such an explanation is not satisfactory. Leviticus 21:1-6 forbids priests to defile themselves by coming into contact with the dead, but the passage does permit them to mourn for blood relatives, i.e., parents, siblings, and offspring. The passage further specifies that priests may not shave their heads and gash their bodies for mourning in the Canaanite fashion, but there is no indication that Ezekiel is to gash himself here. Indeed, the shaving of the head does not appear to be a mourning exercise in this instance. Rather, the often noted intertextual relationship between this passage and Isaiah's depiction of Judean prisoners of war in Isaiah 7:20 appears to present a better explanation for Ezekiel's symbolic action. Isaiah 7:20 depicts Judean captives with shaved heads, genital areas, and beards as they are about to be led away into captivity by the Assyrians. Indeed, Sennacherib's famous palace relief depicting his siege of Lachish in 701 BCE shows impaled Judean prisoners, some of whom have had their heads and bodies shaved prior to execution. Ezekiel's shaved head and body appear to symbolize the fate of the people of Jerusalem who are about to die in the siege of the city and be exiled to all the corners of the earth in the aftermath of the siege and the destruction of the city.

YHWH's oracle concerning judgment against Jerusalem then appears in Ezekiel 5:5-17 in the form of an expanded prophetic judgment oracle, which typically includes a section devoted to the grounds for judgment followed by another segment, generally introduced by the Hebrew term *laken*, "therefore," that announces the punishment against the judged party. The present oracle employs several versions of the prophetic judgment oracle and its constitutive elements to make its point.

The first segment of the oracle appears in Ezekiel 5:5-6. These verses present a first statement of the grounds for judgment. The segment is introduced by the messenger formula *koh 'amar 'adonay yhwh*, "thus says my lord, YHWH," which functions as a means to designate an oracle spoken by a prophet as a direct quote of a message from YHWH. YHWH states how Jerusalem was placed in the center of the nations, apparently articulating the view that Jerusalem and the temple constitute the holy center of all creation. YHWH initially states the grounds for judgment by asserting that Jerusalem had rebelled against YHWH's laws and acted more corruptly than the nations around her. No details are given at this point, so the present charge functions as the general statement for the more detailed charges to follow.

The second segment appears in vv. 7-9. This segment begins with the term *laken*, "therefore," followed once again by the messenger formula *koh 'amar 'adonay yhwh*, "thus says my lord, YHWH." This combination of terms both links the present segment to the preceding verses and reiterates the claim that this is a direct quotation of YHWH. The conjunction with vv. 5-6 ensures that the present segment is viewed as both a continuation and development from the preceding material. It is a self-contained example of the prophetic judgment speech. The grounds for punishment are stated in v. 7 in terms that largely repeat the earlier charge, viz., Jerusalem has acted more corruptly than the nations around her. But the oracle develops the point further by stating YHWH's announcement of punishment in vv. 8-9. The announcement of punishment is introduced by *laken*, "therefore," to ensure that the punishment is viewed as a consequence of the stated charges. The judgment is expressed in general terms, however; YHWH simply employs the challenge formula "behold, I am against you," (Hals, 359) and then follows with a promise to execute judgment such as has never been seen before among the nations.

The third segment of the oracle appears in v. 10 in which YHWH develops the preceding announcement of judgment. The segment begins with *laken*, "therefore," again to indicate continuity and development of the preceding material. This time, the announcement of punishment is specified with the claim that parents will eat their children, an act that appears elsewhere in the Hebrew Bible when two Samarian women make a pact to eat their own children when their city is placed under siege (2 Kings 6:24-30). Such an act speaks to the desperate conditions of a city under siege that has run out of food, forcing its inhabitants to engage in despicable behavior simply to survive. YHWH reiterates the promise to bring judgment and adds that the survivors of the siege will be scattered in exile throughout the world.

The final and culminating segment of the oracle appears in Ezekiel 5:11-17, which lays out YHWH's plans to punish Jerusalem in excruciating detail and explains the punishment in relation to Ezekiel's symbolic action outlined in vv. 1-4. Again, the segment begins with *laken*, "therefore," to indicate continuity and development of the preceding material. The oracle itself begins with a combined oath formula *hay-'ani . . . 'im-lo'*, "by my life . . . if [I] do not," combined with the oracular formula *ne'um 'adonay yhwh* "oracle of my lord, YHWH," i.e., "by my life, oracle of my lord, YHWH, if [I] do not . . . ." The combined formulae essentially state, "May I die if I do not act against you." The oracle then proceeds with a basic statement of the charge that the people of Jerusalem defiled YHWH's temple with their abominable actions. The statement does not specify what those actions might be, but it presupposes that the temple is the holy center of creation. Holiness includes both ritual and moral dimensions and so YHWH's charges indicate the contention that sanctuary has been profaned because the people have corrupted it by failing to maintain their own ritual and moral sanctity. YHWH then embarks on a lengthy tirade concerning the consequences for such corruption. YHWH begins by repeating imagery of the initial symbolic action in vv. 1-4, i.e., YHWH will shear the people like sheep led to slaughter and show no pity or compassion in doing so. Taking up the motif of the three-thirds of Ezekiel's sheared hair, YHWH states that one-third of the people will die in the city due to disease and famine, one-third will die by the sword as the city is attacked, and one-third will be scattered, i.e., go into exile, as the sword pursues them. YHWH's anger against the people will constitute a revelatory act, i.e., "they will know that I YHWH have spoken." This formula is an example of the divine self-disclosure formula, which Ezekiel employs extensively to indicate that historical actions, particularly disasters, are to be viewed as deliberate actions undertaken by YHWH so that humans may recognize YHWH as the sovereign G-d of all creation. The point is reiterated when YHWH states that the people will become a mockery among the nations who will in turn recognize YHWH as the sovereign G-d of all creation. The point is made a third time when YHWH states that the people will suffer arrows of famine, wild beasts, disease, bloodshed, etc., all afflictions suffered by a city under siege so that the people will understand that YHWH has spoken. Although many interpreters maintain that YHWH is a vengeful G-d in the Hebrew Bible, such portrayals only account for one side of YHWH. Ezekiel and indeed the Hebrew Bible at large acknowledge that evil as well as good must come from YHWH as the sovereign deity of all creation. By the same token, Ezekiel's vision of restoration in Ezekiel 40–48 points to the merciful side of YHWH. Although the New Testament especially portrays the loving side of G-d through Christ, readers must recall that the revelation of Christ in the New Testament comes in relation to the destruction of the Second Temple by the Romans in 70 CE understood as an act of divine punishment. Rabbinic Judaism takes a similar view; i.e., both judgment and mercy come from G-d, the divine sovereign of all creation.

The Third Oracular Account of Ezekiel's Inaugural Vision: Commission concerning the Mountains of Israel (6:1-14)

Ezekiel 6:1-14 constitutes the third oracular account of the introduction to the book of Ezekiel with its presentation of Ezekiel's oracles against the highlands of Israel (Sweeney 2005d, 129–34; Hals, 37–41). The unit begins with the introductory prophetic word transmission formula in Ezekiel 6:1 "and the word of YHWH was unto me, saying . . . ," which introduces YHWH's instruction speech to the prophet in vv. 2-14 concerning the oracles which he is to speak against the highlands of Israel. The next occurrence of the prophetic word formula appears in Ezekiel 7:1, which introduces the fourth oracular account of the introduction. YHWH's instruction speech begins with YHWH's introductory instruction to speak in vv. 2-3aα, "O, Ben-Adam, set your face to the hills of Israel and prophesy unto them, and you shall say . . . ." The oracular speech that Ezekiel is to speak on YHWH's behalf then follows in vv. 3aβ-14. The oracular speech proper begins with an introductory address in v. 3aβ to the hills to hear the word of YHWH, "O hills of Israel, hear the word of my lord YHWH." Two oracular speeches, each introduced by the messenger formula "thus says my lord YHWH," follow in vv. 3b-10 and 11-14. The first in vv. 3b-10 addresses the mountains of Israel and announces YHWH's punishment against them. The second in vv. 11-14 initially addresses the prophet who is to react with alarm at the announcement of judgment against the mountains of Israel. Both oracles employ the YHWH recognition formula (Hals, 362) to indicate that the scenarios of judgment outlined in each will demonstrate YHWH's power and presence.

The initial version of the prophetic word formula in v. 1 includes no embellishments and simply functions as an introduction to this subunit in keeping with the overall organizational principles of the book of Ezekiel.

YHWH's initial address to the prophet in vv. 2-3aα addresses Ezekiel once again as Ben-Adam, "son of Adam," in keeping with Ezekiel's priestly identity and the role of the Zadokite priesthood as both descendants of Adam and the representatives of humanity before YHWH in the Jerusalem Temple. The command to "set your face unto the hills of Israel" employs a common element of expressive action in the book of Ezekiel (see Hals, 354) that aids in underscoring the oracle to be delivered. The practice of setting one's face against an addressee apparently derives from the prophet's practice of facing the parties to whom he delivers an oracle. The address to the highlands of Israel follows directly from the condemnation of Jerusalem in Ezekiel 5. Insofar as Jerusalem is the site of the temple of Israel, it stands as the holy center of all Israel. If the temple is defiled as charged in Ezekiel 5, then the entire land of Israel—and indeed creation as a whole—suffers the consequences as well. It is striking that Ezekiel addresses the mountains rather than the people of Israel. Priestly thought presumes that human action affects the status of the land or creation on which they dwell; thus, if human action is considered as contrary to the will of YHWH, the land becomes profane or defiled, having lost its sacred character through human misconduct.

YHWH instructs Ezekiel word for word in vv. 3aβ-14 about what he is to say to the highlands of Israel in keeping with the practice of sending messengers or ambassadors in the ancient Near Eastern world. The initial address to the highlands names the addressee and follows with a basic announcement formula to hear the word of YHWH in keeping with the messenger's role to deliver the message word for word.

The first oracle in vv. 3b-10 begins with a typical example of the prophetic messenger formula that signals Ezekiel's role as messenger of YHWH and the following oracle as a direct quote of YHWH's own statements to be conveyed to the mountains, hills, streams, and valleys of Israel. All creation in Israel has been affected and therefore YHWH addresses all the natural features of the land.

The first segment of this oracle begins with the announcement in v. 3bβ, "Behold, I am bringing the sword against you," and it concludes with the recognition formula in v. 7, "And you shall know that I am YHWH." This segment focuses especially on YHWH's/Ezekiel's charges that the cultic practices of the people defy YHWH's will. Charges of idolatry are common in the book of Ezekiel, although readers should bear in mind that those charged never have the chance to speak for themselves in the book. Were the people actually worshipping other gods, or is this simply Ezekiel's view of the matter given his interest in explaining why the Babylonian empire has been able to subdue Israel and exile portions of its population despite YHWH's pledges to defend the people and turn them into a great nation? Various cultic installations are included in Ezekiel's address. The shrines or high places refer to cultic sites around the land. Temples are generally placed on the tops of hills, both to symbolize the heavenly domain of the deities to whom they are dedicated and to serve practically as a place where grain offered by the people might be processed. Winnowing grains requires wind to separate the grain from the chaff, and hilltops provide the best locations to find such wind when processing the grain offered at the sanctuaries. The altars are devoted to the presentation of burnt offerings from the herd and flock as well as agricultural produce, and the incense stands are employed for the offering of incense as part of the worship service. The announcement of punishment against the high places clearly employs the imagery of defilement. The scattering of dead bodies around the shrine represents the deaths of those associated with them, and it symbolizes the shrine's defilement insofar as corpses and the bones of dead bodies are a polluting element that compromises the holiness of any location or person. Ezekiel constantly employs gutter language to describe what he considers to be illegitimate gods, i.e., the term, *gillulim*, often translated as "fetishes" or the like, actually refers to dung. Just as the temple serves as the sacred center of Israel, so the shrines serve as the sacred centers of the towns and settlements in which they are located; once the shrines are destroyed, the towns and settlements themselves are laid waste. Such imagery of destruction appears in the blessings and curses that conclude major legal portions of the Torah in Leviticus 26 and Deuteronomy 28–30. Ancient Near Eastern treaty texts that stipulated the obligations of nations and their kings who entered into treaty relationships with each other typically concluded with blessings and curses that would come upon the parties to the treaty in keeping with their observance of the treaty's terms (Barré, 1992). Pentateuchal law likewise employs blessings and curses that will apply to the people depending on their observance of YHWH's expectations. Ezekiel's announcements of punishment apparently derive from such practice, apparently presupposing that the people have violated YHWH's will and will now suffer the consequences for having done so. The concluding recognition formula "and you shall know that I am YHWH" employs the common formula in Ezekiel for designating such scenarios as revelatory acts that assert YHWH's role as sovereign over Israel and all creation (Zimmerli 1982, 29–98).

The second segment of the oracle appears in vv. 7-10, which shifts from the general condemnation of the cultic practices and installations of the towns and settlements to take up the fate of the remnant of the people who will survive the punishment to be scattered or exiled among the nations. Remnant theology is a characteristic of the book of Isaiah, which envisions the destruction of some ninety percent of the population of Israel before YHWH's judgment is complete (see Isa 6:12-13). Ezekiel is apparently in dialogue with Isaiah insofar as he articulates the fate of the remnant. Like Isaiah, Ezekiel envisions the remnant as the basis for restoration in the aftermath of exile. Unlike Isaiah, Ezekiel focuses on the emotions of both YHWH and the people in the context of a relationship that has been disrupted. Ezekiel speaks of YHWH's broken-heartedness in describing the punishment to be visited upon the people. When speaking of the people, Ezekiel continues to employ invective in v. 9, not only describing their cultic objects as "fetishes," or more literally as "dung," but employing the language of "whoring" to charge the people with abandoning YHWH. In the end, Ezekiel maintains that the people will be disgusted with themselves (Heb., *naqottu*) because of their evil and their abominations. The culmination of this segment appears in v. 10 in which YHWH/Ezekiel claims that the people will ultimately realize that YHWH had good reason to bring punishment upon them, indicating the lengths to which the book of Ezekiel will go to maintain that the people and not YHWH were ultimately responsible for their own suffering.

The second major oracle of the passage appears in vv. 11-14, again introduced by the messenger formula. The oracle begins with an instruction, formulated as a second-person singular command directed to Ezekiel to strike his hands together and exclaim *'ah* over the fate of the people. Although *'ah* is often translated "aha" or the like, it is best left untranslated as "ach!" and should be understood as an impromptu exclamation. Here, the command is an expressive action on the part of Ezekiel to signify his recognition that YHWH's plans to punish Israel are necessary. The oracle then reverts to descriptions of the punishment in v. 10, which recaps the symbolic action of Ezekiel 5:1-4 by stating the fates of three classes of Israelites who would correspond to the three portions of Ezekiel's hair described earlier: those far away will die of disease, those near will die by the sword, and those who escape will die of famine. The recognition formula in v. 13 then turns to a description of the dead corpses of the people strewn about their shrines with the remains of altars and idols about them. The references to green trees and leafy oaks symbolize the role of the fertility goddess, e.g., Asherah, in Canaanite religion, who is responsible for childbirth and represented by verdant trees that produce fruit and nuts. The final statement of the oracle draws once again on Isaiah's image of YHWH's hand stretched out against those who are to be punished (Isa 5:25; 9:11, 17, 20; 10:4), which in turn draws upon the image of Moses' and Aaron's hand or rod stretched out against Egypt in the exodus narratives (Exod 7:19; 8:1, 12; 9:22; 10:12, 21; 14:26; 17:11-13). Diblah is unknown. Most interpreters, beginning with the medieval Jewish exegete, Rashi, emend the text to read Riblah based on the similarity in appearance between the Hebrew letters *dalet* and *resh*. Riblah, situated on the northern border of Israel (Num 34:11), is the location where Pharaoh Necho of Egypt imprisoned King Jehoahaz ben Josiah of Judah after removing him from the throne (2 Kings 23:33) and where Nebuchadnezzar camped during the siege of Jerusalem (2 Kings 25:6).

The Fourth Oracular Account of Ezekiel's Commission concerning Judgment against Israel on the Day of YHWH (7:1-27)

Ezekiel 7:1-27 constitutes the fourth subunit of the account of Ezekiel's inaugural vision with an oracular account concerning Ezekiel's commission to announce judgment against Israel on the Day of YHWH (Sweeney 2005d, 129–34; Hals, 41–45). Ezekiel 7:1 begins with an example of the YHWH word transmission formula "and the word of YHWH came to me, saying . . . ," which introduces the entire subunit. The chronological formula in Ezekiel 8:1 marks the beginning of the next major unit of the book of Ezekiel in Ezekiel 8–11, leaving the recognition formula in Ezekiel 7:27 as the conclusion of the present text. Following the introductory YHWH word transition formula, Ezekiel 7:2aα employs the formula "and you, O Ben-Adam" to formulate Ezekiel 7:2aβ-27 as an address by YHWH to the prophet in which YHWH instructs Ezekiel to announce judgment against the land of Israel. Two oracular units then appear in Ezekiel 7:21-27, each introduced by an example of the messenger formula "thus says my lord, YHWH." The first oracle in Ezekiel 7:2-4 provides a brief announcement of judgment concerning the anticipated "end" (Heb., *qets*) of Israel, and the second oracle in Ezekiel 7:5-27 provides an extended announcement of the same theme that associates the end of Israel with the Day of YHWH tradition.

The Day of YHWH tradition is a well-known motif in the prophetic literature of the Hebrew Bible (Cathcart). Interpreters maintain that the tradition originally functioned in relation to the temple liturgies of the fall New Year festival cycle, including Rosh ha-Shanah, Yom Kippur, and Sukkot, as a means to express YHWH's support for the nation of Israel or Judah and the Davidic monarchy. The fall festivals celebrate the conclusion of the agricultural year and the final ingathering of the fall fruit and olive harvest immediately prior to the onset of the rains. Insofar as YHWH brings fertility and rain to the land, the fall festivals also celebrate YHWH's role as sovereign deity over all creation and humanity centered in Jerusalem as the holy center of creation. Thus the fall festivals of Rosh ha-Shanah, Yom Kippur, and Sukkot are the time when YHWH judges the world and determines what the coming year will bring for all creation, humanity, and the land and people of Israel/Judah. But whereas the Day of YHWH tradition was conceived as a day to recognize YHWH's kingship and promise to secure the nation and the ruling house of David, the prophets of the Hebrew Bible turn the tradition into an element of prophetic critique, arguing that the Day of YHWH is a day in which YHWH will pass judgment against those who act against YHWH's will. Thus Amos 5:18-20 portrays the Day of YHWH as a day of darkness and judgment against the northern kingdom of Israel in which the nation will be punished for the various violations of social justice articulated throughout the book. Zephaniah 1:2-18 employs the threat of judgment against those who adhere to foreign gods as a means to persuade its Jerusalemite and Judean audience to adhere to YHWH by means of King Josiah's program of religious reform and national restoration. The book of Isaiah employs the motif on a number of occasions to portray

YHWH's judgment against all the arrogant of the world, including both Israel and the nations, in Isaiah 2:5-21, against Babylon in Isaiah 13:1-22, and against the nations at large, particularly Edom, in Isaiah 34:1-17. Obadiah likewise employs the motif to condemn Edom, and Joel employs it to condemn the nations that threaten Jerusalem. Jeremiah 46 and Ezekiel 30 portray it as a day of YHWH's judgment against Egypt, and Zechariah 14 portrays it as a day of YHWH's judgment against the nations gathered at Jerusalem.

In the present case, Ezekiel 7 employs the motif as a day of judgment against Israel due to the nation's failure to observe YHWH's will. Insofar as Ezekiel charges that Jerusalem and the temple are corrupted (Ezek 5:5-17), the entire land of Israel is now likewise corrupted because the Jerusalem Temple stood as the holy center of Israel and creation at large. By this means, Ezekiel explains the disaster that overtakes Israel, Judah, and Jerusalem in the late monarchy period; i.e., if Israel, Judah, and Jerusalem suffer invasion in the eighth–sixth centuries BCE, then the people must have failed to observe YHWH's will. Such a strategy is an attempt to defend the righteousness, integrity, and presence of G-d against charges that G-d had failed to uphold the covenant. Such attempts to charge the victims of oppression with responsibility for their own suffering have been recognized as increasingly hollow in the aftermath of the modern experience of the Shoah or Holocaust.

The first oracular instruction in Ezekiel 7:2-4 lays out the basic parameters of YHWH's announcement of judgment against Israel and thereby serves as an introduction to the following oracle. The announcement that the "end" (Heb., *qets*) is coming against Israel appears to draw upon Amos's similar announcement concerning the northern kingdom of Israel (Amos 8:1-3). The announcement clearly charges Israel with abominations (Heb., *to'ebot*), which would have played a role in the earlier charges in Ezekiel 5:5-15 that the temple was corrupted. YHWH's lack of pity is a common motif throughout the book of Ezekiel. The concluding recognition formula indicates that the coming judgment against Israel is a revelation of divine presence and action within the world of creation.

The second oracular instruction in Ezekiel 7:5-27 then functions as the primary oracle concerning the condemnation of Israel. Like vv. 2-4, vv. 5-27 are introduced by the messenger formula in v. 5. Most scholars argue that vv. 5-9 and 10-27 constitute two discrete oracles insofar as each segment concludes with a version of the recognition formula. Many further argue that the present form of the text is very confused and thereby prefer the shorter form of the LXX text as a witness to the original Hebrew. A contributing factor is the observation that vv. 5-9 largely duplicate vv. 2-4, and they thereby indicate textual confusion. But such a view must be rejected on two major grounds. First, the shorter LXX text represents an attempt to make sense out of the longer, repetitive, and more difficult proto-Masoretic text in order to present a coherent and aesthetically pleasing text to an educated Greek-reading audience. The second is the recognition of the rhetorical strategy employed in the Hebrew text. The restatement of the terms and contents of vv. 2-4 is a rhetorical technique by which YHWH or the prophet introduces the issue in vv. 2-4 and then reiterates the charges in vv. 5-9 as a basis for a more extended condemnation in vv. 10-27. Verses 5-9 both repeat themes and language from vv. 2-4 and add to that language to make the point. For example, vv. 5-9 repeat the announcement that the end is coming, but these verses add language to characterize the end as a singular evil brought by YHWH. The "cycle" (Heb., *tsefirah*) has come against Israel (i.e., the cycle of punishment corresponding to the corruption with which Israel is charged), and the end is near (drawing on other expressions of the Day of YHWH, e.g., Isa 13:6). The oracle concludes with repeated statements concerning YHWH's anger, the lack of pity, the punishment for abominations, and the recognition formula as before. Such a rhetorical technique grabs the audience's attention with a truncated announcement in vv. 2-4. With the initial attention secured, vv. 5-9 elaborate and develop the announcement in vv. 5-9 prior to the full description in vv. 10-27.

Ezekiel 7:10-27 then constitutes the most developed form of the oracle. The oracle lacks a messenger formula, which indicates that it is designed to follow immediately upon vv. 5-9. The oracle begins with an announcement, "Behold the day! Behold it comes!" as a means to develop the earlier statements concerning the coming end into a full announcement of the Day of YHWH. Verses 10-11 then follow with general announcements of alarm about the coming day. The statements concerning the blossoming rod, blossoming arrogance, etc., draw upon the imagery of Numbers 17–18 in which YHWH's selection of the tribe of Levi and the line of Aaron to serve as the Levites and priesthood of Israel is signaled by their blossoming rods. The Levitical rod, such as those carried by Moses and Aaron throughout the exodus and wilderness narratives, is a symbol of priestly office and authority; indeed, Hosea 4:12 signals that the priestly rod was employed in relation to oracular inquiry. The use of this imagery here to signal the coming disaster indicates the collapse of priestly authority in the aftermath of the corruption of the temple and the land at large in Ezekiel's view.

Verses 12-13 then indicate consequences for the land and people at large, specifically the collapse of economic and moral life as a result of the corruption of the temple and priesthood. One may observe that Leviticus 19 characteristically combines ritual and moral requirements in a single text that calls for holy action on the part of the people; indeed, Leviticus 19:35-36 calls for just measures in economic life as an aspect of such holiness.

Verses 14-18 make it clear that the coming disaster is internal. These verses employ the imagery of a *shofar* or ram's horn blown to warn the inhabitants of an approaching invader, but the *shofar* warns of an internal threat to the life of the nation that functions more as disease or pestilence that kills just as surely as a sword. Verses 19-22 then make it clear that in the face of such threat, economic resources such as silver and gold are useless in any case. These verses may draw upon Isaiah 2:6-21, which announces that people will throw away their idols of silver and gold on the Day of YHWH's punishment against the arrogant. The imagery of uncleanness in v. 20 employs language referring to menstrual flow, which in the view of priesthood renders both women and men unclean due to the fact that menstrual blood (and emitted semen) is a fluid that is alive within the human body but dies upon emission, rendering one unable to approach the holy precincts of the temple. In order to purify oneself, one must bathe in the ritual bath (see Lev 15:19-30; 18:19; 20:18; cf. Lev 15:1-18).

Verses 23-24 then turn to the language of conquest. The initial statement to "forge the chain" refers to the chains or ropes employed by conquerors to lead away lines of captives. The portrayal of Israelite homes given to the evil ones of the nations is a clear image of foreign invasion and conquest.

Finally, vv. 25-27 conclude the oracle with images of the failure of leadership, including prophets, priests, elders, monarchs, and princes (cf. Isa 3:1-15). The whole concludes with the recognition formula again insisting that the realization of such punishment must be recognized as a revelation of YHWH as sovereign over creation and human life.

Presentation of Ezekiel's Oracles following His Vision of Jerusalem's Destruction/YHWH's Departure from Jerusalem

Ezekiel 8:1–19:14

The second major unit of the book of Ezekiel appears in Ezekiel 8:1–19:14, which presents Ezekiel's initial oracles following upon his vision of the destruction of Jerusalem and the exile of the people (Sweeney 2005d, 125–43). This unit is demarcated at the outset by the introductory chronological formula in Ezekiel 8:1, *wayehi bashanah hashishit bashishi bahamishah lahodesh*, "and it came to pass in the sixth year, in the sixth [month], on the fifth of the month . . . " Ezekiel 20:1 opens with a similar chronological formula *wayehi bashanah hashebi 'it bahamshi be 'asor lahodesh*, "and it came to pass in the seventh year, in the fifth [month], on the tenth of the month," to introduce the following unit of the book. Within Ezekiel 8:1–19:14, examples of the classical prophetic word formula *wayehi debar yhwh 'elay lemor*, "and the word of YHWH was unto me, saying," in Ezekiel 12:1, 12:8, 12:17, 12:21, 12:26, 13:1, 14:1, 14:12, 15:1, 16:1, 17:1, and 18:1 introduce the constitutive subunits of Ezekiel 8:1–19:14. Thus, the presentation of oracles in Ezekiel 8:1–19:14 includes thirteen subunits, each of which addresses an aspect of Jerusalem's coming destruction and exile, viz., the autobiographical vision account in Ezekiel 8:1–11:25, the oracle concerning the symbolic portrayal of exile as reversal of the exodus in Ezekiel 12:1-7, the oracular explanation of Ezekiel's symbolic action in Ezekiel 12:8-16, the oracle concerning Ezekiel's symbolic action in eating and drinking (exodus reversal) in Ezekiel 12:17-20, the oracle concerning the efficacy of the vision in Ezekiel 12:21-25, the oracle concerning the imminent fulfillment of the oracle in Ezekiel 12:26-28, the oracle concerning false prophecy in Ezekiel 13:1-23, the oracle concerning threats against false prophets and diviners in Ezekiel 14:1-11, the oracle concerning individual righteousness in Ezekiel 14:12-23, the oracle concerning the allegory of the useless vine in Ezekiel 15:1-8, the oracle concerning the allegory of Jerusalem as G-d's adulterous wife in Ezekiel 16:1-63, the oracle concerning the allegory of the eagles, the vine, and the cedar in Ezekiel 17:1-24, and the oracle concerning the responsibility of the individual and the demise of the monarchy in Ezekiel 18:1–19:14. The formal structure of the unit may be presented as follows:

II. Ezekiel's oracles concerning his vision of YHWH's departure from the Jerusalem Temple and its significance (Ezek 8:1–19:14)
   A. The autobiographical vision account (8:1–11:25)
   B. The oracle concerning the symbolic portrayal of exile as reversal of the exodus (12:1-7)
   C. The oracular explanation of Ezekiel's symbolic action (12:8-16)
   D. The oracle concerning Ezekiel's symbolic action in eating and drinking exodus reversal (12:17-20)
   E. The oracle concerning the efficacy of the vision (12:21-25)
   F. The oracle concerning the imminent fulfillment of the oracle (12:26-28)
   G. The oracle concerning false prophecy (13:1-23)
   H. The oracle concerning threats against false prophets and diviners: (14:1-11)
   I. The oracle concerning individual righteousness (14:12-23)
   J. The oracle concerning the allegory of the useless vine (15:1-8)
   K. The oracle concerning the allegory of Jerusalem as G-d's adulterous wife (16:1-63)
   L. The oracle concerning the allegory of the eagles, the vine, and the cedar (17:1-24)
   M. The oracle concerning the responsibility of the individual and the demise of the monarchy (18:1–19:14)

Autobiographical Vision Account: Sixth Year (592/591 BCE), Sixth Month, Fifth Day (8:1–11:25)

The first major subunit of Ezekiel 8–19 appears in Ezekiel 8:1–11:25, which presents Ezekiel's account of his vision of YHWH's departure from Jerusalem and efforts to destroy the city (Sweeney 2005c). The chronological formula in Ezekiel 8:1 demarcates the subunit. The prophetic word formula in Ezekiel 12:1 introduces the following subunit. The account of Ezekiel's vision appears in autobiographical form as the prophet describes his divine transport from his house in Tel Aviv to the temple mount of the city of Jerusalem where his angelic guide shows him YHWH's efforts to depart from the city and to bring about its destruction and purging. The subunit presumes throughout that Jerusalem has become corrupted by the removal of its Zadokite priesthood, which was responsible for maintaining the city's sacred character, and the actions of the remaining people who were unable to maintain the city's holiness. The corruption of the city therefore calls for its destruction and purging, which YHWH carries out prior to departing by means of the divine throne chariot depicted in Ezekiel 1:1–3:15.

The purging of the city appears to be constructed as an analogy to the scapegoat ritual employed on Yom Kippur, the Day of Atonement, which is intended to represent the symbolic purging of the nation from sin. According to Leviticus 16, the high priest purges the nation by engaging in a ritual that calls for the presentation of two goats at the temple. One is offered as a *hatta't*, "sin offering," which atones for the sins of the priest and the nation at large. The priest then lays his hands on the second goat, symbolically transferring the sins of the nation to the animal, which is then released into the wilderness where it will symbolically take the nation's sins to Azazel, a mythological demon figure in ancient Judean thought. By analogy, Ezekiel 8–11 portrays the destruction of the old men, the women, the young men and women, and the infants as an analogy to the sacrifice of the goat employed as the *hatta't*, "sin offering," in Leviticus 16. The adult men, who constitute the worshipping community of Jerusalem, are then exiled to Babylonia as an analogy for the goat who is released into the wilderness, where they will then undergo the process of atoning for the sins of the nation. In this manner, Ezekiel interprets the destruction of Jerusalem as an act sanctioned by YHWH and intended to purge the city of its corruption so that it might once again stand as the site of YHWH's holy temple at the center of all creation.

The formal structure of the subunit appears as follows:

Autobiographical Vision Account: Sixth Year (592/591 BCE), Sixth Month, Fifth Day (Ezek 8:1–11:25)
    (1) The initial date and setting of Ezekiel's oracles concerning the destruction of Jerusalem: Ezekiel's house, the elders, and the angelic guide (8:1-2)
    (2) New setting: north gate of Jerusalem: Ezekiel's vision of the offensive image (8:3-6)
    (3) New setting: north gate of the inner court: hole in the wall (8:7-13)
    (4) New setting: north gate of the temple: women wailing for Tammuz (8:14-15)
    (5) New setting: entrance to the temple main hall: Ezekiel's vision of the destruction of Jerusalem and the departure of YHWH (8:16–10:22)
        a. Transport to the temple entrance (8:16aα^{1-7})
        b. Vision report of the abomination in the temple and its consequences (8:16aα^{8}–10:22)

       1.) First episode: twenty-five men face east to worship the sun ($8:16a\alpha^8$-b)
       2.) Instruction report: rhetorical question employed to assert a provocation against YHWH (8:17-18)
       3.) Second episode: the destruction of Jerusalem and the departure of YHWH's divine presence (9:1–10:22)
          a.) Ezekiel's report of YHWH's summons to the officials who will kill the people of Jerusalem (9:1)
          b.) Ezekiel's portrayal of the killing of Jerusalem's inhabitants (9:2-11)
          c.) Ezekiel's description of the preparations to destroy the city with fire (10:1-8)
          d.) Ezekiel's description of YHWH's departure from the city of Jerusalem (10:9-22)
(6) New setting: east gate of the temple disputation oracle sequence concerning the purging of Jerusalem (11:1-23)
    a. Account of YHWH's first oracle: the premise to be refuted (11:1-4)
    b. Account of YHWH's second oracle: affirmation of punishment (11:5-12)
    c. Account of YHWH's third oracle: YHWH's promise of restoration following punishment and exile (11:13-21)
    d. Concluding segment: YHWH's departure from Jerusalem (11:22-23)
(7) New setting: Ezekiel's return to Babylonian exile (11:24-25)

The Initial Date and Setting of Ezekiel's Oracles concerning the Destruction of Jerusalem: Ezekiel's House, the Elders, and the Angelic Guide (8:1-2)

Ezekiel 8:1-2 defines the initial date and setting of Ezekiel's oracles concerning the destruction of Jerusalem. The sixth year refers to the sixth year of Jehoiachin's exile in 592 BCE, and the fifth day of the sixth month refers to the fifth day of Elul, some fourteen months after Ezekiel's inaugural vision. Ezekiel initially sits in his own home in Tel Aviv, where the elders of the nation have gathered to listen to his oracular statements. Some interpreters argue that this setting represents the origins of the synagogue insofar as it portrays a gathering of exiled Jews at the house of a Zadokite priest in exile (cf. Ezek 11:16). Although it is not entirely clear that study or worship takes place at this setting, the prophet functions as a means to illustrate and to communicate divine instruction concerning the significance of the destruction of Jerusalem.

The narrative employs the term "the hand of my L-rd YHWH" to indicate the means of Ezekiel's visionary experience and his supernatural transport from Tel Aviv in Babylonia to Jerusalem. The term typically depicts cases of prophetic visionary experience, such as that of Saul, Elijah, Isaiah, and others. It indicates that YHWH takes possession of the prophet to speak through him and to convey him to the site of the soon-to-be-destroyed Jerusalem Temple.

The use of an angelic guide is increasingly common in priestly portrayals of YHWH's interaction with human beings in the late monarchic, exilic, and early-Persian periods as the priesthood attempted to protect YHWH's sanctity by employing mediators for divine-human encounters rather than face-to-face communication. The angelic guide is described as a fiery presence, Hebrew, *kemar'eh-'esh*, "like the appearance of fire," although Septuagint texts read this phrase as *kemar'eh-'ish*, "like the appearance of a man," in an effort to give the angelic guide a more tangible form. Other descriptors include *kemar'eh-zohar*, "like the appearance of brilliance," employing the term Zohar, which functions as the title of the well-known work of medieval Kabbalah, and *kemar'eh-hahashmalah*, "like the appearance of amber." The Hebrew term *hashmal* is of uncertain meaning, although many believe that it designates a precious stone, such as amber. In modern Hebrew, the term means "electricity." Ezekiel's use of simile and imagery for fire, light, and precious stones represents attempts to avoid describing the presence of YHWH in tangible terms, particularly since such imagery conveys both presence and intangible form. Precious stones in particular refract light and convey shifting shades of color, which provide a suitable imagery to convey the presence of YHWH.

New Setting: North Gate of Jerusalem: Ezekiel's Vision of the Offensive Image (8:3-6)

Ezekiel 8:3-6 portrays Ezekiel's transport from his home in Tel Aviv to Jerusalem at the entrance of the Penimith Gate on the northern side of the city. The Penimith Gate would have been situated along the northern wall of Jerusalem, which would give access to the Temple Mount and the courtyards of the temple. The prophet notes that "the Glory of the G-d of Israel," the phrase employed in Ezekiel and priestly literature to depict the presence of YHWH, also appears at the Penimith Gate just as the divine presence appeared to him in his inaugural vision in Ezekiel 1:1–3:1-15.

YHWH instructs Ezekiel to look northward so that he might see "the offensive image" (Heb., *semel haqqin'ah*, "the image that provokes jealousy/rage") to the north of the Altar Gate. King Nebuchadnezzar of Babylon had already besieged Jerusalem in 598/597 BCE at the time of Jehoiakim's revolt. Upon the submission of the city to the Babylonians, Nebuchadnezzar deported the young King Jehoiachin ben Jehoiakim of Judah as well as many other prominent Judean figures, such as the priest Ezekiel ben Buzi. Normal Babylonian practice would call for the erection of a stele on the site of the subjugated city to announce Nebuchadnezzar's victory, presumably accomplished with the aid of his god, Marduk. Such a stele would have been placed in an area where it would have been seen by all to underscore Nebuchadnezzar's hold on the city and the consequences of defying his rule. The temple courtyard would have been an ideal location for the placement of such an image, because everyone in the city had to come to the temple to present their offerings at the altar. Insofar as the stele would have depicted Nebuchadnezzar and his gods, it would have constituted an offensive image to a priestly figure such as Ezekiel. The presence of such an idolatrous image in the temple courtyard would defile the courtyard and the sanctuary in Ezekiel's view, thereby driving YHWH's holy presence away from the temple.

New Setting: North Gate of the Inner Court: Hole in the Wall (8:7-13)
Ezekiel's angelic guide brings him to the entrance of the temple court in Ezekiel 8:7-13, shows him a hole in the wall, and then instructs him to dig through the wall. The purpose of such an instruction has confounded many interpreters, but it appears intended to emulate the means by which Nebuchadnezzar's soldiers entered the city of Jerusalem during the Babylonian siege of 598/597 BCE. It would be suicidal for an army to storm a thick defensive wall, such as the wall that would have defended Jerusalem's northern border. Instead, Babylonian military practice called for the use of sappers to dig under such walls in an effort to undermine and topple them, enabling Babylonian forces to enter the city with far fewer casualties. The northern border of Jerusalem, where the temple enclosure was located, was built on relatively level ground rather than on a rocky slope. The northern wall would therefore have presented an opportunity for sappers to dig under the northern wall and cause it to collapse. Such action would not have been possible along the western and eastern walls of the city that were built on the rocky slopes of the city of David.

Once inside, the angelic guide instructs Ezekiel to view the abominations allegedly practiced by the people inside the temple compound. Many interpreters assume that this passage depicts corrupt practice and iconography in the Jerusalem Temple, but the portrayal of the various detestable creeping things, beasts, and fetishes of the house of Israel on the walls of the temple hardly means that the temple had been remodeled to include such carvings on its inner cedar walls. As the accounts of the building of Solomon's temple indicate (1 Kings 6–7), the walls of the temple were carved and inlaid with gold images of Garden of Eden imagery, viz., pomegranates, lions, palm trees, cherubs, etc. The cost of replacing this imagery with something different and detestable would have been prohibitive and unlikely in the late seventh or early sixth century BCE. Rather, the imagery suggests that Ezekiel would have seen the same imagery as had been constructed for Solomon's temple, but his perception of the defilement of the temple would have prompted him to understand that imagery differently, viz., no longer is it the wonderful imagery of the Garden of Eden, but now it appears as the vile imagery of idolatry and corruption.

Much the same consideration would apply to the liturgical practice in the temple. The Zadokite priests, such as Ezekiel, had been deported, leaving persons who, in Ezekiel's estimation, were not fully sanctified to conduct the liturgies of the temple. The figure of Jaazniah ben Shaphan among the seventy elders of Israel would be a case in point. The seventy elders of Israel were a well-known and respected institution of the leadership of Israel from the time of the wilderness period on, and Jaazniah ben Shaphan was a scion of the famed ben Shaphan family that had served as King Josiah's advisors (n.b., the scribe Shaphan oversaw Josiah's Temple renovation in 2 Kings 22) and the prophet Jeremiah's supporters (Ahikam ben Shaphan delivered Jeremiah from charges of sedition in Jer 26, Elasah ben Shaphan conveyed Jeremiah's letters to Babylon in Jer 29, and Gemariah ben Shaphan reviewed Jeremiah's scroll in Jer 36). But neither the seventy elders of Israel nor Jaazniah ben Shaphan were Zadokite priests, so they were unqualified to present incense before YHWH in the temple. Consequently, Ezekiel judges their actions to be an abomination akin to the presentation of strange incense by Aaron's sons Nadav and Abihu in Leviticus 10 and Korah in Numbers 16. In Ezekiel's view, such defilement drives YHWH's holy presence away from a now corrupted temple.

New Setting: North Gate of the Temple: Women Wailing for Tammuz (8:14-15)

When Ezekiel's angelic guide brings him to the north gate of the temple itself, he sees women weeping for Tammuz. Tammuz is the Babylonian god of fertility who dies and goes to the underworld at the beginning of the dry summer season. According to the Babylon myth "The Descent of Ishtar to the Underworld," Ishtar descends to the underworld in the late summer to bring her dead consort back to life so that the fall rains might commence and restore fertility to the land. Weeping for Tammuz becomes part of the liturgy for this time of the year so that Ishtar might make the journey to restore the dead god to life. Mourning rituals during the late summer are also typical of Judaism, as indicated by the mourning practices associated with Tisha b'Av, "the Ninth of Av," in the late summer as the rainy season inaugurated by Sukkot approaches in the fall. We do not know that ancient Judean women actually started to worship Ishtar during the Babylonian period, but any late summer mourning rituals would have prompted the Babylonian-bound Ezekiel to draw such a conclusion.

New Setting: Entrance to the Temple Main Hall: Ezekiel's Vision of the Destruction of Jerusalem and the Departure of YHWH (8:16–10:22)

Ezekiel's movement to the inner court before the entrance to the temple itself initiates the portrayal of the destruction of the temple and the city of Jerusalem and YHWH's departure from the city in Ezekiel 8:16-10:22. Following the notice of Ezekiel's transport to the temple entrance in Ezekiel 8:16aα^{1-7}, Ezekiel 8:16aα^{8}–10:22 then turns to Ezekiel's vision report of the abominations that corrupted the temple in Ezekiel's view as well as the process by which the temple and city are destroyed as YHWH departs.

Transport to the Temple Entrance (8:16aα^{1-7}). Ezekiel's location in the inner court places him close to the altar that stands before the temple, and it enables him to see into the temple structure itself back to the holy of holies, where the Ark of the Covenant, representing YHWH's divine presence, would be situated.

Vision Report of the Abomination in the Temple and its Consequences (8:16aα^{8}–10:22). The vision proceeds in three components, viz., the first episode, which portrays twenty-five men facing east to worship the sun in Ezekiel 8:16aα^{8}-b; an instruction report in Ezekiel 8:17-18, which employs a rhetorical question to assert that the worship of the twenty-five men is a provocation against YHWH; and a second episode in Ezekiel 9:1–10:22, which portrays the destruction of Jerusalem and the departure of YHWH from the city.

First Episode: Twenty-Five Men Face East to Worship the Sun (8:16aα^{8}-b). Ezekiel observes twenty-five men facing to the east with their backs to the temple as they bow down to the rising sun. As in the preceding passages, Ezekiel understands this act to be an act of apostasy in which the men worship the sun. But again, the narrative is formulated in a visionary context that would portray men standing before the temple at sunrise to begin the temple's morning service at sunrise. Ezekiel views the men as apostate and portrays them accordingly, but we readers do not know what these men actually intended by their act. Was it an act of apostasy or was it preparation for a standard temple morning service that Ezekiel interprets as corrupt because of the infuriating image he had seen earlier in the temple courtyard and the removal of the Zadokite priesthood, which oversaw temple worship?

Instruction Report: Rhetorical Question Employed to Assert a Provocation against YHWH (8:17-18). Following upon Ezekiel's vision of the twenty-five men in the inner court of the temple, YHWH asks Ezekiel a rhetorical question designed to assert that their actions are an abomination that corrupts the temple's sanctity and provokes YHWH's anger. YHWH asks Ezekiel if he has seen these abominations. Ezekiel can only answer in the affirmative. YHWH's question therefore functions rhetorically as a claim that these actions are indeed abominations. The portrayal of the land as "lawless" (Heb., *hamas*, "violence") underscores the role that the temple plays in ensuring both the sanctity and the stability of the surrounding land at large, viz., if the temple's sanctity and purity remain uncompromised, the land enjoys stability. But if the temple's sanctity and purity are compromised, the land descends into chaotic violence. YHWH's statement employs the imagery of a branch thrust before YHWH's nose to portray the provocation that YHWH feels in the face of such abominations. Many interpreters have interpreted this image as a reference to an offensive act of bodily emission or sexual conduct, but such interpretations have largely come from the interpreters' overactive imaginations. A branch shoved in one's face is provocative enough in and of itself! YHWH's refusal to show mercy or compassion in the face of such provocation indicates YHWH's frustration with a population that purportedly has turned to foreign worship and corrupted the temple. It is disturbing in that it holds out no possibility of repentance on the part of the people, whether they actually committed the provocations or not. In Ezekiel's view, YHWH has made the decision to destroy the temple and the city of Jerusalem.

Second Episode: The Destruction of Jerusalem and the Departure of YHWH's Divine Presence (9:1–10:22). Ezekiel's portrayal of the destruction of the temple and the city prior to YHWH's departure proceeds in four major segments. First is the report of YHWH's summons to the officials who will carry out the killings of the people in Ezekiel 9:1. Second is Ezekiel's portrayal of the killing of the city's inhabitants in Ezekiel 9:2-11. Third is Ezekiel's description of the preparations to destroy the city with fire in Ezekiel 10:1-8. Fourth is Ezekiel's description of YHWH's departure from the city of Jerusalem in Ezekiel 10:9-22.

Ezekiel's Report of YHWH's Summons to the Officials Who Will Kill the People of Jerusalem (9:1). Ezekiel recounts YHWH's summons to those who will carry out the slaughter of the people in the city of Jerusalem. The Hebrew term *pequddot* is often translated as "officials," but properly indicates anyone designated for an official task. The use of the term here indicates YHWH's appointment of these figures to carry out the slaughter of the people of Jerusalem. Each carries a destructive weapon (Heb., *mashhit*) in his hand. YHWH's decision to kill the people of the city indicates an irreversible decision to purge the city as a result of the temple's corruption. Because the land and creation at large have been undermined in Ezekiel 8:17 as a result of the corruption of the holy center of creation, the people are no longer able to sustain themselves.

Ezekiel's Portrayal of the Killing of Jerusalem's Inhabitants (9:2-11). Ezekiel's portrayal of the killing of Jerusalem's inhabitants begins with a description of the six figures who will carry out the slaughter and of a seventh figure, dressed in white linen with a writing case on his waist, who will supervise them. The six men enter the scene from the upper gate at the north of the temple's courts, indicating that they come from the same direction as the Babylonian invaders of Jerusalem, who would have entered the city and temple compound from the north, the side of the city that is most susceptible to assault. The dress of the six men is not indicated, but their threatening nature is quite clear in that each carries a weapon (*mappats*). The seventh figure wears white linen, which is the characteristic dress of a priest serving at the altar of the temple, and the writing case he carries was necessary to record those killed or spared. The purpose of this imagery is to draw a direct analogy between the slaughter of Jerusalem's inhabitants and the role of animal offerings in maintaining the stability of the created order. Humans were allowed to slaughter animals as an outlet for their capacity for violence, but restrictions were placed on the slaughter of animals. Only certain types of animals could be slaughtered and their blood had to be treated properly as a means to control the violence that had been unleashed by the privilege of eating meat. Humans were not allowed to eat the blood of animals, as the blood contained life and was meant to be returned to the earth in a symbolic burial of the slain animal (Gen 9:1-6; Lev 11; Deut 14). But when the temple becomes corrupted and the land is consequently filled with violence (Ezek 8:17), the lives of the human beings who live in the land then come under threat as creation itself become unsustainable. Thus, the slaughter of the people is portrayed as an analogy to sacrifice, viz., if the animal offerings that played a role in maintaining the sanctity of the temple and the stability of creation were no longer possible, then human beings themselves are subject to sacrifice. Thus, the figure overseeing the slaughter is dressed like a priest who officiates at sacrificial offerings, and he carries a writing case to record those who are so slaughtered, just as the priests would record the offerings made on behalf of the people. The proximity to the bronze altar built by Solomon (1 Kings 8:64) underscores the analogy of the slaughter of the people to the offerings of animals during the course of the temple liturgy.

Ezekiel portrays YHWH's presence in motion as YHWH issues commands for the destruction of the people. YHWH emerges from atop the cherub built upon the Ark of the Covenant to the lintel of the temple, which means that YHWH has departed from the holy of holies where the ark resides to the door of the temple itself. YHWH's movement indicates intent to depart the temple altogether. YHWH commands the man dressed in white linen to pass through the city and mark the foreheads of those men who moan and groan over the abominations committed in it. The mark, Hebrew *taw*, is an X that later developed into the letter T. Early Church Fathers interpreted the mark as the sign of the cross (Lalibert and West, 29), but the mark is simply a means to designate those who will be spared in the slaughter. Interpreters have struggled to see in the description of the men to be spared some indication of wrongdoing in their moaning and groaning, but the intent of their moaning and groaning is unclear. Insofar as men constitute the worshippers in the temple of Jerusalem, perhaps their moaning and groaning is intended to depict their efforts at worship. In any case, the following portrayal of slaughter indicates that the men are to be spared. Instead, YHWH orders the slaughter of the old men, the young men and the young women, the women, and the children, but no one who bears the mark is to be killed. Insofar as those bearing the mark are men of the age of majority, the very men who constitute the worshipping community of the Jerusalem Temple, YHWH's commands indicate the responsibility that the men have for maintaining the sanctity of the temple and thus for the lives of those who depend upon them. The killing of course completes the defilement of the temple insofar as blood is a defiling agent that requires purification.

As the appointed figures go out to fulfill YHWH's command, Ezekiel is left alone to plead before YHWH, asking whether YHWH intends to destroy the entirety of Israel and Jerusalem. YHWH's answer that the iniquity of Judah and Israel is great provides a statement of rationale for the destruction, particularly YHWH's charge that the people believed that YHWH would never see what they had done. Indeed, this statement serves as an affirmation that YHWH sees all and punishes all iniquity without compassion. At the same time, Ezekiel's corporate view of human wrongdoing leaves no room for recognizing acts of righteousness among the population. All the while, the man dressed in white linen records the slaughter.

Ezekiel's Description of the Preparations to Destroy the City with Fire (10:1-8). Ezekiel's description of the preparations to destroy Jerusalem begins with the formulaic first-person statement *wa'er'eh wehinneh*, "and I looked, and behold," as he continues to adopt the stance of an observer who reports the event to his audience. The prophet's account initially returns to a focus on YHWH's divine presence, here portrayed in relation to the cherubs who bear the divine throne through the heavens. Readers have already been introduced incidentally to a cherub figure in Ezekiel 9:3, but here it becomes clear that the cherubs (Heb., *kerubim*) are identified with the living beings (Heb., *hayyot*) who bore the divine throne in the inaugural vision of Ezekiel 1:1–3:15. By shifting terminology in this manner, the book of Ezekiel employs a strategy of progressive revelation in its portrayal of YHWH's divine presence and the surrounding retinue. Ezekiel notes "the expanse" (Heb., *haraqi'a*) that appears above the heads of the cherubs. The Hebrew term *raqi'a* had previously been employed in Ezekiel 1:22 to portray the divine presence of YHWH, and it does so again in the present context. But the text further elaborates on the term by adding comparative references to two images. The first is "like a stone of sapphire" (Heb., *ke'eben sappir*), which aids in embellishing the imagery of the "firmament." In Genesis 1:6-8, the *raqi'a* or "firmament" functions as the foundations for the heavens, which would indicate an association with the blue appearance of the sky. Sapphire stones are likewise known especially for their blue appearance, sometimes mixed with red, but they are also known for the amorphous character of the color scheme within the stone that refracts light and suggests a reality beyond normal visual perception. Such a quality makes the sapphire ideally suited to function as an analogy for describing the amorphous presence of YHWH and of the heavens. The association with YHWH's divine presence is then confirmed by the following reference to the simile of "the throne" that appears over the heads of the cherubs. Insofar as the Ark of the Covenant serves as the throne of YHWH (see, e.g., 1 Sam 4:4; Isa 66:1), Ezekiel's description continues to identify YHWH's divine presence with the imagery of the Ark of the Covenant.

YHWH's command in Ezekiel 10:2 to the figure dressed in white linen initiates a sequence of action that will result in the destruction of the temple and the city of Jerusalem. The first command, "Enter between the wheelwork under the cherubs, and fill your hands with coals of fire from between the cherubs, and scatter them over the city," begins the sequence of destruction. As Ezekiel looks on, he describes the movement of YHWH's divine presence. Initially situated to the south of the temple, YHWH's presence moves to the lintel (Heb., *miftan*) of the temple as the figure dressed in white linen goes in between the cherubs to fulfill the command. The figure's approach to the cherubs recalls the movement of the high priest as he would approach the Ark of the Covenant in the holy of holies of the temple at Yom Kippur, but YHWH's movement to the lintel of the temple signals that the temple is about to be destroyed, not purged as one would expect at Yom Kippur. As a result of YHWH's movement, the interior of the temple fills with smoke, much as it would fill with smoke from the temple incense burners to represent the divine presence during times of worship. The sound of the cherubs' wings, here compared to the divine voice of El Shaddai, would be represented by the sounds of the air movement through the upper windows of the temple structure as the hot air of the incense smoke would rise and the cooler air entering through the upper windows would sink to take its place. The effect would represent a whirlwind as the smoke circulated through the interior of the temple structure.

Ezekiel's account of YHWH's second command in Ezekiel 10:6 to the figure clothed in white linen both reiterates and demonstrates the fulfillment of the first command. The role of the cherub in handing the figure a coal from the fire recalls the role of the seraph who touched a hot coal to Isaiah's mouth in Isaiah 6:6-7 to purify Isaiah so that he might serve as a prophet of YHWH. But in the present context, the role of the fire will be to purge the temple and the city of Jerusalem by destroying them altogether. The reference to the cherub's hand recalls Ezekiel's earlier description of the living beings in Ezekiel 1:8.

Ezekiel's Description of YHWH's Departure from the City of Jerusalem (10:9-22). Ezekiel's description of YHWH's departure from Jerusalem begins once again with the formulaic first-person introduction *wa'er'eh wehinneh*, "and I looked, and behold," in Ezekiel 10:9. At this point, Ezekiel focuses on the four *'opannim*, the four "wheels," which are associated with each of the four cherubs. The focus on the wheels thereby signals concern with the movement of YHWH's divine presence as it prepares to depart from the site of the temple. The derivation of the term *'opan*, "wheel," is uncertain, although some have speculated that it is associated with the root *pnh*, "to turn," and the noun *panim*, "face." The noun is believed to be derived from the verb root *pnh*, signifying that a face is turned toward a particular direction. In this case, the association with face would also denote a sense of the presence of the four cherubs/living creatures, each of which has four faces and moves simultaneously in the four directions of each of its faces. Insofar as the cherubs/living creatures have bodies of burnished bronze, the four "wheels" gleam like a stone of beryl (Heb., *'eben tarshish*, lit., "a stone of Tarshish"). The term Tarshish may well refer to a city or location in the western Mediterranean, but it also refers to the precious stone beryl which frequently appears with a yellow or green hue, thereby making it a suitable simile for the bronze overlaid features of the cherubs and the divine throne chariot. Again, the ability to refract light enables the stone to represent a simultaneously tangible and intangible reality that serves as an appropriate representation of the intangible presence of the divine.

The description turns to the structure of the "wheels" in vv. 10-14. The portrayal of the wheels as each representing "a wheel within a wheel" (Heb., *ha'opan betok ha'opan*) has prompted considerable confusion among interpreters. Some argue that the image represents a hubbed wheel; others imagine a structure by which one wheel is set within another, which of course is practically impossible. In fact, the image is deliberately intended to be impossible insofar as it represents divine movement beyond that which is possible for earthly creatures. The wheel within a wheel is meant to represent a wheel that may move in any or all directions at once, much as the four cherubs move in the directions of all of their four faces at once without veering away. The portrayals of the backs, hands, wings, and wheels all covered with eyes likewise has presented interpreters with difficulties, many of whom imagine the eye of the divine presence looking throughout the world. Such a suggestion is not entirely wrong, but the dynamics by which such eyes are represented are not well understood. Insofar as the cherubs and other features of the divine throne are overlaid with burnished bronze, they offer a reflective presence. When placed before the ten menorahs or candelabras of the temple, each with seven lamps, such a structure would reflect the light of seventy lamps, thereby giving the impression of fiery divine eyes looking out from the midst of the apparition. Verse 14 concludes the subunit with a slightly modified reiteration of the four faces of the cherubs/living creatures from Ezekiel's inaugural vision, viz., the face of the cherub (in place of a bull), the face of a human, the face of a lion, and the face of an eagle, each representing the divine qualities of strength, intelligence, royalty, and mobility (see Ezek 1:10).

Verses 15-17 portray the ascent of the cherubs prior to YHWH's departure from the city. The text carefully distinguishes the cherubs from the presence of YHWH so as not to confuse the two and thereby prompt readers to identify the cherubs with YHWH per se. The clear association between the *'opannim*, "wheels," and the cherubs is maintained throughout to convey the unified movement of the apparition.

The departure of the divine presence then follows in vv. 18-22. YHWH's departure from the lintel of the temple signifies YHWH's departure from the temple altogether, leaving it subject to destruction as portrayed throughout Ezekiel 10. The movement to the eastern gate of the temple reverses the movement of YHWH's entrance into the temple each morning, insofar as the morning service held at sunrise would see the illumination of the interior of the temple, signifying YHWH's presence and the daily repetition of the act of creation, beginning with light, each morning (cf. Levenson 1988, 53–127). The concluding statements of the passage reiterate the identification of the cherubs with the living creatures of Ezekiel's inaugural vision by the Chebar Canal as well as their movement in the direction of all four of their faces at once.

New Setting: East Gate of the Temple Disputation Oracle Sequence concerning the Purging of Jerusalem (11:1-23)

A new setting appears in Ezekiel 11:1-23 when a divine wind transports Ezekiel to the east gate of the Jerusalem Temple. The east gate is the main gate of the temple, which faces east toward the rising sun. It therefore serves as the main point of entry and departure for the temple, and thereby serves as the location at which YHWH announces the purging of the temple together with the departure of the divine presence. The passage takes the form of an account of a disputation oracle in which YHWH, speaking through Ezekiel, challenges the people's understanding that they are to be destroyed like sacrificial meat in a pot. The first segment in Ezekiel 11:1-4 presents YHWH's account to Ezekiel of the twenty-five men and their leaders who employ the analogy of a pot and meat to portray their understanding of their hopeless future. The second segment in Ezekiel 11:5-12 presents a second oracle by YHWH affirming the people's view that they will suffer judgment like meat in a pot. It develops the image by indicating the exile of the people and the execution of many on the border of Israel. The third segment appears in Ezekiel 11:13-21 in which YHWH refutes the viewpoint of the leaders by portraying the purging of the city as a prelude to its eventual restoration. The fourth segment appears in Ezekiel 11:22-23 in which the divine presence departs from the purged city.

Account of YHWH's First Oracle: The Premise to Be Refuted (11:1-4).
Ezekiel 11:1-4 presents the first stage in the account of YHWH's disputation oracle concerning the sacrificial role of the city of Jerusalem. The segment begins with the initial notice in Ezekiel 11:1 concerning Ezekiel's divine transport to the east gate of the temple and his report of the twenty-five men who were standing there. The east gate of the temple is the main entrance to the temple, which is open to view by the people who would be gathered for holy worship. The main gate of the temple faces east because this is the direction from which the rising sun might be seen each morning. Insofar as the morning sun would shine into the open east gate of the temple, the daily morning service would replicate the first act of creation in Genesis 1:3-5 by allowing light to illumine the interior of the temple each and every morning. The twenty-five men standing at the east gate have been noted before in Ezekiel 8:16, where they were charged with illicit worship of the sun, although it is likely that they were actually engaged in morning prayers at the temple. At this point, they are noted primarily for the presence of their leaders, Jaazniah ben Azzur and Pelatiah ben Benaiah. Ezekiel 8:16 does not name these men. Their designation as leaders of the people (Heb., *sarey ha'am*) indicates no priestly role. The Hebrew term *sar*, "captain, prince, officer," merely indicates a political or administrative role rather than any sort of sacred appointment as a priest in the temple.

YHWH's statement to Ezekiel in Ezekiel 11:2-4 instructs Ezekiel to prophesy against this group on the grounds that they plan iniquity and counsel evil in the city of Jerusalem (cf. Nah 1:9, 11). The basis for YHWH's charge is the statement these men make that there is no need to build houses as the city has become a pot and all of the inhabitants are meat in that pot. This statement takes up the prophet Jeremiah's advice to build houses and bear children despite the realities of exile as a means to prepare for a Jewish future beyond the downfall of Jerusalem and Judah (see Jer 29:5-7; cf. Jer 1:10; 12:14-17; 18:5-10; 24:6; 31:28, 40; 42:10; 45:4). The nihilistic viewpoint of these leaders is confirmed by their claims that Jerusalem is a pot and its inhabitants are meat. The nihilism of the image of cooking dead meat should be obvious in and of itself, but it is also noteworthy that it builds upon the imagery of offerings and sacrifice at the temple in which portions of sacrificial meat are cooked for sacred meals on the temple premises. In the view of these leaders, Jerusalem and its inhabitants have no chance; they will be sacrificed to and by YHWH, just as surely as the offerings brought to the temple. The segment concludes with YHWH's instructions to Ezekiel that he should prophesy concerning this viewpoint.

Account of YHWH's Second Oracle: Affirmation of Punishment (11:5-12).

Ezekiel 11:5-12 follows with the presentation of a second oracle from YHWH in which YHWH gives a first response to the statement made by the leaders of the people in v. 3. The initial reference to the spirit of YHWH that falls upon Ezekiel in v. 5 characterizes the oracle as the result of ecstatic possession of the prophet. The oracle per se is formulated as a disputation that takes up the statement made by the leaders and then begins to explicate its meaning. Although disputations typically attempt to refute the initial premise, the refutation will not appear until a third oracular report in Ezekiel 3:14-21. YHWH's response affirms the analogy comparing the city and its inhabitants with the pot and the meat, but it turns the leaders' statement against them by charging that they in fact are responsible for the piling of corpses in the city. Such a charge supports Jeremiah's contentions that Jerusalem should not revolt against Babylon in the first place (see Jer 27–29). YHWH's oracle then continues to develop the judgmental understanding of the pot and meat analogy by promising that the people will be taken out of the pot, i.e., exiled from the city. Afterwards they will be handed over to the invaders for judgment and execution by the sword at the border of Israel. This oracle then concludes in v. 12 with another instance of the YHWH revelation formula, which identifies this scenario of judgment as a revelatory act of YHWH, but it follows by charging the people and their leaders with disobeying YHWH's statutes and laws and behaving in the manner of the nations that surround Israel.

Account of YHWH's Third Oracle: YHWH's Promise of Restoration following Punishment and Exile (11:13-21). The account of YHWH's third oracle in Ezekiel 11:13-21 begins with a notice in v. 13 that Pelatiah ben Benaiah dropped dead. Such a notice typically appears as part of a prophetic confrontation narrative (e.g., Isa 26–37; Jer 27–28; Amos 7:10-17) in which the death signals the validity of the oracle of YHWH as spoken by the prophet in question. In the present instance, it signals the point at which YHWH's oracles will refute the viewpoint of the people and their leaders as presented in Ezekiel 11:3. Ezekiel's own exclamation that YHWH is wiping out the remnant of Israel underscores the point to be refuted, viz., that the people will be destroyed. Ezekiel's role is to serve as a foil for YHWH's counterargument as well as the conduit for the oracle.

The account of the oracle per se then follows in vv. 14-21. At the outset of the oracle, YHWH reformulates the viewpoint of the people by portraying them as having stated they should keep far from YHWH and reiterating that the land is given to them as a possession. Such a statement indicates their rejection of YHWH's second oracle as presented in Ezekiel 11:5-12, i.e., they will not be judged and will remain secure in the land. YHWH's response to this characterization reaffirms the scenario of punishment by stating that the people will indeed go into exile, but it adds a note that YHWH will serve as "a small sanctuary" (Heb., *miqdash me'at*) for the people while they are exiled in foreign lands. This statement has prompted considerable debate, viz., does the phrase refer to the diminished size or character of YHWH's presence among the nations, or does it refer to the relatively brief period of time that the people will be exiled? Indeed, Jewish exegesis takes it as a constituent reference to YHWH's continued support for the people even as they are in exile, and characterizes the *miqdash me'at* as a precursor to the later Hellenistic-rabbinic period institution of the synagogue as a house of study and worship for Jews living outside the environs of Jerusalem. Here, the *miqdash me'at* functions as a means to see to the restoration of Jews once the punishment is over as YHWH promises to gather the people from the countries where they have been exiled and to restore the land of Israel to them. In return, YHWH expects that the people return and cleanse the land from the various abominations of the past. YHWH further promises to remove the heart of stone from the people and to replace it with a heart of flesh so that they will observe YHWH's statutes and laws. The statement that "they will be my people and I will be their G-d" is a formulaic statement of covenant renewal (Rendtorff; cf. Ezek 14:11; 36:28; 37:23; Jer 7:23; 31:33; 32:38; Hos 2:23; Zech 8:8). The oracular account concludes with YHWH's vow to punish those whose hearts are still set on the abominations.

Concluding Segment: YHWH's Departure from Jerusalem (11:22-23).
The account of YHWH's disputation oracle concludes with the portrayal of YHWH's departure from Jerusalem in Ezekiel 11:22-23. The purging of the city announced by YHWH begins with the removal of YHWH's holy presence so that the final desecration may begin, thereby paving the way for the restoration. The movement of the divine presence to the hill east of the city retraces the route by which YHWH, symbolized by the rising of the sun (cf. Hab 3; Ps 104), enters the sanctuary each morning.

New Setting: Ezekiel's Return to Babylonian Exile (11:24-25)
Ezekiel 8–11 concludes with a notice of Ezekiel's return to his home in the exile community of Babylonia. His task is to inform the exiles of everything he had seen in the vision as recounted in Ezekiel 8–11. Insofar as the vision recounts what will take place, it functions as an account and interpretation of the coming destruction of Jerusalem in 587 BCE and the exile of the surviving inhabitants of Jerusalem and Judah.

Oracular Account: Symbolic Action concerning the Exile as Reversal of the Exodus (12:1-7)

Ezekiel 12:1-7 constitutes an oracular account of Ezekiel's compliance with YHWH's instructions to perform a symbolic action (Sweeney 2012). In this instance, YHWH instructs Ezekiel to perform a symbolic action that portrays the coming exile of the nation as a reversal of the exodus. The passage begins with an introductory prophetic word transmission formula in v. 1, "and the word of YHWH came to me," which introduces Ezekiel's account of YHWH's instructions in vv. 2-6. Ezekiel's account of his compliance with YHWH's instructions appears in v. 7. The following unit begins in Ezekiel 12:8 with another example of the prophetic word transmission formula.

The account of YHWH's instructions to the prophet begins in v. 2 with a statement of the premises that undergird the proposed symbolic action. YHWH addresses Ezekiel as "son of Adam" to underscore his identity as a priest and his role in representing humanity before YHWH in the Jerusalem Temple. YHWH then follows with accusations that Ezekiel lives among a rebellious people, who "have eyes to see, but they do not see, and [who] have ears to hear, but they do not hear, for they are a rebellious house." The basis for such charges are not specified, but the previous vision account in Ezekiel 8–11 makes it clear that YHWH charges the people with corrupting the temple with foreign worship, which in turn necessitates punishment as part of the overall scenario of purging the temple. This charge has clear intertextual connections with Jeremiah 5:21, "Hear this, O foolish people without sense, [who] have eyes, but they do not see, [who] have ears, but they do not hear," and Deuteronomy 29:3, "And YHWH has not given you a mind to know, eyes to see, and ears to hear until this day." Both passages presuppose the earlier account of Isaiah's commission as a prophet in Isaiah 6, in which his task was to make sure that the people did not see, hear, or understand YHWH's will lest they repent and avoid the punishment that YHWH intended for them. In this respect, Ezekiel builds on a tradition that views disaster as a result of both the rebelliousness of the people who do not see, hear, or understand the divine will and the will of YHWH per se, insofar as YHWH has ensured that the people will not see, hear, or understand in order to carry out the punishment of Jerusalem as part of a divinely ordained plan to reveal YHWH's presence and sovereignty over the world at large. Such a view raises moral questions concerning divine action, insofar as the teleological or goal-oriented approach to divine revelation and action entails an ontological moral problem in that generations of the people are deliberately consigned to punishment to serve the divine agenda. In Ezekiel's view, G-d thereby takes on an autocratic character as a deity whose will be done no matter what the cost to the people affected.

YHWH's instructions to Ezekiel in vv. 3-6 include commands to prepare for exile in vv. 3-4a and to go into exile in vv. 4b-6. The instructions to prepare for exile include instructions to carry baggage on the shoulder so that all the people will see and to break through the wall of the city and depart at night. Both of these instructions deliberately take up elements of the exodus narrative. Exodus 12:34 relates how the Israelites left Egypt with their kneading bowls on their shoulders so that they could hurriedly bake bread while on the march out of Egypt. Exodus 12:12 emphasizes that the exodus from Egypt take place at night when YHWH strikes down the firstborn of Egypt. In both cases, YHWH's instructions are designed to evoke the exodus, but of course, the context differs. Whereas the exodus is conceived as a divine act of liberation from Egyptian slavery, Ezekiel's symbolic action is designed to portray a divine act of punishment and exile.

Ezekiel 12:7 concludes the unit by relating how Ezekiel complied with YHWH's instructions.

Oracular Account: Ezekiel's Explanation of the Symbolic Action (12:8-16)

Although an introductory prophetic word transmission formula in Ezekiel 12:8 formally demarcates Ezekiel 12:8-16, the unit nevertheless builds upon the instructions to perform a symbolic action in Ezekiel 12:1-7. The prophetic word formula again introduces an instruction speech by YHWH in Ezekiel 12:9-16 in which YHWH instructs Ezekiel to explain the meaning of the action to the people by focusing on the image of the exiled king.

YHWH's instruction speech again begins with the address form "son of Adam" and is followed by a rhetorical question in v. 9 in which YHWH asks Ezekiel if the house of Israel had asked Ezekiel, "What are you doing?" The people's question entails an explanation for Ezekiel's action as described in Ezekiel 12:1-7.

YHWH's instructions to Ezekiel concerning his response then follow in vv. 10-16. YHWH introduces the response in v. 10 with an instruction to speak to the people. The answer begins with an example of the prophetic messenger formula "thus says my L-rd, YHWH," here vocalized as "Thus says my L-rd, G-d," which in turn introduces a statement of YHWH's basic point, viz., that this oracle pertains to the "prince" (Heb., *hannasi'*) and all the people in the midst of the city of Jerusalem. Ezekiel typically identifies the king of Judah not as "king" (Heb., *melek*) but as "prince" (Heb., *nasi'*) to emphasize the king's subservience to YHWH. Ezekiel 12:11 emphasizes that Ezekiel's actions are meant to represent those of the king and the people, viz., that they are about to go into exile. Ezekiel 12:12-13 emphasizes that the king is going into exile, in large measure to highlight that the exile will affect the entire nation. He emphasizes that the king must carry his baggage like everyone else and he employs standard Babylonian imagery concerning the entrapment of captives with a fishing net (cf. Hab 1:14-17; cf. Marduk's use of a net to defeat Tiamat in the Babylonian creation epic, *ANET* 60–72). Ezekiel 12:14 emphasizes that all the king's entourage will be scattered as well so that there will be no one to help him. Finally, Ezekiel 12:15-16 points to the revelatory significance of both the symbolic action and its fulfillment by employing the self-revelation formula "and they shall know that I am YHWH" to explain that YHWH's exile of the nation is intended as a means to reveal YHWH's power and sovereignty to the house of Israel.

Oracular Account: Symbolic Action concerning Eating and Drinking (Exodus Reversal) (12:17-20)

The prophetic word transmission formula in v. 17 demarcates Ezekiel 12:17-20, but this text continues to reflect upon the symbolic actions of the previous two oracular accounts. The account of YHWH's instruction speech begins in v. 18 with an instruction to eat and drink in trembling and apprehension. Such a portrayal modifies the hurried manner in which the escaping Israelite slaves would eat in the time of the exodus (see Exod 12:11), but again, the people in Ezekiel's time go into captivity whereas those from the time of the exodus escaped from captivity. YHWH's instructions to explain the act to the people in vv. 19-20 make it clear that the people will eat with trembling and apprehension because their land is devastated. Indeed, the portrayal of the devastated land draws intertextually on the scenario of devastation in Isaiah 6:11-12. Again, the concluding self-revelation formula at the conclusion of YHWH's instruction emphasizes that this scenario reveals YHWH's presence and power.

Oracular Account: Disputation concerning the Efficacy of the Vision (12:21-25)

Ezekiel 12:21-25 again begins with an example of the prophetic word transmission formula, but the unit nevertheless builds on the previous units in Ezekiel 12:1-7, 12:8-16, and 12:17-20. Following the prophetic word transmission formula in v. 21, YHWH's instruction speech in vv. 22-25 takes the form of a disputation. A disputation is designed to challenge a prevailing view or premise by persuading the audience to adopt another view (Graffy, 52–56; Murray).

YHWH's instruction speech addresses Ezekiel as "son of Adam" and then employs a rhetorical question in v. 22 to introduce the premise to the people that YHWH is about to challenge. YHWH quotes the people's statement, "The days go on, and every vision perishes," which expresses the people's belief that the prophetic visions sent by YHWH to the people through the prophets, such as Ezekiel, come to nothing. YHWH instructs Ezekiel to refute this assertion in vv. 23-25 by emphasizing that every one of YHWH's prophetic visions will be fulfilled. The passage concludes with YHWH's emphatic statement, "I will speak a word, and I will do it."

Oracular Account: Concerning the Imminent Fulfillment of YHWH's Oracles (12:26-28)

Ezekiel 12:26-28 is once again demarcated by the prophetic word transmission formula, but it nevertheless concludes the sequence of oracular accounts in Ezekiel 12:1-7, 12:8-16, 12:17-20, and 12:21-25. Following the prophetic word formula in v. 26, YHWH's instruction speech in vv. 27-28 is once again formulated as a disputation (Graffy, 56–58; Murray). YHWH again addresses Ezekiel as "son of Adam" and quotes a somewhat different premise in v. 27 from the previous unit: "The vision that he sees is for many days and for distant times he prophesies." In this instance, the people maintain that YHWH's oracles pertain to a distant future, not to the immediate present. YHWH instructs Ezekiel to respond in v. 28 with the statement, "My entire word will no longer be delayed; when I speak a word, it will be done." The oracular formula "oracle of my L-rd YHWH" (vocalized as "oracle of my L-rd G-d") concludes the statement and verifies it as a word of YHWH.

Oracular Account: Concerning False Prophets (13:1-23)

Ezekiel 13:1-23 is demarcated initially by the prophetic word formula in v. 1. Verses 2-23 then constitute an instruction speech by YHWH to Ezekiel in which YHWH instructs Ezekiel to deliver two oracles concerning false prophets. The instruction speech includes two parts, each of which begins with YHWH's address to Ezekiel as "son of Adam" in vv. 2 and 17. The first portion of YHWH's instruction speech in vv. 2-16 instructs Ezekiel to deliver two interrelated prophetic judgment speeches against the false prophets who would deceive the people of Israel by claiming that they had spoken on behalf of YHWH when in fact they had not. The second portion of YHWH's instruction speech in vv. 17-23 complements the first by focusing on the women prophets who likewise prophesy falsely. Once again, YHWH instructs Ezekiel to deliver a prophetic judgment speech against these women whom YHWH charges with lying to the people. A similar rhetorical strategy of condemning both the male leaders of the people and the women of Jerusalem appears in Isaiah 3:1–4:5 (Sweeney 1996, 105–12).

The first portion of YHWH's instruction speech to Ezekiel in vv. 2-16 begins with YHWH's address to the prophet in v. 2a-bα. YHWH addresses Ezekiel as "son of Adam" in keeping with Ezekiel's status as a priest who represents humanity's attempt to stand once again before YHWH's holy presence by reentering the Garden of Eden as represented by the holy of holies of the Jerusalem Temple. YHWH's introductory instruction includes two elements. The first is a very general instruction to prophesy to "the prophets who prophesy" in v. 2a, and the second is a specified instruction to say to those who prophesy out of their own hearts in v. 2bα. The reason for the two-fold address is to build the case for YHWH's charges by first addressing prophets in general and then by identifying the specific addressees by charging them with prophesying their own messages rather than those of YHWH. Such a charge, of course, undermines the credibility of these purportedly false prophets.

The oracles that Ezekiel is to speak to these prophets then follow in vv. 2bβ-16. The prophet's oracular speech is to begin with two elements of prophetic technical language. The first is the call to attention in v. 2bβ in which Ezekiel will introduce his speech by demanding that his audience hear the word of YHWH (Hos 4:1; Amos 3:1; Mic 6:1; Isa 1:10; Ezek 6:3; cf. Judg 5:3; Prov 7:24). The second is the prophetic messenger formula in v. 3aα, "Thus says my L-rd YHWH," read in Hebrew as "Thus says my L-rd G-d," which certifies Ezekiel as YHWH's spokesperson and the oracle as YHWH's own. The two-part oracle follows in vv. 3aβ-16.

The first portion of the oracle appears in vv. 3aβ-9 as a typical example of a prophetic judgment speech formulated as a "woe" oracle. The accusations against the false prophets appear in vv. 3aβ-7. The accusations employ the "woe" oracle form in which the address to the condemned party begins with the interjection, "Woe!" (Heb., *hoy*), which warns the addressee of an impending disaster or judgment (Amos 5:18-20; Isa 5:8-24; Hab 2:6-20). A characterization of the prophets then follows in vv. 3aβ-b, which charges the prophets with acting as "foolish" or "disingenuous" (Heb., *nebalim*) prophets who speak out of their own spirits or minds without ever having seen a vision of YHWH. The oracle then turns to a set of direct accusations of wrongdoing and dishonesty on the part of these prophets in vv. 4-7. The first compares the prophets with jackals scampering around ruined buildings in search of any morsels of food or carrion that they might happen to find. The second charges that these prophets did nothing to defend the people against assault by a foreign army insofar as they did not help in repairing the walls of the city so that they might resist attack. The reference to the Day of YHWH draws upon a well-known tradition in which YHWH assaults the people or an enemy of Israel for wrongdoing that defiles the nation (Isa 2:6-22; 13:1-22; Amos 5:18-20; Zeph 1:7-18). By citing such a tradition, the oracle makes it clear that had these prophets acted properly, they might have saved the people from the judgment that YHWH has brought upon them. The oracle continues by charging these prophets with relating false visions and engaging in lying divination by quoting the oracular formula "oracle of

YHWH" (Heb., *ne'um yhwh*) when in fact YHWH did not speak the oracles that these prophets had given to the people. Verse 7 emphasizes this last point by stating it as a rhetorical question, "Did you not see a false vision and speak a lying divination, saying 'oracle of YHWH,' when I did not speak?"

The announcement of punishment against the false prophets follows in vv. 8-9. The announcement is introduced by the particle *laken*, "therefore," which typically connects the announcement of punishment to the accusation in the prophetic judgment speeches to make clear that the judgment is understood to be a consequence of the actions laid out in the accusation portion of the speech. The prophetic messenger formula appears once again to underscore the validity of the oracle that Ezekiel is to deliver. A restatement or summation of the accusation then appears, "because you spoke falsely and you envisioned lies . . . " and introduces the announcement of judgment per se. A second example of the particle *laken*, "therefore," underscores the judgment once again, and the formula "behold, I am against you" and the oracular formula "oracle of my L-rd YHWH/G-d" further emphasize and authenticate the announcement of punishment. The announcement of punishment states that YHWH's hand will be against these false prophets in judgment, that they will never stand in the council of YHWH or YHWH's royal court in the manner presumed of a true prophet (1 Kings 22:19-23; Isa 6; Jer 23:9-40, esp. v. 18), that they shall not be inscribed among the house of Israel, and that they will not enter the land of Israel. Whereas the first two consequences challenge the ability of these false prophets to function as prophets, the second two emphasize that they will no longer be considered a part of the nation of Israel. The oracle concludes with the YHWH self-revelation formula to indicate that these prophets will know YHWH once the judgment against them has been carried out.

The second portion of the oracle then follows in vv. 10-16. Although these verses are constituted as a discrete prophetic judgment speech, they build on the first judgment speech by employing the imagery of a poorly built wall to illustrate the consequences of a poorly conceived prophecy concerning YHWH's intentions.

The accusation or statement of the grounds of punishment appears in vv. 10-12, which begin by charging that the false prophets have led the people astray by announcing that there will be peace when in fact no such peace will occur. This is the first point at which the oracle discloses something of the substance of the charges of false prophecy. Given the historical setting of Ezekiel during the last years of the kingdom of Judah, the prophets to be condemned may well have been those who supported Josiah's reform prior to his death, e.g., Jeremiah, Nahum, and Zephaniah, as well as earlier prophets whose oracles were read in support of the reform, e.g., Isaiah, Hosea, Amos, and perhaps Micah. Alternatively, they may have included prophets who supported King Jehoiakim's or King Zedekiah's efforts to resist the Babylonian empire by relying on Egypt for support, e.g., Hannaniah (see Jer 27–28). Having stated the premise of the oracle, it then turns to the analogy of a poorly built wall to be plastered over, thereby masking the poor construction that will inevitably result in its collapse when rains and wind batter it down. Such an analogy emphasizes that the so-called false prophets themselves have so-to-speak plastered over the problems of Israel by declaring a future of peace when in fact war and defeat resulting in Israel's (or better Judah's) collapse is inevitable. An underlying element of the oracle builds on a pun with the Hebrew noun *tepel*, "plaster, whitewash," which is remarkably similar to the verbs *yippol*, "it (the outer wall) will fall (masculine singular)," and *tippolnah*, "they (the hailstones) will fall (feminine plural)," in v. 11. The final rhetorical question, "Will it not be said to you, 'where is the plaster that you applied?'" of course suggests the underlying question, "Where are the prophets who prophesied peace to you?"

The announcement of judgment then follows in vv. 13-16 introduced by the particle *laken*, "therefore," and the prophetic messenger formula "thus says my L-rd YHWH/G-d," as in v. 8. The announcement continues the analogy of the poorly built wall by depicting YHWH as the one who will unleash hailstones and rain to cause the wall's collapse. Of course, the razed wall represented the people who will endure punishment from YHWH because the false prophets led them astray. The oracle closes by making the analogy clear, viz., just as the wall and its plasterers are gone, so are the false prophets who prophesied peace when no peace was coming. The oracular formula "oracle of my L-rd YHWH/G-d" concludes the oracle.

The second portion of YHWH's address to Ezekiel appears in Ezekiel 13:17-23 in which YHWH instructs Ezekiel to deliver a prophetic judgment speech against the women prophets who prophesy falsely. YHWH's instruction speech again begins with an address to Ezekiel as "son of Adam," but it is reinforced by "and you, O son of Adam" to express continuity with the preceding instruction to address the male prophets as well as disjunction to rivet the attention of Ezekiel and the reader on what is to follow. Interpreters cannot be certain as to the identities of these women. Women prophets, such as Miriam (Exod 15), Deborah (Judges 4–5), and Noadiah (Neh 6:14), were known in Judah and Israel. Huldah, an older contemporary of Ezekiel, announced to King Josiah that he would perish despite his righteousness because YHWH had already decreed the destruction of Jerusalem due to

King Manasseh's wickedness several generations earlier (2 Kings 22:14-20; cf. 2 Chr 34:22-28). Again, YHWH's instructions to Ezekiel in vv. 17-18aα[1] emphasize that these women prophets also speak oracles of their own invention rather than those of YHWH.

The accusations or grounds for punishment appear in vv. 18aα[2]-19. Again, the accusations are formulated with the prophetic messenger formula to validate the oracle as an oracle of YHWH and with the "woe" (Heb., *hoy*) oracle form to indicate the warning of impending disaster. The characterization of the women, however, differs from that of the men in that the present oracle focuses on the distinctive garments of the women prophets that trap people into believing in their oracles. Such a strategy constitutes a play on the view that women prophets somehow seduce their clients into believing in them. Interpreters do not fully understand the nature of the garments; one is some sort of an arm- or wristband and the other appears to be some sort of veil or head covering that would have been recognized in ancient Judah as the distinctive features of a woman prophet. By engaging in such entrapment, YHWH charges that these women have profaned YHWH's holy name among the people, which indicates that they have falsely represented YHWH. The reference to the handfuls of barley and pieces of bread indicate that prophecy was a profession in the ancient world insofar as prophets were paid for their services, generally in produce (1 Kings 14:3; Amos 7:12). The accusations indicate that these women have announced death for those who will not die and life for those who will not live, and that their pronouncements therefore constitute lies.

The announcement of punishment then follows in vv. 20-23, which again begin with *laken*, "therefore," to establish the connection between accusation and consequence, and the prophetic messenger formula to validate the announcement as an oracle of YHWH. The announcement per se once again focuses on the distinctive garments of the women prophets. The scenario employs imagery of sexual violence insofar as YHWH will tear the armbands and veils from the women in an act that suggests that they are being stripped by their enemies, something that would likely have happened when an enemy conquered a city and assaulted the women. Here, YHWH's assault of the women is portrayed as an act of deliverance for the people by which YHWH is revealed to the people at large. YHWH's concluding statements reiterate this stance by charging that the women's demoralization and misguidance of the people with their lies will be cause to prevent them from ever prophesying or divining again. Once again, YHWH claims to save the people so that they will know YHWH.

Oracular Account: Threats against False Prophets and Diviners (14:1-11)

Ezekiel 14:1-11 breaks the normal pattern by beginning with a notice in v. 1 that some of the elders of the people of Israel came to him and sat down before him, presumably to pose an oracular inquiry. The standard form of the prophetic word formula immediately follows in v. 2 to indicate that vv. 1-11 stand as a structural block much like the other oracular accounts in Ezekiel 12–19. The prophetic word formula in Ezekiel 14:12 marks the beginning of the next unit. The reason for the deviation from the typical form is to highlight the parallel to Ezekiel 8–11, which likewise begins with a notice that the elders of Israel sat before Ezekiel in his home as he recounted his visionary journey to the Jerusalem Temple to portray its destruction (contra Renz, 72). Whereas the earlier vision account focused on the purging of the city of Jerusalem and its people, the present account builds upon the preceding unit by focusing on the purging of those among the people of Judah living in exile whom Ezekiel charged with turning to idolatry. Much like those portrayed in the vision of Ezekiel 8–11, we do not know if these persons actually turned to idolatry, but Ezekiel charges them with such conduct and condemns them for it. Although many interpreters presuppose that these elders have turned to Babylonian or other Mesopotamian deities and practices, the oracle gives no indication as to the identities of the gods to which these people turn or the nature of the practices in which they engage. They could just as easily turn to other Judean or Israelite prophets who might convey a different understanding of YHWH and YHWH's purposes from that of Ezekiel. Jeremiah after all engages in polemics with Judean prophets whom he labels as false, such as Shemaiah the Nehelamite noted in Jer 29:29-32. In a situation of exile, any number of prophets might call for the return of the exiles to Jerusalem and the land of Judah, but Ezekiel emphasizes that further judgment, destruction, and exile lie ahead.

YHWH's oracle per se appears in vv. 3-11 in the form of an instruction speech to Ezekiel. As usual, YHWH addresses Ezekiel as "son of Adam" to account for his status as a Zadokite priest. But the first portion of the oracle in vv. 3-5 begins with a rhetorical question posed to Ezekiel in which YHWH first charges that these men have turned to idolatry and then asks Ezekiel if it is appropriate to respond to him. The polemical nature of the inquiry is clear from the use of the terms "fetishes" (Heb., *gillulim*) and "stumbling block of their guilt" (*mikshol 'awonam*) to refer to the practices of these men. The Hebrew term *gillulim*, often rendered as "fetishes" or "idols," actually means "dung balls," and the Hebrew expression *mikshol 'awonam*, "the stumbling block of their guilt," makes it clear that their practices are wrong and defiling. YHWH's question to Ezekiel, "Shall I really respond to their inquiry?" (Heb., *ha'iddarosh 'iddaresh lahem*, "Shall I surely be sought to/by them?"), employs the verb root *drsh*, "to seek, inquire," in both infinitive absolute and imperfect Niphal forms to indicate a setting of oracular inquiry. The answer to YHWH's question is obviously, "No!" given the charge of idolatry.

But vv. 4-11 present the two responses to these rhetorical questions, each of which begins with the particle *laken*, "therefore," in vv. 4-5 and 6-11. In vv. 4-5, YHWH instructs Ezekiel to tell the people that YHWH will indeed respond to such inquiries by passing judgment against anyone who engages in such idolatrous practice. YHWH certifies the oracle by employing the messenger formula "thus says my L-rd YHWH/G-d" in v. 4 and follows it up with an example of a case law form drawn from ritual instruction (e.g., Lev 17:3-7, 8-9, 10-12, 13-14; cf. Greenberg 1983, 248; Allen 1994, 205). The purpose of such case law is to specify the consequences for anyone who commits an illegal or defiling act (Liedke, 106–43). In the present instance, YHWH specifies that the consequence of such oracular inquiry will indeed be an answer from YHWH in which YHWH will pass judgment on the person in question.

The second response in vv. 6-11 reiterates this point by emphasizing that YHWH will indeed punish anyone who makes such an inquiry. But vv. 6-8 also call upon the people to repent of such practice and to return to YHWH. Such a concern indicates that the entire oracular sequence in vv. 3-11 is intended to call for repentance. Following the particle *laken*, "therefore," vv. 6-8 begin with YHWH's instructions to Ezekiel to address the house of Israel. Again, YHWH employs the messenger formula to certify that the oracle is from YHWH. The address to the people begins with a call to repentance in v. 6aβ-b, but it follows in vv. 7-8 with reiterations of the points made in vv. 4-5, viz., YHWH will respond directly with punishment to anyone who reveres idols, engages in defiling practice, or consults prophets associated with idolatry. In the end, YHWH's judgment will be revelatory in that those who suffer the punishment will know YHWH.

Verses 9-11 then turn to the question of the prophet who would be consulted by persons charged with idolatry. The passage makes it clear that such a prophet will suffer punishment, but it presents the issue in somewhat confused terms in its efforts to demonstrate that YHWH is the ultimate sovereign G-d. The passage begins in v. 9 with another statement of case law that takes up the issue of what will happen to a prophet who has been seduced into such illicit oracular inquiry. The verb *pth*, "to be simple," may be employed for those who are simple-minded (Hos 7:11; Prov 20:19); those who are enticed or deceived (Deut 11:16; Job 31:27); women who are seduced by men (Exod 22:15; Hos 2:16); or even prophets who are deceived or seduced by G-d (1 Kings 22:20; Jer 20:7). The oracle makes it clear that YHWH deceived the prophet in question and that the prophet will now suffer punishment for his or her action along with the person who made the oracular inquiry. Such an assertion protects YHWH's power as sovereign deity of the universe, but it also raises troubling theological questions about YHWH's role in setting up the deception in the first place and then executing punishment against the deceived parties (cf. YHWH's hardening of Pharaoh's heart in Exod 7:3 and YHWH's instructions to Isaiah in Isa 6:10 to render the people blind, deaf, and dumb so that they might suffer punishment). In the end, the punishment is intended to demonstrate YHWH's sovereignty and power to the people and thereby to bring them back to YHWH. The concluding statement, "And they shall be my people and I will be their G-d," is the standard covenant formula that binds the people of Israel and YHWH together (cf. Ezek 11:20; 36:28; 37:23; Jer 7:23; 31:33; 32:38; Hos 2:23; Zech 8:8; Exod 6:7; Lev 26:12; Rendtorff).

Oracular Account: Concerning Individual Righteousness and Guilt (14:12-23)

Ezekiel 14:12-23 begins with a typical example of the prophetic word formula in v. 12, which serves as the introduction to the next oracular account in the sequence concerning the guilt and righteousness of individuals. The appearance of the next prophetic word formula in Ezekiel 15:1 marks the beginning of a new unit. The oracular account in Ezekiel 14:12-23 is designed to demonstrate that the guilty do not escape punishment even if the righteous intercede for them.

YHWH's address to Ezekiel appears in vv. 13-23 once again in the form of an instruction speech addressed to Ezekiel as "son of Adam." The purpose of the instruction is to demonstrate to Ezekiel that those who suffered punishment deserved their fates as a consequence of their own actions and that those who survived the destruction of Jerusalem did so because they merited mercy because of their own righteousness.

YHWH makes this point in the first part of the instruction speech in vv. 13-20 by holding up three well-known figures as examples of righteous men who would be able to save themselves in the coming disaster because of their righteous characters but who would otherwise be unable to save others.

The three are Noah, Daniel, and Job; each was a righteous man who in the past was able to save the lives of others, but in the present circumstances, even these men would not be able to save others. All three must be known to Ezekiel and his audience, although it is not entirely clear that all are known to Ezekiel from biblical literature. Noah and Job are known in the Bible. Noah's righteousness prompts YHWH to save Noah and his family; during the flood Noah saves his family and the animals of the world by taking them on board the ark constructed at the direction of YHWH. Job likewise was a righteous man (Job 1–2) who suffered affliction; in the end, he was able to save the lives of his three friends, who had been wrong in their characterization of YHWH as a righteous deity who punishes the wicked and rewards the righteous and of Job as one who must be guilty (Job 42). Daniel presents a conundrum, however. Although Daniel is known in the book of Daniel as a wise and righteous man, it is not clear that he saves the lives of others. Indeed, the biblical book of Daniel was not composed until the second century BCE, some four centuries following Ezekiel. It appears, however, that Ezekiel 14:12-23 does not have the biblical figure Daniel in mind; instead, it presupposes the Canaanite figure Dan-El, a wise and righteous man who intercedes with the gods for the life of his son, Aqhat, in the Ugaritic legend of Aqhat. Biblical readers assume that the biblical figure Daniel is intended here, but close attention to the form of the name Daniel in the passage confirms that the Canaanite figure is intended. Although the name is vocalized as Daniel (Heb., *dani'el,* as in the book of Daniel), the consonantal text reads *dn'l,* not *dny'l,* in accordance with the Canaanite or Ugaritic rendering of the name. YHWH lays out four scenarios of punishment, viz., famine, wild beasts, sword, and pestilence, that would be brought against the land to punish it for the sins of its people, but in each instance YHWH states that the righteousness of these three men would not suffice to deliver the guilty land from its punishment; Noah, Daniel, and Job would only be able to save themselves by their righteousness, not their presumably guilty sons, daughters, or anyone else.

In the second part of the instruction speech in vv. 21-23, introduced by the messenger formula "for thus says my L-rd G-d/YHWH," YHWH points to the survivors of the disaster as an example of divine mercy that will comfort Ezekiel. The purpose of this demonstration is to point out that there will be survivors who survived on account of their deeds. Such a contention conflicts with the portrayal of judgment in Ezekiel 8–11 and indicates some shifting of opinion in the book as it struggles with the question of divine punishment and human accountability.

Oracular Account: The Allegory of Jerusalem as a Useless Vine (15:1-8)

Ezekiel 15:1-8 appears in typical form with an example of the prophetic word formula in v. 1, which introduces the oracular account. The oracular account per se appears in vv. 2-8, which focus on comparing Jerusalem to a useless grapevine, good only for tinder, to demonstrate that Jerusalem will be burned like the rest of Judah. The prophetic word formula in Ezekiel 16:1 marks the beginning of the next unit in the sequence.

The oracular account appears in the form of an instruction speech in which YHWH addresses Ezekiel as "son of Adam" and then poses to him in the first part of the oracular account in vv. 2-5 rhetorical questions concerning the useless character of the wood of a grapevine. Such wood is generally thin and twisted which renders it useless for anything except for tinder. YHWH's three initial questions in vv. 2-3 establish that such wood is no better than any other type of wood and that it is useless insofar as it is not even suitable for making pegs on which a vessel might be hung. But YHWH takes the questions further in vv. 4-5 by positing that the two ends of a piece of grapevine wood might be burnt when it is used as fuel for a fire, rendering it even more useless.

The second portion of the oracular account in vv. 6-8 then applies the allegory of the grapevine wood to the projected destruction of the city of Jerusalem. This segment opens with the particle *laken*, "therefore," to establish that these verses present the conclusions to be drawn from the allegory presented in vv. 2-5. The image of useless wood that has been burned aids in setting up the point of the allegory, viz., that the people of Jerusalem are no better than the people of any other city in Judah or Israel and that it, too, will suffer burning and destruction from YHWH. Such a premise is important for two basic reasons. First, Jerusalem is the holy center of Judah and Israel insofar as the temple of YHWH marks Jerusalem as YHWH's holy city that together with the house of David will be protected by YHWH forever (see 2 Sam 7; Ps 2; 46; 47; 48). Second, Jerusalem had been spared destruction during the Assyrian invasion of Judah in 701 BCE. The Assyrians assaulted and burned every city in Judah at that time. Jerusalem was besieged, but it was never taken by Sennacherib's forces (see 2 Kings 18–20; Isa 36–39; *ANET* 287-88). Instead, Sennacherib was compelled to withdraw from Judah, leaving King Hezekiah on the throne and Jerusalem intact, in order to put down the Babylonian revolt that broke out in conjunction with Hezekiah's action. Hezekiah was clearly defeated, but his ability to remain on the throne and Jerusalem's survival played a role in building a scenario of divine protection for both the Davidic monarchy and the Jerusalem Temple. The purpose of the oracle is to dispel any such conceptions of Jerusalem's special status as YHWH's protected city. Indeed, YHWH promises punishment for the inhabitants of Jerusalem on account of the trespass for which YHWH charges them. The oracular formula "oracle of YHWH" (Heb., *ne'um yhwh*) closes the unit and certifies it as an oracle of YHWH.

Oracular Account: The Allegory of Jerusalem as YHWH's Adulterous Wife (16:1-63)

Ezekiel 16:1-63 opens in typical form with an example of the prophetic word formula in Ezekiel 16:1. Despite its length, this oracular account employs a rather standard form of the prophetic judgment speech, including a lengthy account of the grounds for punishment in vv. 2-34 followed by an elaborately structured announcement of punishment and subsequent restoration in vv. 35-64. The latter section begins in v. 35 with a call-to-attention formula addressed to the "harlot" Jerusalem and linked to the preceding material by the particle *laken*, "therefore." An example of the prophetic messenger formula "thus says my L-rd, G-d" in v. 36aα$^{1-4}$ then introduces the first announcement of judgment in vv. 36aα^5-42, which presents a lurid portrayal of Jerusalem's exposure and punishment for her alleged crimes. A second section announcing consequences for Jerusalem then follows in vv. 43-66. Although this segment begins with a brief announcement of punishment in v. 43, its use of a rhetorical question, "And have you not committed depravity together with all your abominations?" then leads to a renewed set of accusations in vv. 44-52 concerning Jerusalem's licentious conduct far beyond that committed by her sisters, Samaria and Sodom. But this set of accusations, linked to the preceding material by a conjunctive *waw* in v. 53, leads to a qualified announcement of restoration for Jerusalem, Samaria, and Sodom in vv. 53-58. This segment in turns leads to the final subunit of the passage, an announcement concerning YHWH's restoration of the covenant with Jerusalem in vv. 59-63, linked to the preceding by a conjunctive *ki* and the prophetic messenger formula "for thus says the Lord, G-d" that is intended to shame Jerusalem into remembering her relationship with YHWH. The appearance of the prophetic word formula in Ezekiel 17:1 marks the beginning of the next unit of the book.

Following the introductory prophetic word formula in v. 1, Ezekiel 16:2-34 metaphorically lays out the accusations leveled by YHWH against the city of Jerusalem. The passage begins in vv. 2-3aα^1 with YHWH's instructions to Ezekiel to announce Jerusalem's wrongdoing to her. The accusations that Ezekiel is to level against Jerusalem begin with YHWH's statement of the prophetic messenger formula in v. 3aα$^{2-6}$, "Thus says my L-rd G-d to Jerusalem," which identifies YHWH as the speaker of the following accusations.

The first segment of YHWH's accusation appears in vv. 3aα^{7}-14 and metaphorically portrays YHWH's beneficent acts for Jerusalem, depicted here as an unwanted baby girl who was left to die by her parents. Such abandonment of infant girls was all too common in the ancient world as daughters were viewed as an expense, viz., daughters would have to be provided with a dowry at the time of their marriage into another family whereas sons would remain in the family, inherit and work family land, receive the dowry of the women they would marry, and father sons who would one day inherit the land after the passing of their parents. YHWH identifies Jerusalem as the Canaanite daughter of an Amorite father and a Hittite mother. This should come as no surprise as Jerusalem is identified as a Jebusite city conquered by David without loss of life to its population. Ironically, Jerusalem would form the core population for Judean/Jewish identity as the population of the surrounding Judean countryside was frequently killed off or driven away by foreign invaders, such as the Assyrians in the late eighth century or the Babylonians in the late seventh and early sixth centuries BCE. The portrayal of Jerusalem as the hybrid daughter of Amorite and Hittite parents makes sense, insofar as Jerusalem was situated in a crossroads region between Asia Minor to the west, where the Hittite empire was located until ca. 1300 BCE, and Mesopotamia to the east, where the Semitic Amorite population emerged as the dominant force in a formerly Sumerian culture during the second millennium BCE. The metaphorical portrayal as an abandoned baby girl apparently presupposes the circumstances of the period following the battle of Kadesh in 1300 BCE in which the Hittites defeated the Egyptians and drove them out of western Asia, but were too weakened by the battle to follow up on their victory and take control of the land of Canaan. Mesopotamia for its part was also unable to dominate the region, leaving the conditions ripe for the emergence of smaller states, such as Israel/Judah, Philistia, Aram, Ammon, Moab, Edom, and others, during the transition from the Bronze to the Iron ages.

The portrayal of Jerusalem as an abandoned baby girl presupposes the political vacuum in western Asia that led to the formation of Israel/Judah and the other smaller states that emerged in the region at the outset of the Iron Age. The abandoned infant does not receive even basic care; her umbilical cord is not cut and her body is not rubbed with salt and wrapped in the manner typical in ancient times when such procedures were employed to remove the traces of the placenta and to protect the newborn baby during her first forty days of life. YHWH appears as a passerby who sees the baby kicking in her placenta and takes action to save her life and raise her to maturity. In a mark of patriarchal perspective, the baby is considered to be grown up when she reaches puberty; i.e., when she has grown breasts and pubic hair and is therefore ready for marriage.

The passage employs the motif of YHWH's marriage to the bride Jerusalem (cf. Zeph 3:14-20; Isa 49–54) to portray YHWH's actions to support Jerusalem. At the time of puberty—and therefore marriage—YHWH cleans her, clothes her, and decks her out in jewelry as part of the establishment of a marriage relationship in which the groom is expected to provide the bride with support and clothing (cf. Exod 21:10). With a self-congratulatory flair, YHWH opines that Jerusalem emerged as a rare beauty, recognized by all the nations and fit for royalty.

Having laid out the care lavished upon the once-abandoned girl, YHWH turns to accusations in vv. 15-29 that the bride Jerusalem acted as a harlot among the other nations of the world. Such a charge reflects the sociopolitical realities of Israel's and Judah's position as a crossroads region through which travelers and traders from Egypt, Asia Minor, Mesopotamia, and Arabia would pass on their way to engage in international trade. Indeed, the strategic position of Israel/Judah played an important role in developing Solomon's wealth and power in the tenth century BCE and it also played a role in attracting the major powers of the day, Egypt, Assyria, and later Babylonia, who sought to dominate the trade routes upon which Israel and Judah sat and from which they prospered. YHWH employs the metaphor of a harlot to express Jerusalem's relations with foreigners. The various gifts of YHWH the husband, e.g., clothing and tapestries, gold and silver, food items, and even the children born to Jerusalem, became items that facilitated Jerusalem's "harlotry" with the nations with which she would engage in trade. Jerusalem's actions appear to represent pagan religious rituals represented by the nations of the world, such as sacrificing children as offerings to the gods in times of emergency and building high places outside of Jerusalem to serve as open-air sanctuaries for the worship of foreign gods. The prudish YHWH expresses horror and disgust at Jerusalem's actions with her neighbors, portraying the large penises of the Egyptians and the shock of the Philistine women at Jerusalem's actions. Assyria, Canaan, and Chaldea (Babylonia) are also mentioned as partners for Jerusalem, which makes eminent sense as the Mesopotamian powers were generally motivated by an interest in dominating the trade routes of western Asia that led to Egypt.

The last segment of YHWH's portrayal of Jerusalem in vv. 30-34 focuses on the licentiousness of Jerusalem, i.e., Jerusalem was so anxious to engage in relations with the nations of the world that she reversed the normal activities of prostitute. Whereas a prostitute is normally paid for her services, YHWH depicts Jerusalem as paying the nations to engage in relations with her; such a metaphor likely symbolizes the tribute that Jerusalem had to pay as a vassal to her suzerain overlords, Aram and Israel in the ninth to the eighth centuries, Assyria in the eighth to seventh centuries, and Babylonia in the seventh to the sixth centuries BCE.

Following the delineation of accusations in vv. 2-34, Ezekiel 16:35-63 turns to the announcement of the consequences that will follow from Jerusalem's alleged abominations. The call to attention in v. 35 begins with the particle *laken*, "therefore," which establishes the causal relationship between Jerusalem's alleged wrongdoing and the consequences that will follow. YHWH addresses Jerusalem as *zonah*, "whore," to underscore the charges leveled against her. The call-to-attention formula "hear the word of YHWH" then introduces the following oracular material.

YHWH's lengthy speech to Jerusalem, which announces judgment and then restoration for Jerusalem, follows in vv. 36-63. Following the prophetic messenger formula in v. 36aα "thus says my L-rd G-d," the passage comprises two major announcements of judgment or consequences in vv. 36aβ-42 and 43-63, each of which begins with a formulaic accusation, *ya'an ki*, "because you . . . ," which then lays out a brief accusation against Jerusalem followed by YHWH's statement of the consequences to be leveled against the bride/city.

The first announcement of judgment in vv. 36aβ-42 continues the earlier motif of charging Jerusalem with sexual misconduct in v. 36aβ-b, but vv. 37-42 begin with the particle *laken*, "therefore," to emphasize that the consequences are to be considered as YHWH's punishment against Jerusalem for her conduct. The Israelite legal penalty for willful adultery is death by stoning (Deut 22:22-24). Jerusalem is therefore given over to be stoned to death by all of her alleged lovers and even those whom she refused. But the penalty appears to go beyond a simple execution in that the treatment of the alleged adulteress Jerusalem is portrayed almost as though it were a rape scene, insofar as she is stripped before the crowd and given to them to vent YHWH's fury (cf. Galambush, 124, who correctly labels the scene as pornographic; Wong, 32–57). In this respect, it is striking that none of her alleged lovers is punished, particularly since Deuteronomy 22:22-24 calls for the stoning of both the man and the woman in such cases. The metaphorical nature of the punishment is made clear in that Jerusalem's alleged "lovers" will also pierce her with swords and burn her houses as the invading Babylonians would do when they conquered and destroyed the city. The passage concludes with a statement that once the punishment is over, YHWH will then be quiet and display anger against Jerusalem no more.

The second subunit in vv. 43-63 develops the motifs of the first, but after it has elaborated upon the accusations against Jerusalem in vv. 43-52, it projects YHWH's actions to restore Jerusalem in vv. 53-63. The elaborations enable a comparison of Jerusalem with the experience of her neighbors, Samaria and Sodom, that allows YHWH to charge that she is even worse than they were. It also enables YHWH to bring the cycle full circle to restore Jerusalem, thereby honoring the eternal nature of the covenant made with Jerusalem.

Ezekiel 16:43-52 begins with the accusation "because you did not remember the days of your youth, and you infuriated me with all these things" as a basis to elaborate on the nature of Jerusalem's alleged sins. The claim that Jerusalem's mother was a Hittite (see v. 3) becomes a basis for charging Jerusalem with depravity, as the Hittites are among the seven Canaanite nations with which Israel is not to intermarry because of their idolatry. YHWH begins by quoting the proverb "like mother, like daughter" to make this point, but turns to Jerusalem's metaphorical sisters, Samaria and Sodom. Samaria is chosen because it was destroyed by the Assyrians in 722–721 BCE, so it serves as a paradigm for the experience of Jerusalem at the hands of the Babylonians insofar as Samaria's destruction was viewed as YHWH's punishment for its alleged sins (see 2 Kings 17). Sodom is chosen because it is the quintessential and paradigmatic sinful city in biblical literature that was likewise destroyed by YHWH because of its sins (Gen 18–19). The references to the daughters of both cities refer to the other cities that make up their respective spheres of influence. Unlike the modern nation state, ancient states were comprised of cities and spheres of influence that were tied to the capital city by treaties that bound them together in kingdoms such as the northern kingdom of Israel. The comparison with these cities enables YHWH to charge that Jerusalem is even worse than Samaria and Sodom, and so Jerusalem deserves even greater punishment.

Ezekiel 16:53-58 then states YHWH's intentions to restore Samaria and Sodom as a prelude to restoring Jerusalem. This proposal defines the purpose of the punishment meted out to each city in the previous subunits, viz., the punishment is intended as a corrective that will purge the city of her alleged crimes and render her fit for a restored standing in the world and relationship with YHWH. Indeed, such a scenario of purging Jerusalem and creation at large lies at the center of the portrayal of Jerusalem's destruction in Ezekiel

8–11 and its restoration in Ezekiel 40–48. It is based on the notion that temples must be purged—or cleansed, as the case may be—to render them holy once again after they have been defiled by improper practice (see the accounts of temple restoration in 2 Kings 18:1-8; 23:1-25; 2 Chr 29–31; 1 Macc 4:36-51). They are purged by means of the *hatta't*, "sin offering" (Lev 4:1–5:13), together with the removal of the corrupting items from the temple and the correction of the offending behavior. The sacrifice of the *hatta't* symbolizes the purging insofar as it is offered on the altar as a fire offering to YHWH. Until such purging takes place, Jerusalem must endure the mockery of her neighbors, Aram and Philistia, who are portrayed as laughing and mocking her as she undergoes her punishment.

Finally, Ezekiel 16:59-63 addresses the issue of the restoration of the eternal covenant. The passage is joined syntactically to the preceding material by an introductory *ki*, "for," and the prophetic messenger formula in v. 59aα. YHWH promises to remember the eternal covenant with Jerusalem, which Jerusalem is charged with having violated. Once Jerusalem is restored, she will receive her former sisters, Samaria and Sodom, as daughters, indicating that she will rule over the former northern Israel and the territory of Edom. The passage reveals a sense of anxiety about the Zion-covenant tradition, which is understood to be eternal, but nevertheless comes into question when the Babylonian empire destroys Jerusalem and the temple of YHWH. Ezekiel's portrayal of Jerusalem's punishment as a purge brought about by YHWH becomes a means to resolve the dilemma of an eternal covenant in which Jerusalem is destroyed and exiled, and thereby lays the basis for visions of restoration at the end of the book. YHWH's statement in v. 62, "I will establish my covenant with you, and you shall know that I am YHWH," is a modified version of the self-revelation formula that appears throughout the book. The statement is based on the premise stated in v. 63 that YHWH will forgive Jerusalem, thereby indicating YHWH's acceptance of Jerusalem as a *hatta't* offering.

Oracular Account: The Allegory of the Eagles, the Vine, and the Cedar (17:1-24)

The prophetic word formula in Ezekiel 17:1 opens the presentation of the allegory concerning the eagle, the vine, and the cedar in Ezekiel 17:2-24 and identifies it as an oracle from YHWH. Although a second example of the prophetic word formula appears in v. 11, it does not open a new unit within the literary structure of Ezekiel 8–19. Rather, the question in v. 12, "Do you not know what these things are?" referring to the allegorical images in vv. 2-10, indicates that the prophetic word formula in Ezekiel 17:11 introduces the second major portion of the oracular account in Ezekiel 17:1-24. Consequently, Ezekiel 17:2-10 presents the images of the allegory, whereas Ezekiel 17:12-24 presents the interpretation of these images. Overall, the allegory portrays King Jehoiachin's exile to Babylon in 597 BCE (2 Kings 24:6-16), the installation of his uncle, Zedekiah, as king (2 Kings 24:17-20), and Zedekiah's demise when he allies himself with Egypt and revolts against Babylon (2 Kings 25:1-30).

Ezekiel 17:2-10 presents the imagery of the allegory. The segment begins in typical fashion with YHWH's address to Ezekiel as "son of Adam" to indicate the identity of the priest as the descendant of Adam and the representative of humankind in the temple before YHWH. Ezekiel 17:2 presents YHWH's basic instruction to Ezekiel to present a riddle (Heb., *hidah*) and an allegory (Heb., *mashal*). The following instruction to present the allegory appears in two portions, each introduced by a second person singular example of the verb "to say," followed by the prophetic messenger formula "thus says my L-rd, G-d" in vv. 3 and 9, which present two different aspects of the allegory.

The first component of the allegory in Ezekiel 17:3-8 begins in vv. 3-6 with the depiction of a large eagle with huge wings and pinions, full plumage, and brilliant colors that goes to the Lebanon Range, plucks off the top of a cedar, carries it to the land of traders, sets it in a city of merchants, takes some of the seed of the land to a fertile field, and sets it beside abundant waters, where it grows into a low vine that spreads out with many branches. The eagle refers to the Babylonian empire, led by King Nebuchadnezzar, which was often symbolized by an eagle. Nebuchadnezzar exiles King Jehoiachin in 597 BCE to Babylon following his father's unsuccessful revolt. Nebuchadnezzar placed Jehoiachin's uncle, Zedekiah, on the throne as a puppet ruler and later destroyed Jerusalem and exiled Zedekiah in 587 BCE when revolt broke out a second time. The Lebanese cedar refers to the house of David, which was known for its royal palace lined with cedar wood and called "the House of the Forest of Lebanon" (1 Kings 7:2-5; cf. Isa 22:8). The land of traders (Heb., *kenaʿan*) is a double entendre as the Hebrew word *kenaʿan* refers to both traders and Canaan, where the land of Israel is located. The reference to the city of merchants (Heb., *rokelim*) likewise constitutes a double entendre as the Hebrew term *rokelim* signifies both merchants and tale-bearers or bearers of gossip, slander, and defamation (Lev 19:16). These images draw upon Solomon, who made a fortune in trade with the nations but imported foreign religious worship into Israel when he married foreign wives (1 Kings 4–5; 11). The reference to taking seed from the land and planting it in fertile fields signifies Nebuchadnezzar's first deportation of Jehoiachin and many other prominent and skilled Judeans to Babylon, which is located by the Euphrates River that waters Babylon's fields (cf. Ps 137:1). The reference to the low-growing vine and its many branches refers to Zedekiah, whom Nebuchadnezzar placed on the throne to serve Babylonian interests. The book of Isaiah employs tree and vine imagery to portray Davidic monarchs (Isa 11:1-9), based on Mesopotamian imagery that portrays the monarch as a tree growing from heaven.

The second component of the allegory in vv. 7-8 refers to a second great eagle, identified as Pharaoh Psamtek (Psammetichus) of Egypt to whom Zedekiah turned for support in his 588 BCE revolt against Babylon.

The second portion of YHWH's instruction to the prophet in vv. 9-10 poses a set of rhetorical questions that are designed to assert the downfall of Zedekiah. Will the vine thrive? Of course not, as the eagle (signifying Nebuchadnezzar) will tear it to pieces! And even if it is transplanted, the east wind will wither it. The east wind refers to the Hamsin or Sharav, a dry desert sirocco that appears during the transition from the dry summer season to the wet winter season much like the Santa Ana winds of Southern California. The east wind is a common metaphor for YHWH's power (see Fitzgerald 2002), e.g., in dividing the Red Sea (Exod 14–15) or in defeating enemies and transforming creation (Joel 4). The reference to the east wind here indicates that if Nebuchadnezzar does not destroy Zedekiah, YHWH will.

Ezekiel 17:11-24 then turns to the interpretation of the allegory. The interpretation appears in vv. 12-24, which are formulated as an instruction speech by YHWH to Ezekiel introduced at two points by the imperative formula "say, please (Heb., *'emor-na*) to the rebellious house" in v. 12a and again by the imperative formula "say (Heb., *'amor*)" in v. 12b. The first imperative introduces YHWH's question to the prophet in v. 12a, "Do you not know what these things are?" The question clearly ties the explanation to the preceding material in vv. 3-10 in which YHWH described the imagery of the allegory, and it also functions as a means to invite an explanation of their symbolism. The second imperative then introduces the explanation proper. It begins in vv. 12b-14 with a basic identification of the king of Babylon as the referent for the eagle in the allegory, and then follows with a portrayal of Nebuchadnezzar's initial actions against King Jehoiachin of Judah when he invaded Judah in 598/597 BCE. Nebuchadnezzar exiled Jehoiachin to Babylon together with large numbers of Judeans who held high positions and possessed useful skills and training. Nebuchadnezzar replaced Jehoiachin with his uncle, Mattaniah ben Josiah, who was renamed Zedekiah upon ascending the throne. Zedekiah's task was to ensure a tranquil Judah's submission to its suzerain, Babylon. The passage emphasizes the covenant or treaty made between Nebuchadnezzar and the two kings. The covenant and oath imposed on Jehoiachin would have called for sanctions in the event that Judah violated its treaty with Babylon. Jehoiachin's deportation would have been based on treaty clauses that would have been invoked when his father, Jehoiakim, violated the covenant to revolt against Babylon. The covenant enacted for Zedekiah would have stipulated penalties should Zedekiah revolt against Nebuchadnezzar.

Verses 15-24 then turn to Zedekiah's revolt against Babylon and the consequences that he will suffer for having done so. The passage is formulated as a prophetic judgment speech in which the bases for action against Zedekiah are laid out in v. 15 and the consequences in vv. 16-24. This passage does not begin with imperatives such as those found in v. 12, but the shift in the narrative to a description of Zedekiah's revolt against Babylon—and YHWH—is clear. This portion of the passage begins in v. 15 with a basic statement of the monarch's revolt against Babylon by sending envoys to Egypt to seek support against the Babylonians. Egypt thereby emerges as the referent of the second great eagle mentioned in vv. 7-8 above. Again, rhetorical questions point to the basic issues of the passage: will he succeed, will he escape, will one who breaks a covenant escape? The third formulation of the question raises a fundamental issue, viz., one who breaks a treaty cannot escape the consequences.

Verses 16-24 then present the consequences of Zedekiah's revolt. Verses 16-18 begin with a presentation of YHWH's answers to these questions: he will not escape. These verses begin with an oath formula spoken by YHWH, which makes it clear that YHWH will enforce the consequences for breaking the treaty. YHWH's initial statement reiterates the fact that Jehoiachin broke his covenant with Nebuchadnezzar, and it states that the consequence for having done so is that Zedekiah will die in exile in Babylonia. YHWH further states that the Pharaoh of Egypt will not come to Zedekiah's aid once Jerusalem is placed under siege. Verse 18 reiterates the fact that Zedekiah broke his covenant with Babylon and that he will therefore suffer the consequences.

Verses 19-21 then make clear the consequences that YHWH will bring against Zedekiah for having violated his covenant. This segment begins with another example of the oath formula in v. 19, which functions as a foundation for YHWH's announcement of punishment against Zedekiah. Verse 19 begins with the particle *laken*, "therefore," which typically introduces the consequences in a prophetic judgment speech, and an example of the prophetic messenger formula, which identifies the following oracle as a speech by YHWH to the prophet. Using imagery typical of the Babylonians, v. 20 states that YHWH will trap Zedekiah, carry him off to Babylon, and judge him there for committing a trespass against YHWH. Verse 21 makes it clear that Zedekiah's soldiers will also suffer. An example of the self-revelation formula at the end of v.21 points to these acts as proof that YHWH has spoken.

Finally, Ezekiel 17:22-24 concludes this segment with an oracle of restoration for the house of David as the ultimate consequence of the process described above. The oracle begins with another example of the prophetic messenger formula, and it employs earlier imagery concerning the plucking of the top of a cedar to signal the restoration of the Davidic house. Isaiah 11:1-9 employed similar imagery to portray the rise of a righteous Davidic monarch. Together with Ezekiel 37:15-28, this passage demonstrates that Ezekiel envisions a restoration of the Davidic house, in contrast to the book of Isaiah which envisions a Persian monarch to rule over Israel (Isa 44:28; 45:1) and the Davidic covenant granted to the people (Isa 55:3), and to the Masoretic version of the book of Jeremiah, which envisions the Davidic covenant applied to the city of Jerusalem (Jer 33:14-26; see Goldman, 9–64).

Oracular Account: Concerning the Responsibility of the Individual and the Demise of the Princes of Israel (18:1–19:14)

The prophetic word formula in Ezekiel 18:1 introduces the final subunit of Ezekiel 8–19 concerned with the moral responsibility of the individual and the demise of the princes of Israel. Many interpreters argue that Ezekiel 18:1-32 and 19:1-14 constitute discrete literary units because of their differences in form and content, but the presence of the prophetic word formula in Ezekiel 18:1—and not in 19:1—marks them as a single unit within the overall synchronic literary form of the book of Ezekiel, even if they were composed at different times and for different sets of concerns. Such a feature demands that the two chapters form a single unit and that they be read in relation to each other. Insofar as Ezekiel 18:1-32 argues that each individual generation is judged righteous or wicked depending upon its actions, it sets the stage for the lament over the princes of Judah in Ezekiel 19:1-14. Insofar as Ezekiel 19:1-14 metaphorically portrays the fates of some of the last kings of Judah, viz., Jehoahaz, Jehoiakim, and Jehoiachin, the unit maintains that each of these monarchs was judged according to his actions.

The first segment of this unit is the prophetic word formula in Ezekiel 18:1, which introduces the whole. The second segment is Ezekiel 18:2-32, which is formulated as a disputation speech in which YHWH challenges a belief apparently common among the people of the time that they suffered at the hands of the Babylonians because of the sins of previous generations. A disputation speech typically includes three major elements: a premise or thesis to be disputed, an alternative premise or thesis to be supported, and argumentation designed to demonstrate the validity of the alternative premise or thesis (see Murray; cf. Graffy, 58–64).

The statement of the thesis to be disputed appears in v. 2. Here, YHWH questions the validity of a proverb that has been circulating among the people, "Fathers have eaten sour grapes, and the teeth of the sons are set on edge." The proverb metaphorically maintains that the people of the present generation suffer for the sins of their ancestors. Grapes are a common agricultural product in the land of Israel in antiquity and they must be harvested when they are ripe. Grapes harvested too early before they mature will produce a sour taste that causes one to clench one's teeth upon tasting them. In Ezekiel's lifetime, the subjugation of Judah first to Egypt following the death of King Josiah in 609 BCE and then to Babylonia following the Babylonian defeat of Egypt in 605 BCE would have constituted the major source of national suffering following the reign of King Josiah. Josiah after all attempted to restore Judean political power and religious integrity as the power of the Assyrian empire waned. Many Judeans at the time apparently understood the reversal of Judean fortunes to be the result of divine punishment for past sins. Indeed, such a perspective appears in the Ten Commandments (Exod 20:5-6, which promise punishment to the third and fourth generation of those who reject YHWH and mercy to the thousandth generation of those who accept YHWH; cf. Exod 34:6-7). Such a perspective also underlies the narratives of the Former Prophets, viz., Joshua, Judges, Samuel, and Kings, which argue that northern Israel was destroyed because the people followed the illicit religious policies of King Jeroboam ben Nebat. Following the Babylonian exile, the Former Prophets would also argue that Jerusalem was destroyed because of the sins of King Manasseh, who died in 642 BCE, some fifty-five years prior to the destruction of Jerusalem in 587/586 BCE. YHWH, speaking through Ezekiel in Ezekiel 18:2-32, will argue against this view. Indeed, this proverb also appears in Jer 31:29-30 where it is employed to describe a future when everyone is punished for their own sins rather than for the sins of their ancestors.

The statement of the counterthesis appears in Ezekiel 18:3-4. YHWH's statement begins with an oath formula in which YHWH swears by YHWH's own life that this proverb will no longer endure among the people of Israel. YHWH makes the point that all lives, those of parent and child alike, belong to YHWH. Such a statement implies that YHWH will decide upon the life or death of the person in question. YHWH then explicitly states the counter thesis, viz., "the person who sins will die," viz., people do not suffer for the sins of their ancestors; they suffer because of their own sins. Such a counterthesis is designed in the first instance to defend the notion of YHWH's righteousness. By arguing for such a principle, YHWH maintains that there is moral cause for human suffering and that YHWH is the arbiter for such issues. In this respect, the dispute at hand may be considered as an example of theodicy insofar as it maintains that YHWH is righteous in deciding who will suffer and who will not (see Matties 1990). From Ezekiel's standpoint, human beings are accountable for their own suffering (Joyce 1989, 35–41). Although many interpreters argue that this statement supports the notion of Western individualism and moral accountability, this understanding is true only to a qualified extent. As the argumentation for this counterthesis in vv. 5-32 demonstrates, YHWH employs a generational paradigm in citing the examples that prove the point. YHWH's point in this passage is not simply a matter of individual moral accountability. Rather, it is a matter of generational moral accountability. The following argumentation only takes up examples of fathers and sons; it does not take up the case of brothers.

The argumentation for this dispute appears in vv. 5-32. YHWH argues the case by employing examples of three different individuals, each representing a subsequent generation of father, son, and grandson, respectively, in vv. 5-9, 10-13, and 14-19. A fuller statement of the counterthesis appears in v. 20. Verses 21-23 and 24 respectively take up examples of persons who change their moral behavior from wickedness to righteousness in the first instance and from righteousness to wickedness in the second. Verses 25-29 defend YHWH's position against charges that it is unfair, and vv. 30-32 conclude the subunit with a restatement of YHWH's principle of moral accountability that is employed to call upon the people of Israel to repent from any evil and to adhere to righteous action.

The first example describes the actions of a man who is righteous (Heb., *tsaddiq*) and does what is lawful (Heb., *mishpat*) and just (Heb., *tsedaqah*). The concern with righteousness and justice signals a forensic aspect of this demonstration; indeed, the example is written in a form that is typical of ancient Israelite or Judean case law, which cites both a case or set of acts that would be considered by a court of law followed by the decision of the court as to how to resolve the case at hand. The case or set of facts to be considered appears in vv. 5-9a, introduced by the formula "and if a man is righteous and does what is lawful and right . . . ." A series of conditions that state lawful and just actions then follow to demonstrate his righteous character. The series of stipulations appear to be derived primarily from the so-called

Holiness Code of Leviticus 17–26 that defined righteous and holy behavior in Israel, although provisions from other law codes also appear. Some argue that Ezekiel's series is analogous to those that appear on Egyptian temples (Weinfeld) or in the biblical entrance liturgy psalms that define the qualities necessary for one who would enter the sacred precincts of the Jerusalem Temple (Ps 15; 24). The requirement that he not eat on the mountains refers to the requirement to eat only meat that has been slaughtered according to the holy laws of temple sacrifice so that the blood, which embodies the life of the animal, is properly removed from the animal (see Lev 17; 19:26; cf. Gen 9:1-6). The requirement that he not lift his eyes to the idols (Heb., *gilluley*, "dung balls of") of the house of Israel employs Ezekiel's usual colorful language to refer to idolatrous worship (Exod 20:4-6; Lev 19:4). Defiling another man's wife of course refers to adultery, which renders both the man and the woman morally and ritually unholy (Lev 19:20-22; 20:10). Approaching, i.e., having relations with, a menstruating woman likewise renders a man unholy. Blood is a living substance that dies when it is emitted from the body, and contact with death renders one unholy (Lev 15:19-24). The stipulation that a man not wrong (Heb., *yoneh*, "oppress, cheat") anyone introduces instances of economic conduct (see Exod 22:25-27). The return of the pledge of a debtor refers to the requirement that a lender return an item given in pledge for a loan when the loan is repaid. The reference to robbery (Heb., *gezelah*, "robbery") refers to any dishonest economic action. The requirement to give food to the hungry and clothing to the naked states a basic principle of Jewish righteousness to care for those in need. Lending at advanced interest (Heb., *neshek*, "interest," derived from the verb, "to bite") or accrued interest (Heb., *tarbit*, "interest, increase") are absolutely forbidden in biblical law (Exod 22:25; Lev 25:35-38). The final statements of principle indicate a summation of the righteous man's character insofar as he returns his hand or avoids evil, does true justice with everyone, and observes YHWH's statutes and laws to do what is true. The final declaration that "he is righteous" (Heb., *tsaddiq*) is a legal declaration of innocence in court (Exod 23:7, 8; Deut 16:19; 25:1; 2 Sam 4:11; 1 Kings 2:32; 8:32; 2 Kings 10:9). As a result of his righteous action, the man is allowed to live. Such a declaration constitutes a moral premise here, i.e., righteous action results in life whereas unrighteous action results in death. The passage closes with the oracular formula "utterance of my L-rd, G-d" (Heb., *ne'um 'adonay 'elohim*) to certify a statement by YHWH.

Ezekiel 18:10-13 then considers the case of the son of the above-noted righteous man, but the son is described as evil. The Hebrew term *ben-parits*, literally "a son of outbreak," refers to a disreputable character who habitually breaks the law and social norms. The term is specified by the charge that he spills blood, which is both murder and a defiling act, and that he commits any of the following crimes. The list of crimes avoided by his above-mentioned righteous father then follows. The passage is careful to label these acts "abominations" (Heb., *toʻebot*), which refers to crimes that defile one morally and ritually. The result is a legal death sentence, "He shall surely be put to death" (*mot yumat*), and a statement that the responsibility is his own, his blood shall be upon him.

Ezekiel 18:14-19 then takes up the case of the son of the evil man who has acted righteously like his grandfather. Verse 14 emphasizes that the son/grandson understands the consequences of his behavior by a repeated use of the verb "to see," i.e., "behold he fathers a son, and he sees (Heb., *wayyar*) all the sins of his father, and he understands (Heb., *wayyir'eh*, lit., 'and he sees'), and he does not do any of them." The list of crimes avoided by the son/grandson then follows in vv. 15-17a. But the passage emphasizes in v. 17b that the son shall not be put to death for the crimes of his father; rather, he will live. After repeating that the father would be put to death for his crimes in v. 18, v. 19 then poses a rhetorical question from the audience, "And you say, 'Why does the son not bear the iniquity of the father?'" in an effort to demonstrate the point of the dispute. The question presumes that the son must be put to death because of the sins of the father, but v. 19b reiterates the son's innocence as a basis for declaring that he will be allowed to live.

Ezekiel 18:20 then states YHWH's counterthesis in the disputation, viz., the person who sins is subject to a sentence of death, but the child of a guilty person is not subject to death for the crimes of the parent. Each is judged in accordance with his or her actions, i.e., the righteous person is accounted as righteous and the wicked person is accounted as wicked, and each will be treated in accordance with his or her own actions.

Ezekiel 18:21-23 turns to the question of repentance. YHWH raises the possibility that a wicked person might repent of wrongdoing and take up a righteous life instead. In such a case, a repentant person will be considered righteous and allowed to live. Past transgressions will not be remembered. On the face of it, such a decision grants mercy to the repentant, but one must remember that true repentance must be envisioned here, not a cynical attempt to justify or clear past crimes by later adopting righteous behavior.

Ezekiel 18:24 then turns to the opposite case, viz., a righteous person who turns wicked. By the same token, such a person will be held accountable for the crimes and sentenced to death. Past righteousness will not save a person who turns to crime.

The disputational context emerges once again in Ezekiel 18:25-29 in which YHWH responds to the charge that these decisions are unfair (Heb., *lo' yittaken*, "not measured, regulated"). Here YHWH simply restates the above conclusions without true debate, viz., a wicked person will die for crime, and a person who turns from crime will save his or her life. This segment concludes with the retort in v. 29 that it is not YHWH's ways that are unfair; rather, the audience's ways are unfair.

Finally, Ezekiel 18:30-32 concludes this segment of the passage with an appeal for repentance, which seems to constitute the major point of this subunit. YHWH has laid out an argument for repentance by positing that the wicked will suffer and the righteous will live, and then positing that those who repent will live and those who turn from righteousness to crime will suffer the consequences. The reference to a new heart and a new spirit reinforces the attempt to convince the audience to change its ways. YHWH's final statement that YHWH desires that everyone live—by making the correct choices—likewise attempts to motivate the audience to make the right choice.

The third major segment of this unit is Ezekiel 19:1-14, which continues YHWH's speech to Ezekiel in Ezekiel 18:2-32. But Ezekiel 19:1-14 is demarcated at the outset by an introductory instruction by YHWH to the prophet in Ezekiel 19:1-2aα^1, "And you shall lift up a dirge concerning the princes of Israel, and you shall say . . . ," and at the conclusion by the statement in v. 14b, "It is a dirge, and it has become [functioned as] a dirge." Although this last statement may be an editorial comment, it functions as part of YHWH's speech as a means to identify the character of the composition that Ezekiel is instructed to speak in Ezekiel 19:2aα^2-14a.

A dirge is a specific liturgical form that is employed in cases of mourning for the dead or in poetry that employs the motif of mourning for the dead. It is characterized by its typical 3/2 metric pattern, in which the first stanza has three major beats, but the second stanza has only two (the basic study of the dirge form is Jahnow, esp. pp. 197–210, which treat Ezekiel 19:1-9, 10-14. Hedwig Jahnow, a student of Hermann Gunkel, was murdered by the Nazis at Theresienstadt in 1944 because her father was Jewish). Such a metrical pattern would correspond with the slow-paced, plodding step that would be employed in a funeral procession or mourning ritual in which those carrying the body or processing to the site of a burial would walk in a halting march for three steps and then for two as they proceeded to the gravesite. An example of such a march would be the so-called limping dance of the 450 prophets of Baal at Mt. Carmel in 1 Kings 18:25-29, esp. v. 26. Here, the 450 prophets of Baal were invoking the name of Baal in their contest with the prophet Elijah in an effort to raise Baal from the underworld and put an end to the drought at the end of the dry summer season in Israel. In the present instance, the dirge form signals mourning for the Judean kings portrayed in Ezekiel 19:1-14, viz., Jehoahaz, Jehoiakim, and Jehoiachin, who met their respective demises in different ways. King Jehoahaz ben Josiah was deported to Egypt by Pharaoh Necho shortly after he succeeded his father in 609 BCE (2 Kings 23:31-34; 2 Chr 36:1-4). His older brother King Jehoiakim ben Josiah was placed on the throne by Necho to serve as an Egyptian puppet, and died of unknown causes when he revolted against Babylon in 598 BCE (2 Kings 23:34-35; 24:1-7; 2 Chr 36:5-8; cf. Jer 21:11–22:10). King Jehoiachin ben Jehoiakim was deported to Babylon in 597 BCE for the rest of his life as a consequence of his father's revolt against Nebuchadnezzar (2 Kings 24:8-17; 2 Chr 36:9-10).

The first portion of the dirge in vv. 2aα^2-9 portrays the respective fates of the three above-mentioned kings in metaphorical form. The reference to the lioness employs the symbol of the tribe of Judah from which the royal house of David had come (Gen 49:8-12), but it presents her as a female lion to facilitate the imagery of the kings as her cubs to whom she had given birth. The reference to the first cub points to Jehoahaz, who was exiled to Egypt after serving as king for only three months. Ezekiel 19:3-4 describes him as having been raised to become a great beast who hunted prey and devoured humans, but he was caught in a snare by the nations and carried off with hooks to Egypt. The portrayal of the second cub in vv. 5-9 refers jointly to Jehoiakim, who revolted against Babylon, and to his son Jehoiachin, who was deported to Babylon following his father's unexplained death. Again, the dirge portrays the mother lion selecting one of her cubs to become a great beast who hunts prey and devours humans. Some have argued that the reference to knowing his widows in v. 7 should be emended to knowing his fortresses, but such an emendation is unnecessary. The reference to knowing widows stands in parallel to laying waste cities, and together these images provide the basis for the contention that the land and everyone in it were appalled at his actions. Although the imagery is obscure, Jehoiakim was known for suppressing pro-Babylonian elements in Judean society as he prepared for his revolt against Babylon (see Jer 7, 26-29, and 36, which portray Jehoiakim's attempts to suppress the anti-Egyptian Jeremiah, who called for alliance with Babylon). The dirge portrays the nations arrayed against him, which fits with his revolt against Nebuchadnezzar in 598. But Jehoiakim died when Nebuchadnezzar besieged Jerusalem under circumstances that are never made clear. Nebuchadnezzar's deportation of his eighteen-year-old son and successor, Jehoiachin, is portrayed in vv. 8b-9, which describe how the nations spread their net upon him, caged him, carried him off to Babylon, and imprisoned him in a fortress so that he never returned to Jerusalem again for the rest of his life.

The second portion of the dirge in vv. 10-14a employs the imagery of a vine to portray Judah's subjugation to Babylon and the loss of her monarchs. The medieval Jewish Bible commentator Radaq (R. David Kimhi, 1160–1235 CE) and many interpreters after him have argued that the passage refers to the demise of Zedekiah ben Josiah (2 Kings 24:18–25:7; 2 Chr 36:11-21), the last king of Judah, but the passage contains no specific references to him. Verses 10-11 portray Judah's greatness and might. The reference in v. 10 to "your mother like a vine in your blood" (Heb., *bedameka*) appears to represent a later reference to the portrayal of Jerusalem in her blood in Ezekiel 16:6. Many scholars therefore emend the reference to "your mother like a vine in your vineyard" (Heb., *karmeka*) based on the similar forms of the letters beth and kaph and the letters dalet and resh in Hebrew. Indeed, the portrayal of Israel or Judah as a vineyard picks up the well-known metaphor of Isaiah 5:1-8. The reference to mighty waters and luxuriant boughs and branches emphasizes Judah's well-being and leads the reader to the imagery of the mighty rod and the scepter of rulers in v. 11, which portrays the might of Judah's kings. But vv. 12-14a portray the downfall of once-great Judah from her high position beside mighty waters to a low position in a waterless desert. The reference in v. 12 to the east wind employs a common motif that signals YHWH's actions to bring down an opponent, such as Egypt at the Red Sea (Exod 14–15). The east wind is the dry desert sirocco, known in Hebrew as the Sharav and in Arabic as the Hamsin, analogous to the Santa Ana winds of southern California that appear at times of seasonal transition. Insofar as the Sharav dries out the land and frequently blows in with exceptionally destructive force, it is identified with YHWH's actions against enemies in ancient Israelite and Judean culture. Here, it symbolizes YHWH's actions against Judah herself (Fitzgerald).

Ezekiel's Oracles concerning the Punishment of All Israel

Ezekiel 20:1–23:49

Ezekiel 20:1–23:49 constitutes the third major textual block of the book of Ezekiel. The oracular accounts included in this unit focus on the bases for the punishment of all Israel. The unit begins with the chronological formula in Ezekiel 20:1, *wayehi bashanah hashebi'it bahamishi be 'asor lahodesh*, "and it was in the seventh year, in the fifth month, on the tenth of the month," which would be the tenth day of Av, 591 BCE. The tenth of Av is also the date that Nebuchadnezzar destroyed the temple in Jerusalem five years later. (See Jer 52:12-13; contra 2 Kings 25:8-9, which dates the destruction to the seventh day; rabbinic tradition reconciles the discrepancies by stating that the Babylonian general, Nebuzaradan entered the temple on the seventh of Av, burned it on the ninth, and the fire continued through the tenth [*b. Ta 'anit* 29a]. Judaism observes the anniversary of the destruction of the temple on *Tisha b'Av*, i.e., the ninth of Av.) As in previous units, the prophetic word formula *wayehi debar-yhwh 'elay le'mor*, "and the word of YHWH was unto me, saying," introduces each of the individual oracle reports that constitute the subunits of this text. Following the introductory chronological formula in Ezekiel 20:1, the subunits of this text include Ezekiel 20:2-44, an oracular account concerning Ezekiel's assessment of Israel's past and future; Ezekiel 21:1-5, an oracular account concerning Ezekiel's prophecy against the Negev; Ezekiel 21:6-12, the first oracular account concerning YHWH's sword; Ezekiel 21:13-22, the second oracular account concerning YHWH's sword; Ezekiel 21:23-37, the third oracular account concerning YHWH's sword; Ezekiel 22:1-16, an oracular account concerning bloodshed in Jerusalem; Ezekiel 22:17-22, an oracular account concerning the smelting of Jerusalem; Ezekiel 22:23-31, an oracular account concerning the leadership and people of Jerusalem; and Ezekiel 23:1-49, an oracular account concerning Oholah and Oholibah. The chronological formula in Ezekiel 24:1 marks the beginning of the fourth unit of the book. The formal structure of the unit is as follows:

III. Ezekiel's oracles concerning the punishment of all Israel (Ezek 20:1–23:49)
   A. Introduction (20:1)
   B. The oracular account: concerning Ezekiel's assessment of Israel's past and future (20:2-44)
   C. The oracular account: concerning Ezekiel's prophecy against the Negev (21:1-5)
   D. The first oracular account: concerning YHWH's sword (21:6-12)
   E. The second oracular account: concerning YHWH's sword (21:13-22)
   F. The third oracular account: concerning YHWH's sword (21:23-37)
   G. The oracular account: concerning bloodshed in Jerusalem (22:1-16)
   H. The oracular account: concerning the smelting of Jerusalem (22:17-22)
   I. The oracular account: concerning condemnation of the leadership and people of Jerusalem (22:23-31)
   J. The oracular account: concerning Oholah and Oholibah (23:1-49)

Introduction (20:1)

The introductory chronological statement in Ezekiel 20:1 functions as the introduction for all of the constituent subunits in Ezekiel 20:2–23:49. As noted above, it dates these oracles to the tenth of Av, 591 BCE, some five years to the day prior to the destruction of the Jerusalem Temple. The tenth of Av also appears in the introduction to the next unit of the book in Ezekiel 24:1, albeit in the ninth year. The ascription of the oracles to this date may be a deliberate attempt to tie them to the day of the destruction of the temple itself either by Ezekiel or a later editor of his work. This verse portrays oracular inquiry of Ezekiel by some of the elders of Israel. As in Ezekiel 8:1, the oracular inquiry likely would have taken place at Ezekiel's house.

Oracular Account: Concerning Ezekiel's Assessment of Israel's Past and Future (20:2-44)

As noted above, Ezekiel 20:2-44 begins with an example of the prophetic word formula in v. 2, *wayehi debar-yhwh 'elay le'mor*, "and the word of YHWH was unto me, saying," which introduces the oracular account by identifying it as a word spoken by YHWH to Ezekiel.

The entirety of Ezekiel 20:3-44 is formulated as YHWH's instruction speech to Ezekiel, which instructs him to speak YHWH's oracle to the elders of Israel seated before him. It begins in typical form with the address, "O son of Adam," to identify Ezekiel as the descendent of Adam who has been ordained as a priest to represent all humanity, viz., the children of Adam, before YHWH in the Jerusalem Temple.

The address to Ezekiel as son of Adam is then followed by YHWH's first instruction statement to Ezekiel in v. 3aα that he should speak these words to the elders of Israel. The content of the initial statement appears in v. 3aβ-b. It begins with the prophetic messenger formula *koh 'amar 'adonay 'lhym*, "thus said my L-rd, G-d," to identify YHWH as the source of the following statement to the elders. The statement abruptly conveys YHWH's refusal to speak with them. It begins with the rhetorical question, "Have you come to inquire of me?" YHWH follows up the question immediately with an example of the oath formula *hay 'ani*, "as I live," and the statement "I will not respond to you" (lit., "I will not be inquired by you"). The reason for YHWH's refusal of the elders' inquiry is not immediately stated, but it will be the subject of the following elements of the oracular account. This brief segment concludes with the oracular formula *ne'um yhwh*, "utterance of YHWH," to identify it as YHWH's oracular statement.

YHWH's second instruction speech to Ezekiel begins in vv. 4-5aα$^{1-2}$ with "Will you judge them? Will you judge them, O son of Adam?" Although translators often render these questions as declarations by YHWH, e.g., "Arraign, arraign them, O Mortal!" (NJPS), the Hebrew interrogative form is deliberate in that it requests Ezekiel's assistance in accusing the people of Israel of failing to abide by the terms of the covenant that binds them to YHWH. YHWH's following explanation, "Inform them of the abominations of their ancestors (lit., "fathers"), and you shall say to them," makes it clear that Ezekiel's task is to accuse the ancestors of the people of abominable behavior that betrayed their covenant with YHWH.

The first portion of YHWH's speech that Ezekiel is to convey to the elders appears in vv. 5aα^3-26. It begins with the prophetic messenger formula to indicate that it is a speech by YHWH to be delivered to its recipients, but it is formulated throughout as a speech to Ezekiel that describes the behavior of the ancestors of Israel. Insofar as the speech is designed to demonstrate that the ancestors' behavior violated their covenant with YHWH, it functions as the first portion of a prophetic judgment speech in which the speaker presents the basis for the judgment that is to be announced against the offending party. But as the following segments of the chapter will demonstrate, YHWH's purpose is not simply to announce judgment, but also restoration for Israel once the period of judgment is completed.

YHWH begins the speech with a reference to choosing Israel, which signals the covenant relationship between YHWH and Israel that underlies this entire text. The covenant background is highlighted repeatedly throughout the speech in YHWH's references to raising "my hand" (see vv. 5, 6, 15, 23). The portrayal of YHWH's raised hand is an idiom intended to indicate that YHWH raised the divine hand to swear adherence to the covenant that binds YHWH and Israel together. It is further highlighted by YHWH's repeated references to deeds done on behalf of Israel as part of that relationship, i.e., bringing the people out from Egypt, leading them through the wilderness, revealing to them statutes and laws by which human beings might live, granting them the most beautiful land of all flowing with milk and honey, and granting them the Shabbat or Sabbath to function as the sign of the covenant so that they might be sanctified in their relationship with YHWH and so that they will know YHWH. Scholars have noted that YHWH's speech presupposes many elements of the Pentateuchal exodus and wilderness traditions, especially in the books of Exodus and Numbers. Although many interpreters have attempted to argue that this account of Israel's wilderness sojourn must be late because of its priestly perspective, readers must bear in mind that ancient Israel's and Judah's major religious institutions were temples overseen by the various lines of the priesthood. The mere presence of priestly concerns does not point necessarily to a late text or concept. This applies especially to the references to the Shabbat or Sabbath, which is already known in Isaiah 1:13. Although many elements of the exodus and Numbers wilderness narratives are labeled as late priestly writings, the major criterion for such decisions is the presence of priestly or ritual concerns; but it is not always clear that these elements presume late dating.

This portion of YHWH's speech also lays out Israel's rebellion against YHWH in the wilderness. YHWH charges that each member of the wilderness generation refused to abide by YHWH's demands to cast away the detestable things of his eyes (*shiqqutsey 'enayw*, lit., "excrements of his eyes") and the fetishes of Egypt (*gilluley mitsrayim*, lit., "turds of Egypt"). Ezekiel's use of profanity here is deliberate. On the one hand, the language conveys the fact that the foreign idols defile the people in the ritual sense of rendering them unholy, and on the other it conveys the hygienic sense of rendering them unclean, disgusting, and filthy. But such strong language also conveys the intensity of YHWH's emotions in bringing judgment against the people as YHWH pours out fury upon the people for their refusal to listen to YHWH or to abide by YHWH's requirements. YHWH describes the near destruction of Israel in the wilderness in vv. 13-16, i.e., how YHWH nearly brought Israel to an end altogether, but acted instead for the sake of

YHWH's name so that it might not be profaned in the sight of the nations. The summary here presupposes Moses' challenges to YHWH, i.e., that YHWH could not kill all Israel and make a new people out of Moses' line, as such an act would be immoral in light of the covenant and in the eyes of the nations (see Num 14:11-19; cf. Exod 32:9-14). After Moses challenged YHWH's plans to destroy Israel, YHWH instead resolved to destroy only the wilderness generation and to bring only their offspring to the land of Israel instead. Verse 17 acknowledges YHWH's decision by claiming that YHWH had pity upon them. But vv. 18-26 relate how despite instructions to the descendants of the wilderness generation to observe YHWH's covenant, they likewise refused to abide, prompting YHWH to pour out divine wrath upon them as well. Ironically, YHWH claims in vv. 25-26 to have given the people statutes that were not good and laws by which people could not live. The reference to the firstborn indicates a question over early Israelite practice. Exodus 22:28 (cf. Exod 34:19) demands that Israel give its firstborn sons to YHWH. Such a law may well presuppose a period of human sacrifice, although Exodus 34:19 makes it clear that firstborn sons are to be redeemed. Statements by YHWH to Moses in Numbers 3:6-13, 3:40-51, and 8:13-19 indicate a prior practice of having the firstborn serve as priests in Israel until they were replaced in this role by the Levites. Such statements suggest that there was a prior law concerning the treatment of the firstborn that was replaced by the decision to use Levites as priests in the book of Numbers.

YHWH's third instruction speech to Ezekiel begins in v. 27aαβ, "Therefore, speak to the house of Israel, O son of Adam, and you shall say to them . . . ." The particle *laken*, "therefore," signals transition in YHWH's instruction speech to Ezekiel. Whereas vv. 4-26 laid out the grounds for YHWH's judgment against Israel, vv. 27-29 and 30-44 will lay out the basis on which YHWH will redeem at least some elements of Israel. The speech itself appears in vv. 27aγ-29, and relates how Israel would present offerings to YHWH at any high hill or leafy tree. Such features are considered Canaanite symbols for Baal and Asherah, the Canaanite male and female deities of fertility. YHWH sarcastically refers to the high places (Heb., *bamah*) with the pun, "what (Heb., *mah*) is this high place (Heb., *bamah*) to which you come (Heb., *ba'im*, singular *ba*)? Its name shall be called Bamah until this day." In making such a joke, YHWH eases the transition to the following statements concerning Israel's restoration in vv. 30-44.

YHWH's final instruction speech in this unit appears in vv. 30-44, which are introduced by the command "Therefore, say to the house of Israel" in v. 30aα$^{1-5}$. The particle "therefore" again signals transition. The speech per se begins in v. 30aα$^{6-9}$ with the prophetic messenger formula "thus says my L-rd G-d" to certify it as a speech by YHWH. YHWH begins in vv. 30aβ-31 with a rhetorical question that asks if YHWH should answer their oracular inquiry if the elders continue to defile themselves as their ancestors had done. The answer of course is no, YHWH will not answer. Although some critics see this statement as the end of the original oracle, they miss the significance of YHWH's statement, i.e., YHWH lays out a circumstance which results in the failure of the inquiry, but this is a circumstance that must change. Verse 32 affirms such failure by indicating what the elders have in mind shall never come to pass. But YHWH in vv. 33-38 lays out a different course of action that will result in the restoration of some of the people. This portion of YHWH's speech reiterates the covenant imagery of raised hand noted earlier in the passage, but it changes the hand to a well-known image of YHWH's judgment against the Egyptians during the exodus, viz., the strong hand and the outstretched arm (e.g., Deut 4:34). YHWH's arm here is not used to punish Israel, but to gather them from the lands to which they have been exiled. The people will be returned to the wilderness once again where YHWH will enter into judgment with them face to face, recalling the judgment of the earlier wilderness period. By bringing the people under the "shepherd's staff" to be counted (cf. Lev 27:32), YHWH will choose those who still adhere to the covenant and winnow out those who do not. Such a process will reveal YHWH to the people.

The final segment of YHWH's speech in vv. 39-44 then lays out the process of restoration. Those who continue to worship the idols and fetishes will no longer be allowed to defile YHWH's holy name with their offerings. The only acceptable worship for YHWH will take place on the site of the Jerusalem Temple, i.e., YHWH's holy mountain, where YHWH will be sanctified by Israel's holy offerings in the sight of all the nations. At that point, when the exiled people have been restored to the land of Israel, they will recognize YHWH. Just as YHWH refrained from putting Israel to an end in the wilderness, so YHWH will restore the people of Israel to the land of Israel for the sake of YHWH's holy name.

Oracular Account: Condemnation of the Negev (21:1-5)

The brief oracular account in Ezekiel 21:1-5 begins with a typical example of the prophetic word formula in v. 1, which introduces YHWH's instruction speech to Ezekiel in vv. 2-5 concerning the condemnation of the Negev wilderness region of southern Judah. The oracular account begins with YHWH's typical address to Ezekiel as "son of Adam" to acknowledge his status as a descendant of Adam and priest who represents all of Adam's descendants before YHWH in the temple. It continues with a threefold instruction to Ezekiel to speak to the South, i.e., the Negev. The first is an instruction to set his face against Teman, a term that generally means "south" but has later come to designate Yemen in Hebrew. Given the interest in the Negev in this oracle, it seems likely that it simply refers to the southern regions of Judah to the west and south of the Dead Sea. The second is YHWH's instruction to Ezekiel to "preach" to Darom. The Hebrew term *hattef* means, literally, "to drip," but it is employed idiomatically in biblical and rabbinic Hebrew to describe forms of discourse associated with speaking on behalf of YHWH or expounding a scriptural text. The term Darom refers to the south, much like Teman. The third is an instruction to prophesy against the Negev. The Hebrew term *negev* also generally denotes the south, but it is also the name of the wilderness area in the southern portion of Judah south of the Judean hill country and west and south of the Dead Sea. The reason for Ezekiel's interest in the Negev is that Nebuchadnezzar apparently had an alliance with the Edomites that facilitated his conquest and destruction of Jerusalem. Insofar as Edom is located to the south and east of the Dead Sea, an alliance with Edom would have granted Nebuchadnezzar's forces access to southern Judah (cf. Ezek 25:12-14).

The oracle in vv. 3-4 that Ezekiel is to communicate begins with the call-to-attention formula "hear the word of YHWH" followed by the prophetic messenger formula "thus says my L-rd G-d" to certify the oracle of YHWH. The content of the oracle basically states YHWH's intentions to kindle the Negev so that its trees and brush will be entirely consumed, thereby revealing YHWH's action to the entire world. But v. 5 includes an unusual feature, viz., Ezekiel's retort to YHWH that the people will simply call him a speaker of riddles, allegories, or proverbs (Heb., *memashel meshalim*, "a purveyor of proverbs") to indicate that the meaning of this oracle will not be clear to them and will not be taken seriously. The subunit closes with Ezekiel's objection.

The open-ended nature of this subunit indicates that the three following subunits in Ezekiel 21:6-12, 21:13-22, and 21:23-37, each of which presents an oracular account concerned with YHWH's sword, are meant to specify and elaborate upon the destruction of the Negev announced in Ezekiel 21:1-5. Scholars generally argue that these oracles were composed independently, as they presuppose different periods during the process of the Babylonian conquest of Judah (e.g., Zimmerli 1979, 419–51; Allen 1990, 16–29; Block, 659–99). Although this conclusion may be correct for the composition of these oracles, they nevertheless function together in the present form of the book, albeit as discrete subunits, each introduced with its own prophetic word formula, to specify the initial oracle concerning the destruction of the Negev in Ezekiel 21:1-5.

Oracular Account: The First Oracle concerning YHWH's Sword (21:6-12)

The first oracular account concerning YHWH's sword in Ezekiel 21:6-12 begins with the usual introductory prophetic word formula in v. 6. YHWH's word to Ezekiel begins with the typical address form "son of Adam," followed by instructions to set his face against Jerusalem, to preach against its sanctuaries (on the Hebrew term, *hattef*, "to drip, preach," see Ezek 21:1-5 above), and to prophesy against the land of Israel. As noted in the introduction, Ezekiel always presumes that Jerusalem is the holy center of the entire land of Israel, not only the land of Judah, as well as of all creation.

YHWH's instructions to speak the oracle per se appear in vv. 8-12. Verse 8aα introduces the oracle with an instruction to address the land of Israel and the prophetic messenger formula. The first portion of the oracle in vv. 8aβ-10 announces YHWH's intentions to unsheathe the sword and use it to destroy both the righteous and the wicked together from south to north. Again, such an act is considered revelatory of YHWH's presence and action to the entire world.

At one level, such an oracle would envision a Babylonian scorched-earth policy in which all the inhabitants of the land of Israel would fall victim to the Babylonians. Despite Babylonian brutality, however, it is clear that they did not wipe out the entire population of the land of Israel. At this point, the second portion of the oracle in vv. 11-12 is instructive. YHWH is still the speaker, but YHWH instructs Ezekiel to sigh in grief before the people in an effort to elicit their response. When the people ask what he is doing, Ezekiel is to respond that he is mourning for the coming destruction that will encompass all the people. Ezekiel's sighing over the complete destruction of the people points to another dimension of the text, viz., its intertextual relationship with the narrative concerning YHWH's intentions to destroy Sodom and Gomorrah in Genesis 18. Here, YHWH informs Abraham of the intention to destroy the entirety of Sodom and Gomorrah, and it is left to Abraham to object to YHWH's plan, asking YHWH if the righteous will be destroyed along with the wicked (see esp. Gen 18:22-32). YHWH of course answers that the righteous will not be destroyed. But as the following subunits in Ezekiel 21:13-22 and 21:23-37 indicate, no such reprieve will come as YHWH wields the sword against the people of Israel and Ammon.

But then Genesis 18–19 indicated complete destruction for Sodom and Gomorrah, as no righteous people were present to be delivered apart from Lot and his family.

Oracular Account: YHWH's Second Oracle concerning the Sword (21:13-22)

The second oracular account concerning YHWH's sword begins in the usual manner with the prophetic word formula in v. 13. YHWH's address to Ezekiel as son of Adam, the instruction statement, and the prophetic messenger formula all follow as usual in v. 14a. The oracle that Ezekiel is instructed to speak appears in vv. 14b-22.

The oracle per se employs the same imagery and a similar message to that of Ezekiel 21:6-12. It appears to be based on the observation of a smith who has just completed a sword or who is simply polishing and sharpening a sword that is already made. The oracle focuses specifically on the purposes for which the sword is to be used, i.e., the destruction of the people and princes of Israel. We can never know the image on which the oracle was based; perhaps Ezekiel saw the smith making or sharpening and polishing the sword in Babylonia.

The first portion of the oracle in vv. 14b-18 begins in v. 14b by focusing on the finishing of the sword, particularly its sharpening and polishing. Verse 15 takes up the purpose for which it is to be used, slaughter, and the language pertaining to the sharpening and polishing adds reference to the lightning or flashing character of the hardened metal of the sword as light and perhaps sparks flash off of it as it strikes. Although the language of v. 15b is enigmatic, it appears to suggest that Ezekiel is to address his audience, here personified as "my son" in typical wisdom instruction style, to rejoice at producing a weapon that will defeat any rod or tree that might stand in its way. But v. 16 emphasizes that the sword is not just to be used against wood: it is to be placed in the hand of a killer. This observation then leads to YHWH's command to Ezekiel to cry and wail because the people of Israel and its princes are to be cast before this sword. The sword that YHWH is fashioning for use against Israel is more powerful than the rod that YHWH used against Egypt during the exodus (see the use of Moses' rod in Exod 6–15) or against Assyria during the time of Isaiah (see the use of the outstretched hand and the rod against Israel and Assyria in Isa 9:7–10:34). This segment of the oracle ends with the portrayal of Ezekiel's audience slapping their thighs in recognition of the coming suffering that the will endure.

The second portion of the oracle in vv. 19-22, introduced by the address form "and you, O son of Adam, prophesy!" transitions from the imagery of striking hands to the striking sword. It specifies that the sword has been sharpened and polished for slaughter as it flashes while turning right and left to destroy everyone. YHWH, too, will strike hands as the slaughter proceeds in accordance with YHWH's word.

Oracular Account: The Third Oracle concerning YHWH's Sword (21:23-37)

The third oracle concerning YHWH's sword again proceeds in typical form with the prophetic word formula in v. 23, the address to Ezekiel as "son of Adam" at the beginning of v. 24. The oracle that Ezekiel is instructed to speak proceeds in three portions, each defined at the outset by the address form "and you" in vv. 24, 30, and 33.

The first portion of the oracle in vv. 24-29, addressed to Ezekiel, focuses on the approach of the king of Babylon to a fork in the road. One branch will take him to Jerusalem and the other to Rabbath Ammon, the capital of the Ammonites who were an ally of Judah during the revolt against Babylon (see Jer 27:3). Rabbath Ammon is located on the site of modern-day Amman, Jordan. When the Babylonian king reaches the fork, he engages in several divinatory acts to inquire of the gods which branch of the road he should take, to Jerusalem or to Rabbath Ammon? He shakes arrows as one device, consults teraphim or idols of family gods, and inspects a liver. All of these actions are known acts of divination. The fall of the arrows indicates an answer to the question posed; consulting gods was a typical divinatory act; and reading livers was a well-known procedure. The question would be posed to a sacrificial animal and its liver would be read after it was slaughtered. Depending upon the location of a small finger or protrusion in the liver, the answer to the question would be found. In this case, the results of the divination point the king of Babylon to lay siege to Jerusalem with battering rams, siege mounds, and siege towers. Verse 29, introduced by *laken*, "therefore," and the prophetic messenger formula, makes it clear that in Ezekiel's and YHWH's eyes, Jerusalem is guilty of transgression and therefore the suffering is a form of punishment.

The second address in vv. 30-32 is addressed to "the profaned, wicked prince of Israel." This would have to be King Zedekiah ben Josiah, the nephew of the legitimate King Jehoiachin ben Jehoiakim, who had been exiled to Babylonia in 597 BCE. Zedekiah was placed on the throne as a puppet and his task was to keep Judah submissive to Babylon. He was never viewed as the legitimate king of Judah, and he obviously failed in his task when revolt broke out in 588 BCE. The oracle portrays the removal of the royal turban and crown, as Zedekiah will be brought to ruin. The oracle envisions the return of the legitimate monarch, presumably Jehoiachin or one of his descendants.

The third address appears in vv. 33-37, again addressed to Ezekiel as son of Adam. This portion of the oracle makes it clear that although the king of Babylon will focus his attack on Jerusalem, Rabbath Ammon will be destroyed as well by YHWH's rampaging sword. The oracle presumes that the Ammonites had concluded that they would not be invaded, perhaps because the divinatory acts of the king of Babylon had pointed to Jerusalem and not to Rabbath Ammon. But the sword will nevertheless be wielded against Rabbath Ammon as well.

Finally, the sword will be placed back into its sheath and returned to the land of its creation, i.e., Babylon, where YHWH will judge it as well. Such a model appears in Isaiah where the Assyrian king is employed as YHWH's agent to punish Israel and Judah and then he too is judged and punished after having threatened Jerusalem (see esp. Isa 5–11; 36–37). But whereas the Assyrian king Sennacherib was in fact assassinated by his own sons, it is never clear that Nebuchadnezzar died of anything but natural causes.

Oracular Account: Concerning Bloodshed in Jerusalem (22:1-16)

A typical example of the prophetic word formula in Ezekiel 22:1 introduces this oracular account concerned with bloodshed in Jerusalem. Although the unit may well have been composed together with Ezekiel 22:17-22 and Ezekiel 22:23-31, it functions as a discrete subunit within the synchronic literary structure of Ezekiel 20–23.

The concern with bloodshed in this passage does not presuppose crimes of murder that have taken place in Jerusalem. Instead, it presupposes the sanctity of blood as a fundamental concept in priestly thought. Blood is a living substance in a living body, but blood dies when it is shed. Insofar as death is the ultimate antithesis of sanctity in the conceptualization of the priesthood, the issue of shed blood serves as a key entrée into understandings of what is sacred and what is profane in Judean priestly thought. The concern with the proper treatment of blood in Leviticus 17 therefore introduces the so-called Holiness Code in Leviticus 17–26, which takes up a variety of issues concerning moral and ritual sanctity, including improper sexual relations (Lev 18), a moral and ritual overview (Lev 19), improper sexual relations again (Lev 20), the sanctity of the priesthood (Lev 21), sacred offerings (Lev 22), sacred times (Lev 23), sacred features of the sanctuary (Lev 24:1-9), blasphemy against G-d (Lev 24:10-23), the Jubilee Year (Lev 25), and the blessings and curses associated with the observance of such sacred instruction (Lev 26). Ezekiel 22:1-16 likewise employs the concern with the improper treatment of blood as a leitmotif for the various issues of sanctity addressed in the passage, most of which correspond to those of the Holiness Code. Although most scholars date the Holiness Code to the late Babylonian exile, there is a significant minority who date it to the pre-exilic period (e.g., Milgrom, 1361–64). Whether or not Leviticus was composed in its present form during Ezekiel's lifetime, he appears to be intimately familiar with the issues and language that are features in the Holiness Code. The passage also presupposes Isaiah's charges that Jerusalem had been defiled by bloodshed (Isa 1:10-17 [see esp. vv. 15, 16-17] and Isa 1:18-20) and needed to be purged (see Isa 1:21-26). Like Ezekiel and the Holiness Code, Isaiah employed bloodshed as a general motif to signal the absence of sanctity expressed in a variety of different charges made against Jerusalem. Consequently, Ezekiel 22:1-16 appears to be heavily dependent on the oracles of Isaiah 1:10-26 as well (for treatment of the Isaian texts, see Sweeney 1996, 78–86).

Ezekiel 22:2-16 appears in the form of YHWH's instruction speech addressed to the prophet in which YHWH challenges Ezekiel to judge the city of Jerusalem. YHWH's speech to Ezekiel begins in v. 2 with the address "son of Adam" to signify his priestly status as a representative of humanity before G-d. It continues with the dual question "Will you judge? Will you judge the city of bloodshed?" Although expressed in interrogative terms, YHWH's questions clearly function rhetorically in that they are designed to prompt Ezekiel to render the proper judgment after all of the charges that YHWH is about to make are accepted as true. Such intention is evident in vv. 2b-3aα^1, "make known all its abominations, and you shall say," which introduces the sequence of accusations in vv. 3aα^2 that YHWH intends to make against Jerusalem through Ezekiel. YHWH's accusations begin in v. 3aα^{2-5} with the prophetic messenger formula "thus says my L-rd G-d" to identify YHWH as the authority who spoke the oracle to the prophet. The accusations themselves appear in vv. 3aβ-16, organized in three major sections. Verses 3aβ-5 take up the general accusation of bloodshed, and vv. 6-12, introduced by *hinneh*, "behold," take up the specific accusations. Verses 13-16, introduced by *wehinneh*, "and behold," conclude the oracle with YHWH's statements of the consequences for the alleged crimes of the people.

The first segment in vv. 3aβ-5 focuses on the general accusation of bloodshed as a means to charge that the city has become defiled and has thereby lost its holy status. Leviticus 17 makes it clear that improper treatment of blood compromises holiness due to the exposure to death (see also Lev 19:26). YHWH equates bloodshed with the worship of idols, here called *gillulim*, "turds," to accentuate the disgusting and unacceptable character of the charges that YHWH makes against the people. The statement in v. 4 that the city has incurred guilt recalls the instructions concerning the purging of sin and guilt as prescribed in Leviticus 4–5. YHWH maintains that the time for judgment has come. The references to the mockery of the nations presumes the blessings and curses that appear in Leviticus 26 at the conclusion of the Holiness Code in which YHWH promises to turn the people over to their enemies if they do not observe the instructions of Leviticus 17–25.

The second major segment of the passage appears in vv. 6-12, which specifies the various charges that YHWH makes against the people. This segment begins with YHWH's general charges against the "princes of (Heb., *nesi'ey*) Israel," i.e., the kings and leaders of Israel who have led the people into the general crime of bloodshed. Verses 7-12 then give specific examples, including the humiliation of parents (Lev 20:9; Exod 21:17); the cheating of resident aliens (Lev 19:33-34); mistreatment of widows and orphans (Isa 1:17; Exod 22:21; Deut 14:29; 16:11, 14; 24:17-21; 26:12-13; 27:19; cf. Lev 19:9-10); desecration of YHWH's holy things and the Shabbat (Lev 19:3, 30; Isa 1:10-17); the actions of base persons who denigrate others (Lev 19:16); improper treatment of the blood of animals slaughtered on mountains instead of in the sanctuary (Lev 17); sexual depravity, including relations with a father's wife, menstrual women, other men's wives, and female relatives (Lev 18; 20); acceptance of bribes (Lev 19:15; Deut 16:19); charging interest on a loan (Lev 25:36-37); and extortion of a neighbor (Lev 19:15-18, 35-36).

The final subunit in Ezekiel 22:13-16 delineates the consequences of the alleged misconduct of the people of Jerusalem. This segment presupposes the blessings and curses of Leviticus 26 in which YHWH vows to bring consequences against the people should they fail to observe YHWH's instructions for holy conduct. YHWH employs a rhetorical question to taunt the people, viz., "Will your hearts stand firm? Will your hands remain strong when I deal with you?" as a means to persuade the people that they will not be able to endure YHWH's punishments. The purpose of such actions is to purge the people of their impurity as indicated in v. 15 in which YHWH states, "and I will eradicate your impurity from you" as the nations watch. YHWH's speech concludes with the self-revelation formula "and you will know that I am YHWH."

Oracular Account: Concerning the Smelting of Jerusalem (22:17-22)

This brief oracular account begins in typical fashion with the prophetic word formula in v. 17. The oracle is formulated as YHWH's address to Ezekiel, here identified as "son of Adam," to indicate his priestly status. The oracle itself focuses on the smelting of Jerusalem as a metaphor for the purification of Jerusalem from its impurity. The imagery clearly builds on the preceding oracular account concluding with the imagery of purging Jerusalem. Here, the oracle draws upon Isaiah 1:20-26, which employs the imagery of smelting ore to remove its dross and thereby produce purified metal. It identifies a number of metals: silver, copper, iron, lead, and tin. Metal ore is smelted by heat and flame; the application of intense heat to metal ore causes the pure metal to separate from the impure dross, which either burns off or rises to the top of the molten mass so that it can be removed. Such imagery metaphorically portrays the purging of the people who will suffer invasion, exile, and the death of many of their number. Such a construct raises moral questions insofar as it explains the disaster of invasion and exile by arguing that the victims of the invasion deserved their fate rather than by charging that YHWH was unable to defend the nation against its enemies.

Oracular Account: Condemnation of the Leadership and People of Jerusalem (22:23-31)

Ezekiel 22:23-31 begins with a typical example of the prophetic word formula in v. 23, which introduces YHWH's instruction speech to the prophet. Again, YHWH addresses Ezekiel as "son of Adam" to acknowledge his status as a Zadokite priest who represents humanity before YHWH in the temple. YHWH's speech to Ezekiel is formulated as a prophetic judgment speech that begins with the announcement of judgment in v. 24 and then turns to the bases for judgment in vv. 25-31. The reversal of the two major elements of the prophetic judgment speech indicates an analytical stance that begins with the consequences suffered by those judged and then delineates the explanation for the consequences by charging those who suffer with wrongdoing that brought about their suffering as a form of judgment. This oracle draws heavily on both Levitical literature and prophetic literature, especially the work of Isaiah, Jeremiah, and Zephaniah.

Verse 24 announces judgment against the land by claiming that it has become impure and that no rain will fall upon it. Such imagery typifies blessings and curses texts that often appear at the conclusion of a major biblical law code (e.g., Lev 26; Deut 28–30; cf. Isa 24; Hos 4) to define the projected results of the observance of YHWH's laws. The Holiness Code in Leviticus 17–26 is fundamentally concerned with establishing the holiness of the land of Israel and its population. The blessings and curses in Leviticus 26 begin with statements in Leviticus 26:3-5 that YHWH will bring rain to the land to produce food if the people observe YHWH's expectations.

Verses 25-31 then charge the leaders and people of the land with wrongdoing that brought about the covenant curses noted in v. 24. The charges successively indict the major classes of leadership in Judean society. Verse 25 begins by charging the prophets of the nation with wrongdoing. The charges are expressed metaphorically in language that draws upon other prophetic works, viz., they are like roaring lions that devour prey (cf. Zeph 3:3); they seize wealth (Isa 5:8); they make the women widows (Isa 3:25–4:1). Verse 26 then charges the priests with violating YHWH's Torah, thereby profaning YHWH's holy name. Specific charges include the failure to teach the people the differences between what is holy and profane and what is clean and unclean, which is the primary task of the priesthood (Lev 10:8-11), and the failure to observe the Shabbat, which is rooted in creation itself and central to the covenant (Gen 2:1-3; Lev 19:3; cf. Exod 31:12-17). Verse 27 compares Judah's government officials to wolves who tear prey, shed blood, and destroy life for illegal profits (cf. Zeph 3:3). Verse 28 returns to the prophets by metaphorically claiming that they give false prophecy by applying plaster to a wall, i.e., by covering up what lies beneath (cf. Jer 23:9-40; 27-28). Verse 29 charges the people of the land, the landed gentry of Judah that frequently places kings on the throne (2 Kings 11; 21:24; 23:30), with a variety of economic crimes, including fraud, robbery, and oppressing the poor and foreigners in the land (Lev 19:13, 15-16, 33-34). YHWH's final comments focus on searching the land for a righteous man to prevent the destruction of the land. These comments call to mind the decision to destroy Sodom and Gomorrah (Gen 18–19) and Zephaniah's search for the wicked (Zeph 1:12). Verse 31 makes it clear that the suffering of the land is to repay the people for their misconduct.

Oracular Account: Concerning Oholah and Oholibah: Allegorical Portrayal of Judgment against Samaria and Jerusalem (23:1-49)

Ezekiel 23:1-49 begins with the typical prophetic word formula in v. 1, which introduces the entire unit concerning Oholah and Oholibah in vv. 2-49. The unit compromises two instruction speeches spoken by YHWH to the prophet in vv. 2-35 and 36-42 and a response by Ezekiel in vv. 43-49 in which the prophet quotes YHWH's announcement of judgment against Oholah and Oholibah. Oholah and Oholibah are allegorical names applied respectively to Samaria, the capital of the former northern kingdom of Israel, and Jerusalem the capital of the southern kingdom of Judah. Both names are derived from the Hebrew root, *'hl*, which means "tent" in noun forms and "to tent" in verbal forms. The root is chosen here as a reference to YHWH's presence insofar as YHWH is depicted as residing in a tent during Israel's early history prior to settlement in the land of Israel (see e.g., 2 Sam 7:6) and YHWH's sanctuary continues to function as YHWH's tent in later times (Ps 15:1; 66:5). The term for Samaria, Hebrew, *'oholah*, is generally understood as "her tent" presuming that the final *he* is the feminine possessive suffix, and *'oholibah* is generally understood to mean "my tent is in her" (Greenberg 1997, 474). Both names are allegories that presuppose the Israelite/Judean marriage tradition for portraying Israel's or Jerusalem's relationship with YHWH in which YHWH is understood to be the husband and Israel or Jerusalem is understood to be the wife (see Baumann; Abma). Although some cases employ the metaphor as a means to depict the restoration of YHWH's relationship with Israel/Judah after a period of national stress (see Zeph 3:14-20; Isa 54), others portray Israel or Jerusalem as a rebellious bride who has abandoned her husband for other lovers (see Hos 1–3; Jer 2; Ezek 16). The present example functions similarly to Ezekiel 16 to depict Jerusalem's alliances with foreign nations as a rebellion against YHWH. The marriage metaphor here employs some rather misogynistic assumptions and pornographic depictions in its portrayal of Samaria and Jerusalem as the guilty parties at times of national threat and destruction. Such a portrayal constitutes a form of theodicy because it is designed to defend YHWH against charges of impotence, abandonment, and malevolence insofar as YHWH does not defend either Samaria or Jerusalem from their enemies. Much as raped women are often inappropriately blamed for their own suffering, the passage blames Samaria and Jerusalem for their own victimization by charging that they abandoned YHWH to fraternize with other lovers (see esp. Galambush).

Ezekiel 20:1–23:49

YHWH's first address to Ezekiel in vv. 2-35 begins with the typical address "son of Adam" to acknowledge his status as a Zadokite priest. It is an instruction speech that employs the allegory of the two sisters, Oholah and Oholibah, to portray Samaria and Jerusalem as licentious young women who constantly engaged in sexual relations with foreigners. Verses 2-4 lay out the basic premises of the address. Oholah and Oholibah are sisters born to the same mother; they engaged in sexual relations with Egypt while they were very young; they were married to YHWH and bore children to YHWH; and they are identified respectively as Samaria (Oholah) and Jerusalem (Oholibah). The pornographic portrayal of squeezed breasts and nipples is designed to evoke revulsion from the presumably male reading audience of the passage. Historically speaking, the metaphorical portrayal of Samaria's and Jerusalem's relationships with Egypt portray periods when both were allied with Egypt politically. King Solomon of Israel and Judah was known for his alliance with Egypt, particularly insofar as his marriage to the daughter of Pharaoh and other foreign women was viewed as a cause for YHWH's judgment against the kingdom late in his reign and afterwards when the northern tribes revolted against his son Rehoboam (see 1 Kings 3:1; 11–12). King Jeroboam ben Nebat is reported to have fled to King Shishak of Egypt to escape Solomon's attempts to kill him for rebellion (1 Kings 11:40), and Shishak later marched against Jerusalem and plundered the temple treasures (1 Kings 14:25-28). In later times, King Hoshea of Israel allied with Pharaoh So of Egypt in his failed revolt against Assyria (2 Kings 17:4). Likewise, King Jehoiakim of Judah was an ally of Egypt in his failed attempt to revolt against Babylon (2 Kings 23:34-35; 24:1-4), and King Zedekiah of Judah presumably relied on Egypt in his ill-fated attempt to revolt against Babylon a second time (2 Kings 25:1-21).

Verses 5-10 then focus on Oholah/Samaria in an effort to depict her abandonment of YHWH for foreign lovers. She is portrayed as having relations with the Assyrians, again in pornographic terms. The Assyrians are portrayed as various types of governors and officials, clothed in blue, the color of authority and royalty in the ancient world, and mounted on horses. All are portrayed as handsome young men, and Oholah is portrayed as a whore who lusts after the Assyrian idols and gives herself to the Assyrian men in lurid fashion. As for the Assyrians, they seized her sons and daughters and put her to the sword. This portrayal clearly portrays Israel's relationship with Assyria from the late ninth through the eighth centuries BCE, which ultimately resulted in her destruction. In an effort to defend Israel against the Arameans, King Jehu of Israel (842–815 BCE) submitted to Assyria as a vassal (see *ANEP*, 351–55) so that Assyrian power would check any Aramean efforts to invade Israel. The alliance lasted through the reigns of the Jehu kings, including Jehoahaz (815–801 BCE), Jehoash (801–786 BCE), Jeroboam II (786–746 BCE), and Zechariah (746 BCE). Zechariah's assassination was prompted by an attempt to break the Assyrian alliance and establish a new alliance with Aram. The move was countered by Menahem (745–738 BCE), who assassinated Shallum (745 BCE) and restored relations with Assyria during his reign and that of his son Pekahiah (738–737 BCE). But Pekahiah was assassinated by Pekah (737–732 BCE), who allied with Aram and attacked Jerusalem during the Syro-Ephraimitic War. When King Ahaz of Judah (735–715 BCE) appealed to the Assyrian king Tiglath Pileser for assistance, the Assyrians attacked, destroyed Damascus, killed Pekah and subjugated both Israel and Judah, placing Hoshea as king (732–724 BCE) over a much reduced Israel. When Hoshea revolted against Assyria in 724 BCE, he was imprisoned, the land of Israel was devastated, Samaria was destroyed, and the northern kingdom of Israel came to an end as much of its surviving population was exiled to the far reaches of the Assyrian empire (2 Kings 17).

Verses 11-21 depict the rebellion of Oholibah/Jerusalem against YHWH, again in pornographic terms as she abandons her husband YHWH for foreign lovers. She is described as even worse than her sister. She likewise turns to the Assyrians, just as King Ahaz of Judah (735–715 BCE) submitted to Assyrian rule when his country was invaded by Assyria during the Syro-Ephraimitic War (see 2 Kings 16; Isa 7). But Oholibah also turns to the Babylonians whose pictures she saw on walls, apparently a reference to wall reliefs and inscriptions that were commonly used by the Babylonians to portray their power and to intimidate their subjects and enemies. Following the collapse of Assyria in 609 BCE, Judah spent a brief period as an Egyptian vassal during the reign of Jehoiakim (609–598 BCE), but when Babylonia defeated Egypt in 605 BCE, Judah became a vassal of Babylonia. Jehoiakim remained loyal to Egypt, which had placed him on the throne, and attempted revolt against Babylon in 598 BCE. He died during the course of the revolt of unknown causes, and his eighteen-year-old son was left to surrender to the Babylonian king Nebuchadnezzar. Jehoiachin was exiled to Babylon together with Ezekiel and many other Judeans in 597 BCE. Ezekiel's descriptions of Oholibah's lust for the Egyptians with their large organs is again intended to elicit disgust from a male reading audience that apparently harbored fantasies about Egyptian/African men.

Verses 22-35 then present a series of oracles that announce YHWH's intentions to punish Oholibah for her actions. The first in vv. 22-27, introduced by *laken*, "therefore," addresses Oholibah directly with the prophetic messenger formula to introduce YHWH's announcement of punishment. YHWH intends to bring the Babylonians, their Aramean allies from Pekod, Shoa, and Koa, as well as the Assyrians with their chariots, shields, bucklers, helmets, etc., to attack her. Babylonian armies normally included troops from various allies and vassals. After she is stripped of her children, clothing, and jewelry, she will no longer remember Egypt. A second oracle in vv. 28-31, introduced by *ki*, "for," and the prophetic messenger formula, continues the pornographic portrayal of Oholibah's victimization as she is stripped bare and raped. Verse 31 notes that Oholibah will drink from the same cup as her sister, and a third oracle in vv. 32-34 then portrays Oholibah metaphorically drinking from the cup of her sister and suffering the consequences as she chews on its dregs and tears at her breasts in the misery of her suffering. The motif of suffering that results from drinking from a poisoned cup is well known in prophetic literature (see Isa 51:17, 22; Jer 25:15-29; 51:7; Hab 2:16). The fourth oracle in v. 35, again introduced by *laken*, "therefore," and the prophetic messenger formula, charges that Oholiabah/Jerusalem is responsible for her own suffering because she abandoned YHWH for foreign lovers.

Verses 36-49 present a second instruction speech by YHWH to Ezekiel in vv. 36-42 and Ezekiel's response in vv. 43-49. Many interpreters view these verses as a later expansion of the original oracle that was written in the aftermath of Jerusalem's destruction. In the present form of the text, these verses function as a means to elaborate on the guilt of Oholah and Oholibah by claiming that they defiled YHWH's sanctuary (cf. Ezek 8–11).

Verses 36-42 present YHWH's second instruction speech to Ezekiel. It is introduced in v. 36aα by the speech formula, and the speech follows in vv. 36aβ-42. YHWH addresses Ezekiel as "son of Adam" and asks that he judge Oholah and Oholibah because of their abominations. The charge is adultery (Exod 20:14; Deut 5:17; Lev 20:10), which defiles them in priestly thought. Although this metaphor has already appeared in the earlier speech, YHWH extends it to include the charge that the two women have defiled the sanctuary and YHWH's Shabbats. Defilement of the sanctuary is tantamount to defiling all creation insofar as the Jerusalem Temple was conceived to be the holy center of creation in ancient Judean thought, and defilement of the Shabbat functions in a similar manner insofar as the Shabbat establishes the holiness of creation itself in Genesis 2:1-3 and Exodus 31:12-17. The portrayal of the women with eye shadow, bathed, and dressed while waiting for men in the house of YHWH employs a sexual metaphor to depict the defilement of the temple. The set table evokes images of the table placed in the temple for offerings to YHWH, here portrayed as incense and oil.

Incense was offered before YHWH in the ten incense burners of the temple and oil would have accompanied the bread of the presence set on the table before YHWH (see Exod 25:23-30; Lev 2; 1 Kings 7:27-39, 48).

Verses 43–49 present Ezekiel's response to YHWH. The passage begins in v. 43aα^1 with the brief speech formula "and I said" followed by the speech in vv. 43aα^2-49. The first portion of Ezekiel's speech in vv. 43aα^2-45 affirms the charge that Oholah and Oholibah are prostitutes, and maintains that they will be judged as such. The punishment for adultery in Leviticus 20:10 is death, which parallels the punishment for profaning the holy name of YHWH and the holy sanctuary of YHWH (Lev 20:2-5). In the second part of Ezekiel's speech in vv. 46-49, the prophet quotes an oracle by YHWH beginning with *ki*, "for," and the prophetic messenger formula as a means to indicate that the punishment announced is a consequence of the adultery and prostitution identified in vv. 43aα^2-45. The death sentence is carried out through stoning, a common punishment for blasphemy (Lev 24:14; cf. Lev 20:2, 27) and profaning the Shabbat (Num 15:35, 36). The killing of sons and daughters reflects the corporate nature of punishment in the case of Achan (Josh 7). The passage concludes with the YHWH revelation formula to indicate that the realization of such punishment points to YHWH as the ultimate authority.

Ezekiel's Oracles concerning the Destruction of Jerusalem and the Condemnation of Neighboring Nations

Ezekiel 24:1–25:17

Most interpreters argue that Ezekiel 24 concludes a major section of the book in Ezekiel 1–24 concerned with the punishment of Israel and Jerusalem and that Ezekiel 25 marks the beginning of a major section of the book devoted to the oracles concerning the nations in Ezekiel 25–32. Nevertheless, the chronological formulas in Ezekiel 24:1 and 26:1 point to a different conclusion, viz., that Ezekiel 24:1–25:17 constitute a discrete unit within the sequence of chronologically defined subunits that define the book as a whole, and that Ezekiel 26:1 marks the beginning of a new unit within the sequence. The date noted in Ezekiel 24:1, the tenth day of the tenth month in the ninth year, is the date identified in 2 Kings 25:1 and Jer 52:4 (cf. Zech 8:19) as the date when Nebuchadnezzar began his siege of Jerusalem (10 Tevet, 589–588 BCE). The prophetic word formulas in Ezekiel 24:1, 24:15, and 25:1 introduce each of the subunits within Ezekiel 24:1–25:17. Thus, Ezekiel 24:1-14 presents the allegory of the pot as a means to portray YHWH's efforts to afflict or heat up the city of Jerusalem and to purge it from its impurities; Ezekiel 24:15-27 presents YHWH's instruction to Ezekiel that he should not mourn for the death of his wife, just as YHWH will not mourn for the destruction of Jerusalem; and Ezekiel 25:1 presents YHWH's instructions to Ezekiel to condemn Judah's immediate neighbors, i.e., Ammon, Moab, Edom, and Philistia, as Nebuchadnezzar's attack against Judah included these nations as well. By including Judah's immediate neighbors, Ezekiel points not only to the historical dimensions of Nebuchadnezzar's assault, but to the theological dimensions as well. As the holy center of creation, the need to purge Jerusalem calls for the need to purge all creation as well, beginning with Judah's most immediate neighbors.

The formal structure of the unit may be presented as follows:

IV. Symbolic actions concerning the destruction of Jerusalem and the punishment of neighboring nations (Ezek 24:1–25:17)
  A. The Allegory of the Pot (24:1-14)
  B. YHWH's instruction to Ezekiel not to mourn for his wife (24:15-27)
  C. YHWH's instructions to Ezekiel to condemn Ammon, Moab, Edom, and Philistia (25:1-17)

Oracular Account: The Allegory of the Pot (24:1-14)

The prophetic word formula in Ezekiel 24:1 includes a chronological date formula that introduces both the entirety of the unit in Ezekiel 24:1–25:1 as well as the oracular account in Ezekiel 24:1-14. As noted above, the tenth day of the tenth month of the ninth year (10 Tevet, 589–588 BCE) marks the date that Nebuchadnezzar began his siege of Jerusalem (2 Kings 25:1; Jer 52:4; cf. Zech 8:19). The ninth year refers specifically to the ninth year of Zedekiah's reign in 2 Kings 25:1 and Jer 52:4, which corresponds to the ninth year of Jehoiachin's exile. Consequently, the first oracle in the sequence is YHWH's instruction to Ezekiel to perform a symbolic act that will portray the Babylonian siege as an expression of YHWH's efforts to purge Jerusalem of its impurity.

The oracular account per se appears in vv. 2-14 in the form of YHWH's instruction speech to the prophet. YHWH addresses Ezekiel in typical form as "son of Adam" to acknowledge his status as a priest from the Jerusalem Temple, and begins with an instruction in v. 2 to record the above-mentioned date as the beginning of the Babylonian siege of Jerusalem.

YHWH then turns to a second instruction in v. 3aαβ to speak an allegory to the people, here identified not by name but as "the rebellious house." The significance of the name clearly presumes the guilt of the people as the basis for punishment insofar as the term signifies alleged rebellion against YHWH's will. In priestly thought, such rebelliousness constitutes a refusal or failure to observe YHWH's will and thereby renders the people unholy and in need of purging. The allegory (Heb., *mashal*, "proverb, allegory") points to Ezekiel's use of a symbolic action as a means to dramatize YHWH's oracle by expressing it in terms that the people would understand, in this case the procedure for cleansing a pot filled with burnt and caked-on residue, and then applying the lesson to interpret the issue at hand, i.e., Nebuchadnezzar's siege of Jerusalem. The purpose is to point to the siege as an act of YHWH and to justify the siege by claiming that the people had defiled themselves by failing to observe YHWH's will. Nebuchadnezzar's siege then emerges as an act of punishment brought about by YHWH, thereby demonstrating

YHWH's power. Such a symbolic action would thereby be conceived as a means to counter charges that YHWH was powerless to protect the people from the Babylonians.

The choice of the imagery of a dirty pot that needs cleansing makes eminent sense given Ezekiel's identity as a priest. Although the Zadokite priests would normally serve at the altar of the Jerusalem Temple to present the offerings of the people to YHWH, one must consider what happens to the offerings. Although many offerings are either wholly or partially consumed by the altar fire, those portions of the offerings that are designated to be eaten by the priests and the people must be cooked prior to consumption. Among the various means to prepare sacrificial meat for human consumption was the use of pots for boiling meat. The priests were responsible for such meat preparation, and so the symbolic action draws upon Ezekiel's normal experience as a priest.

Following the prophetic messenger formula in v. 3aγ, vv. 3b-5 conveys YHWH's instructions to Ezekiel to carry out the symbolic action. The use of the thigh and shoulder portions indicates choice portions that are normally given to the priests as compensation for their services at the altar (Num 18:12; see also Exod 29:26-28; Lev 7:28-36; 10:12-15; Num 18:18; Gen 32:32). By portraying the cooking of the priests' portions, the symbolic action aims to take an act that would normally be understood as a holy action that would sustain the well-being of Jerusalem, but in the present context it ironically portrays YHWH's intention to purge the city.

Verses 6-8, introduced by the particle *laken*, "therefore," delineate the first set of consequences of the symbolic action, i.e., the defiling nature of the act. These verses constitute a "woe" oracle that condemns Jerusalem for bloodshed by portraying the priests' offerings as improper and defiling. By calling Jerusalem "the city of blood," YHWH points to the city's defilement. Blood is holy as it contains life, but blood dies when it is shed and shed blood thereby defiles. The present scenario presumes that the blood has not been fully removed from the choice meat, i.e., the priests did not properly perform their duties by pouring blood into the ground so that it could return to the earth. As a result, the blood left in the meat burns as scum in the bottom of the pot, thereby defiling the pot and symbolizing the defilement of the city.

Verses 9-14, again introduced by *laken*, "therefore," then elaborate upon the consequences by interpreting the symbolic action in relation to YHWH's intentions to purge and punish the city. Again, the prophetic messenger formula followed by a woe oracle announces the judgment. YHWH portrays a typical means to clean a fouled pot, i.e., heat it up to such an extent that the residue stuck on the bottom of the pot is completely burned up. Such an act thus symbolizes purging the pot and city by fire. Verses 13-14 make it clear that this is an act of judgment brought about by YHWH as punishment for Jerusalem's alleged defilement.

Oracular Account: The Death of Ezekiel's Wife (24:15-27)

Ezekiel 24:15-27 begins with the usual prophetic word formula in v. 15. The oracular account per se appears in vv. 16-27, and focuses on the death of Ezekiel's wife. We do not know her name, her age, or the cause of death, but people often died at relatively young ages in antiquity, and the oracle attempts to employ her death as a means to illustrate YHWH's efforts to bring judgment against Jerusalem.

YHWH's address to Ezekiel in vv. 16-17 begins with the usual reference to the prophet as "son of Adam" to indicate his priestly status. Here, YHWH instructs Ezekiel that he should moan, but he should not formally mourn for the death of his wife and he should dress and eat normally without observing any mourning practices normally associated with the passing of a loved one. He does not sit bare-headed and bare-foot; he does not cover his mouth or face in grief; he does not eat food brought to him by friends and neighbors as would normally be the custom in a house of mourning.

Although many interpreters consider Ezekiel's actions to be insensitive to the extreme, they are based on his identity as a Zadokite priest. Ezekiel's love for his wife is expressed through YHWH's statement that she is "the delight of your eyes." Death is the ultimate defiler of holiness, and Leviticus 21:1-12 defines the means by which the holy priesthood observes the death of close family members. Priests do not come into contact with the dead, but when a blood relative dies, i.e., a parent, a sibling, or a child, they are permitted to come into contact with the dead by mourning and preparing the body for burial. The wife of a priest is not included in the list in Leviticus 21:1-12 because she is not a blood relative; the obligation to mourn for a wife and prepare her for burial belongs not to her husband, but to her children, siblings, and parents. Because Ezekiel cannot mourn for his wife due to his priestly status, his actions then become the basis for a symbolic action that illustrates YHWH refusal to mourn for Jerusalem at the time of its destruction.

Verses 18-24 present Ezekiel's report of the death of his wife and his efforts to explain the significance of the symbolic action to his people. He reports his wife's death in the evening and his compliance with YHWH's instructions before the people in the morning. When they ask why he refuses to mourn, he relates to them YHWH's instructions concerning the significance of his actions. Ezekiel's account of YHWH's instructions in vv. 21-24 begin with the statement that YHWH intends to desecrate the Jerusalem Temple, which YHWH describes in a manner analogous to Ezekiel's wife as "your strong glory, the delight of your eyes, and the desire of your life." YHWH makes sure to accentuate the pain and loss of the people by pointing out that their children will die in the temple when it falls, thereby desecrating it with their own blood. When this happens, the people shall emulate both Ezekiel and YHWH by not mourning. The last statement of this segment makes it clear that the people will grieve for their loss even if they cannot mourn formally.

Verses 25-27 present a final address by YHWH to Ezekiel, introduced by the emphatic "and you, O son of Adam," which announces that a messenger will come to him to inform him of the fall of Jerusalem. On that day, he will end his moaning for the loss of his wife and begin to speak normally again. Apparently, Ezekiel was struck dumb with grief in the aftermath of his wife's passing. When he speaks upon hearing this news, he will become a sign that reveals the presence of YHWH to the people at large.

Oracular Account: Condemnation of Judah's Immediate Neighbors, Ammon, Moab, Edom, and Philistia (25:1-17)

Ezekiel 25:1-17 begins with the customary prophetic word formula in v. 1, which introduces the entire unit. YHWH's address to Ezekiel in vv. 2-17 likewise begins with the usual address form "son of Adam" to signify his status as a Zadokite priest representing all humanity before YHWH in the Jerusalem Temple. YHWH's instruction speech to Ezekiel directs him to speak an oracle against the Ammonites for their alleged support of the Babylonian desecration of the Jerusalem Temple and the destruction of the land of Judah. The oracles concerning Ammon appear in vv. 3aβ-7, but these oracles are followed by oracles against Moab in vv. 8-11, Edom in vv. 12-14, and Philistia in vv. 15-17. Although YHWH's initial instruction includes only the command to speak the oracles against Ammon, the inclusion of the oracles concerning Moab, Edom, and Philistia apparently presupposes their rejoicing at—and perhaps their participation in—Jerusalem's and Judah's defeat. Ancient Near Eastern sources tell us little about the composition of Nebuchadnezzar's army when he invaded Judah first in 598 BCE and later again in 588 BCE, but it is clear that his army would have included forces from his various allies throughout the empire. Jeremiah 27:2-4 suggest that King Zedekiah of Judah attempted to enlist Edom, Moab, Ammon, Sidon, and Tyre in his efforts to resist the Babylonian empire, but it is not clear if any of them joined in the revolt. Jeremiah certainly counseled that both Judah and these nations submit to Babylonian. Although Nebuchadnezzar later laid siege to Tyre, suggesting that it had resisted Babylon, the records do not indicate what Edom, Moab, and Ammon actually did. Second Kings 24:2 indicates that Nebuchadnezzar enlisted bands of Chaldeans, Arameans, Moabites, and Edomites to harass the Judeans as part of his efforts to bring Judah under Babylonian control, and so it makes sense that Ammon, Moab, and Edom sided with the Babylonians, particularly when Nebuchadnezzar's powerful army appeared. Philistia is not mentioned in either of the texts noted above, but it does appear that Philistia remained at least nominally under Egyptian control following Babylonia's defeat of Egypt in 605 BCE (see Wiseman, 230–33). Insofar as Jehoiakim was the ringleader of revolt against Babylon in 598 BCE, as was Zedekiah in 588 BCE, it stands to reason that Philistia would have joined in on any rejoicing and belligerent activity against Jerusalem and Judah once Nebuchadnezzar's army arrived on the scene.

The oracles against the Ammonites in vv. 3aβ-7 begin with the call-to-attention formula "hear the word of my L-rd G-d" in v. 3aβ, which functions as an address form to the party to which the oracle is directed. Ammon is located east of the Jordan River in what is now Jordan, and its capital, Rabbath-Ammon, is the site of modern-day Amman.

The first oracle appears in vv. 3b-5 beginning with the prophetic messenger formula in v. 3bα to identify the following statements as an oracle from YHWH. The oracle is formulated as a prophetic judgment speech. The grounds for judgment appear in v. 3bβ, introduced by the Hebrew particle *ya'an*, "because," with the charges that the Ammonites rejoiced—by saying Aha!—when YHWH's sanctuary in Jerusalem was desecrated, when the land of Israel was desolated, and when the people of Judah were taken off into Babylonian exile. The oracle clearly presupposes the Babylonian destruction of Jerusalem in 587/586 BCE and the subsequent exile of Judah. Such charges against Ammon are particularly galling insofar as Zedekiah apparently viewed Ammon as a potential ally. Indeed, Ammon had been an ally of Judah in the past, particularly during the reign of David when David fled to Ammon for support during Abshalom's revolt against him (2 Sam 15–19). The announcement of judgment then follows in vv. 4-7, introduced by the Hebrew particle *laken*, "therefore." YHWH's intention to deliver the Ammonites to the Kedemites, i.e., "the sons of the east," is a reference to the Arab tribes that inhabited the desert regions east of Ammon, Moab, and Edom. The Assyrians and the Babylonians frequently enlisted Arabs to harass potentially hostile or troublesome border areas to facilitate Babylonian control of the region (Ephal). Rabbah is a reference to Rabbath-Ammon, the capital of Ammon. The scenario depicted here presumes that the Arab tribes will overrun the Ammonites.

The second oracle against the Ammonites appears in vv. 6-7, which is connected to the first oracle by the particle *ki* "for," followed by the prophetic messenger formula in v. 6aα. The oracle per se in vv. 6aβ-7 is also formulated as a prophetic judgment speech. The grounds for judgment in v. 6aβ-b, introduced by the particle *ya'an*, "because," indicated once again Ammon's scornful rejoicing over Judah's downfall. The announcement of judgment in v. 7, again introduced by *laken*, "therefore," indicates that Ammon will be given as booty to the nations. Insofar as the Babylonian army consists of units from the various nations that comprise ancient Babylonia, the judgment is that Ammon will be overrun by the Babylonian army like Judah was overrun. The prophetic proof saying "and you shall know that I am YHWH" indicates that Ammon's punishment will be a revelatory act testifying to YHWH's power in the world.

The oracle against Moab and Seir appears in vv. 8-11. Moab is located immediately to the south of Ammon along the eastern boundaries of the Dead Sea, and Seir is the name given to the south of the Dead Sea that is commonly identified with Edom. The term Seir means "hairy" and likely refers to the desert growth that appears in this region. This region was sometimes dominated by Israel and Judah, but was often at odds with them. In this case, Zedekiah attempted to ally with them, but his efforts were apparently futile once the Babylonian army showed up. The grounds for judgment against Moab and Seir appear in v. 8b, which quotes their statement that Judah is like all the nations. Such a statement indicates Judah's vulnerability to the Babylonian army, which is comprised of troops from various nations, and it further indicates that Judah will be swallowed up by the Babylonians. The view that Judah is like the nations would be anathema to biblical tradition in general and the priest and prophet Ezekiel in particular because of the view that Israel and Judah were enjoined to conduct themselves as the holy people of YHWH, not like the nations that had been expelled from the land before them for conduct that is generally considered to be abominable. The announcement of judgment in vv. 9-10, introduced by *laken*, "therefore," likewise envisions that Moab and Seir will be overrun by the Kedemites or Arab tribes from the east as the vanguard of the Babylonian army. Beth-Jeshimot is located in southern Moab, northeast of the Dead Sea (Num 33:40; Josh 1:3). Baal-Meon is identified with Beth Baal-Meon, located a few miles inland from the Dead Sea (Josh 13:17). Kiritahaim is to the south of Baal-Meon (Num 32:37; Josh 13:19; Jer 48:1, 23). Again, the oracle concludes with YHWH's self-revelation formula to indicate that the anticipated destruction of Moab and Seir will reveal YHWH's power over nations and creation.

The oracle against Edom appears in vv. 12-14. It is introduced by the prophetic messenger formula in v. 12aα, and it is formulated as a prophetic judgment speech like the previous oracles. Edom has a special notoriety in biblical tradition because its eponymous ancestor is Esau, the fraternal twin brother and rival of Jacob (Gen 25–27; 33). Its notoriety also includes a reputation in biblical literature for having participated directly in the Babylonian destruction of Jerusalem and the temple (Ob 1–14; Ps 137:7; Lam 4:21-22). Edom is located south of the Dead Sea to the east of the Judean wilderness of the Negeb. The grounds for judgment appear in v. 12aβ-b, introduced by *ya'an*, "because." This statement indicates Edom's vengeful actions against Judah by which they incurred guilt (see Lev 5:1-13). Such a statement builds up the case that Edom participated willfully in Jerusalem's destruction, and the statement indicating guilt requires ritual purging. In this case, the announcement of punishment in vv. 13-14, introduced by *laken*, "therefore," indicates YHWH's intentions to carry out such purging by destroying the nations. But the punishment against Edom differs from that against Ammon, Moab, and Seir in that the people of Israel will carry out the punishment, not the Babylonian army. The reference to the region from Tema to Dedan takes up most of the territory of Edom (Jer 49:7-8) indicating complete destruction. The YHWH self-revelation formula appears in modified form to indicate that the Edomites will not only know YHWH—they will know YHWH's vengeance. The closing oracular formula *ne'um 'adonay yhwh*, "utterance of my L-rd, G-d," certifies this announcement as a promise of destruction from YHWH.

The oracle against the Philistines in vv. 15-17 begins with the prophetic messenger formula in v. 15aα. Like the other oracles in this sequence, it is formulated as a prophetic judgment speech. The grounds for judgment, introduced by *ya'an*, "because," appear in v. 15aβ-b. The Philistines are located along the Mediterranean Sea coast to the west and south of Judah, and they control the roads that lead to the Sinai and ultimately to Egypt. The Philistines are charged with vengeful action against Judah, which should come as no surprise because they were the traditional local enemy of Judah and Israel from the days of Saul and David (1 Sam 13–2 Sam 5) and throughout much of the monarchic period. As allies of Egypt, they would have jumped at the chance to attack Judah during the time of the Babylonian invasion. The announcement of judgment in vv. 16-17, introduced by *laken*, "therefore," and a repeated example of the prophetic messenger formula, indicates YHWH's intention to destroy the Philistines completely. The scenario of judgment also includes the Cherethites, a term associated with the inhabitants of Crete, generally viewed as the ancestors of the Philistines (Zeph 2:5; cf. 2 Sam 8:18; Amos 9:7). The self-revelation formula at the end of the oracle indicates once again that the punishment will be a revelatory event.

Ezekiel's Oracles concerning Tyre and Sidon

Ezekiel 26:1–28:26

Ezekiel 26–28 constitutes the fifth major unit of the book of Ezekiel. This unit presents Ezekiel's oracle concerning Tyre and Sidon. It is demarcated at the outset in Ezekiel 26:1 by the initial chronological formula and the prophetic word transmission formula that introduce the entire unit. The date presented in Ezekiel 26:1, the eleventh year on the first of the month, is enigmatic because it omits the month. Some read with the LXX, which dates the unit to the twelfth year, on the first day of the first month (see Greenberg 1997, 529 for discussion), but this appears to be an attempt to correct a problematic Hebrew text. The eleventh year of Jehoiachin's exile would date from spring 587 BCE through spring 586 BCE, and would correspond to statements in 2 Kings 25:2 and Jeremiah 52:5, which date Nebuchadnezzar's capture and subsequent destruction of Jerusalem to the eleventh year of Zedekiah's reign—and thus the eleventh year of Jehoiachin's exile. Jerusalem's destruction took place in the summer of 586 BCE, so the present text points to Tyre's rejoicing over Jerusalem's downfall at some point prior to the actual destruction of the city. The Babylonian siege of Tyre began about a year or so later in 585 BCE, and so this oracle announces Tyre's downfall as well.

Although Nebuchadnezzar laid siege to Tyre shortly after the conquest of Jerusalem, he was apparently unable to conquer the city for some thirteen years. His interest in Tyre would have been due to the fact that the city was aligned with Egypt, and therefore constituted an important element in his overall plans to conquer Egypt and thereby secure control over trade and resources throughout the eastern Mediterranean. Unfortunately, there are few Babylonian records concerning the siege, and the statement that it lasted for thirteen years comes from the first-century CE Jewish historian Flavius Josephus (*Ag. Ap.* 1.21, section 156; *Ant.* 10.11.1, section 228). At the outset of the siege, Tyre was ruled by King Ittobaal (Ethbaal) III, whose dates are disputed. The course and outcome of the siege are uncertain, but Nebuchadnezzar's court register indicates that a new king, perhaps to be identified as Baal II, sat on the throne of Tyre ca. 572 BCE, one year after the siege had concluded, and that an earlier king, perhaps to be identified with Ittobaal, was deported to Babylon (*ANET* 308; see also Katzenstein, 295–347; cf. Block, 31).

The chronological and prophetic word formulae in Ezekiel 26:1 introduce the first major oracular account of the passage in Ezekiel 26:2-21. The prophetic word formulae in Ezekiel 27:1, 28:1, 28:11, and 28:20 introduce the subsequence oracular accounts of the passage. Thus, Ezekiel 26–28 includes a sequence of five oracular accounts, each concerned with a different aspect of the condemnation of Tyre and Sidon. Ezekiel 26:1-21 constitutes the first oracular account concerning Tyre. Ezekiel 27:1-36 constitutes the second oracular account against Tyre. Ezekiel 28:1-10 constitutes the third oracular account directed against the prince of Tyre. Ezekiel 28:11-19 constitutes the fourth oracular account against the king of Tyre. And Ezekiel 28:20-26 constitutes the fifth and final oracular account of the unit concerning Sidon and Israel. The concluding oracle in the sequence presumes that the downfall of Tyre and Sidon will lead to the restoration of Israel as part of the overall concern with revealing YHWH to Israel.

Ezekiel 26–28 identifies Nebuchadnezzar's impending conquest of Tyre—as well as the impending conquests of Ammon, Moab, Edom, and Philistia in Ezekiel 25 and Egypt in Ezekiel 29–32—with the revelation of YHWH to Israel and beyond. Within the overall scenario put forward by the book of Ezekiel, YHWH's identification with the Babylonian conqueror facilitates the view that the destruction of Jerusalem and Judah is to be recognized as a purge of the profaned city, people, and sanctuary that prepares for the new temple and the restored nation in Ezekiel 40–48.

The formal structure of the unit may be presented as follows:

V. Ezekiel's Oracles concerning Tyre (Ezek 26:1–28:26)
    A. The first oracular account: concerning Tyre (26:1-21)
    B. The second oracular account: concerning Tyre (27:1-36)
    C. Oracular account: concerning the prince of Tyre (28:1-10)
    D. Oracular account: dirge for the king of Tyre (28:11-19)
    E. Oracular account concerning Sidon and Israel (28:20-26)

The First Oracular Account: Concerning Tyre (26:1-21)

The first oracle concerning Tyre in Ezekiel 26:1-21 is demarcated at the outset by the chronological and prophetic word formulae in Ezekiel 26:1 that introduce the whole. As noted above, the eleventh year refers to both the eleventh year of Jehoiachin's exile and Zedekiah's reign. The month is not indicated and so the date can refer generally to 587/586 BCE, which is when 2 Kings 25:2 and Jer 52:5 date Nebuchadnezzar's capture of the city. Verses 2-21 constitute YHWH's word to Ezekiel, who is here addressed in typical form as "son of Adam" to acknowledge his identity as a Zadokite priest of the Jerusalem Temple, conceived as the holy center of all creation in ancient Jewish thought.

YHWH's address to Ezekiel begins in v. 2 with a statement concerning Tyre's gloating over the downfall of Jerusalem, which then serves as the premise for the balance of the passage. Following the initial address to Ezekiel as son of Adam, v. 2 is formulated as a statement of the grounds of punishment for a prophetic judgment speech. It begins with the particle *ya'an*, "because," to identify the following statement as the cause for the punishment to be announced in vv. 3-21. Tyre's elation at the downfall of Jerusalem appears to be based on the view that Jerusalem competes with Tyre for control of the eastern Mediterranean trade routes. Although Tyre was a major naval power that controlled the coastal sea lanes to Egypt as well as to Asia Minor and beyond, Israel sat astride the land routes between Egypt to the south, Asia Minor to the northwest, and Aram and Mesopotamia to the northeast. Under King Jehoiakim ben Josiah, Judah had been an ally of Egypt, which was forced to align with Babylon following the Babylonian defeat of Egypt at Carchemesh in 605 BCE. The portrayal of Tyre in this passage may be a caricature, however, as Jerusalem's downfall to Babylonia would have indicated that Tyre would be a target as well. Indeed, Nebuchadnezzar began his siege of Tyre shortly after the fall of Jerusalem.

Verses 3-21 are formulated as an announcement of judgment against Tyre in keeping with the prophetic judgment speech genre. Verse 3 begins with the particle *laken*, "therefore," which typically introduces the announcement of judgment in the prophetic judgment speech. Two pairs of oracles then follow in vv. 3-14 and 15-21 concerning the impending downfall of Tyre for having gloated over Jerusalem's demise. The two oracular pairs include two oracles, each of which is introduced by the prophetic word formula "thus says my L-rd, G-d" to certify the oracle as an oracle by YHWH. The second oracle in each pair begins with the particle *ki*, "for, because," which syntactically joins each oracle in the pair together.

The first oracle pair concerning YHWH's or Nebuchadnezzar's assault against Tyre appears in vv. 3-14. The first oracle in the pair appears in vv. 3-6, which describe how YHWH will bring the nations against Tyre. The use of the motif of the nations is particularly appropriate here because Nebuchadnezzar's army would have included units from the many nations that comprised the Babylonian empire. The oracle employs the motifs of sea and bare rock, both of which are particularly important to the characterization of Tyre. Tyre was the major naval power of the ancient world, and so the imagery of the sea attacking Tyre as waves that batter its walls portrays the sea, normally the source of Tyre's power, as the very enemy that threatens Tyre's destruction. The imagery of Tyre battered to bare rock is also particularly appropriate as the name Tyre (Heb., *tsor*) means "rock," insofar as Tyre was an island fortress situated along the coast of Phoenicia. The island fortress was therefore better able to resist assault and to control the surrounding seas. The reference to Tyre as a place for drying nets indicates that the once-powerful city would be used for the most mundane purposes by local fishermen. The portrayal of Tyre together with her towns despoiled by the nations refers to the many coastal towns that were allied with Tyre. Such allies would also be forced to submit to Babylon, most likely when the Babylonian army occupied them during the lengthy siege of the city. The oracular formula *ne'um yhwh*, "oracle of YHWH," appears in the middle of v. 5 to identify YHWH as the source of the oracle. The oracle concludes with YHWH's recognition formula to indicate that the realization of these events would reveal YHWH to the people.

The second oracle of the first pair appears in vv. 7-14, which portray YHWH's bringing Nebuchadnezzar against Tyre. The oracle generally portrays what it means for an ancient city to be placed under siege and overcome by the besieging forces. It begins with a depiction of the approach of the Babylonian army, with its horses, chariots, cavalry, and soldiers that will invade Tyre's coastal allies and then build the various siege engines and mounds that would be employed with shields, battering rams, and swords to attack the city and undermine its walls. The depiction does not appear to be a realistic depiction of the siege of an island nation built on solid rock; rather, it appears to depict common imagery of an assault against an inland city for which horses, chariots, and the downfall of walls and towers would be appropriate. The description of the plundering of the city notes how houses will be torn down and thrown into the sea. It is not clear that this scenario of destruction ever took place, as Tyre seems to have capitulated rather than suffer invasion, but the imagery here must be understood as a depiction of anticipated action rather than a description of a realized event. The oracle concludes with the imagery of Tyre as bare rock used for drying nets and the oracular formula *ne'um yhwh*, "oracle of YHWH."

The second oracular pair appears in vv. 15-21, which depicts the results of Tyre's downfall. The first oracle in the pair is vv. 15-18, which portrays the reactions of the coastlands and their rulers when they witness the downfall of

Tyre. As the primary maritime power of the eastern Mediterranean, Tyre had many clients throughout the Mediterranean world that would react to its demise with fear and apprehension. The oracle portrays the rulers of these coastal nations stepping down from their thrones and removing their royal garments in typical portrayals of mourning in the ancient world. Their dirge (Heb., *qinah*) is formulated as a typical lament psalm with a classical 3/2 beat pattern to emulate the halting march of mourners who bear the body to the grave (for the foundational study of the dirge form, see Jahnow).

The second oracle of the pair appears in vv. 19-21, which describes Tyre's descent to the underworld of death. In ancient Judean thought, the dead went to Sheol, the Pit or the underworld, from whence they would never return. During the monarchic period, there was no concept of heaven where the righteous would reside; such a concept would only develop in the Greco-Roman period and beyond as rabbinic Judaism was influenced by its cultural and religious environment. The oracle concludes with the oracular formula *ne'um yhwh*, "oracle of YHWH."

The Second Oracular Account: Concerning Tyre (27:1-36)

The second oracular account concerning Tyre in Ezekiel 27:1-36 begins in typical fashion with the prophetic word formula in v. 1, which introduces the entire unit. Verses 2-36 are formulated as YHWH's instruction speech to Ezekiel, whom YHWH addresses in the usual manner as "son of Adam." Verse 2 indicates that YHWH instructs Ezekiel to chant a dirge over Tyre. A dirge (Heb., *qinah*) is a mourning hymn that is sung on behalf of those who have died or who may face death (for discussion of the dirge, see Jahnow). It is essentially a funerary psalm that would be typically set in the context of a burial or other mourning ritual. The typical form of the dirge is a 3/2 beat pattern in which the first stanza includes three beats whereas the second stanza includes only two. Such a pattern accompanies a slow, halting funeral procession in which the participants take three steps followed by two as they carry the body to the tomb for burial. The dirge is often employed metaphorically to depict a given party, perhaps an individual, nation, or city, that is subject to judgment or suffering. In the present instance, Ezekiel's use of the dirge to depict Tyre functions metaphorically as a means to indicate YHWH's judgment against the city.

Following the initial statement in v. 3aα$^{1-2}$ "and you shall say to Tyre," vv. 3aα^{3}-36 constitute a dirge that metaphorically portrays the city of Tyre as a beautiful, well-built ship that engages in trade with many nations. But as the dirge continues, Tyre will ultimately be destroyed in a shipwreck that will prompt mourning among her various clients and trading partners. The use of the dirge thereby illustrates Ezekiel's message of judgment against Tyre insofar as the shipwreck is brought about by the east wind, an agent of judgment often employed by YHWH in biblical literature (e.g., Exod 14:21). The dirge includes five major sections, each defined by a shift in content. The first is the initial address to Tyre in v. 3aα^3-b; the second is the metaphorical portrayal of Tyre as a beautiful, well-constructed and well-staffed ship in vv. 4-11; the third is the portrayal of Tyre's trading partners in vv. 12-25a; the fourth is the portrayal of the sinking of the ship in vv. 25b-27; and the fifth is the portrayal of mourning for the doomed ship in vv. 28-36.

The first major section of the dirge appears in v. 3aα^3-b, which constitutes the initial address to Tyre. Tyre is defined through her reputation and function as the major seafaring and trading power of her day. The prophetic messenger formula functions as a means to identify the following metaphorical portrayal of Tyre as an oracle from YHWH.

The second major section is the metaphorical portrayal of Tyre as a beautiful, well-built, and well-handled ship at sea. This segment begins with an address to Tyre, which quotes her own statement concerning her beauty, perhaps to indicate arrogance on her own part as a basis for YHWH's actions against her. The passage describes the careful work of Tyre's builders and the high quality of the materials employed to build her. Cypress from Senir or Mt. Hermon (Deut 3:9) in northern Israel and cedars from Lebanon were known in antiquity as high-grade wood for building ships and lining interior rooms of buildings such as the Jerusalem Temple or the Davidic palace (1 Kings 6–7). The oaks of Bashan, i.e., the region east of the Galilee, were especially well known for strength to fashion oars. The use of the boxwood of the Kittim, i.e., the Greek islands, with inlaid ivory would serve primarily as a decorative touch to enhance the beauty of the ship. Linen from Egypt would have been made from the papyrus that grows in swamps along the Nile. The blue and purple of Elishah, i.e., Cypress, refers to the blue/purple dye that is extracted from shellfish along the eastern Mediterranean coasts. The Greek term Phoenikos, from which Phoenicia is derived, and the Hebrew term Canaan both mean "purple/blue," and indicate the reputation of the dye produced in the region. The crew of the ship is drawn from the Phoenician cities, Sidon, located north of Tyre (Gen 10:15), Arvad, identified as Phoenicia (Gen 10:18), Tyre, and Gebal or Byblos (1 Kings 5:32), which were known for their expertise in seafaring. Tyre is portrayed here as a ship in harbor trading its wares among other ships as was the custom of the day. But Phoenician ships were also employed as warships, and so the crew also includes men from Paras, i.e., Persia, Lud, i.e., Lydia, and Put, i.e.,

Libya, who were well recognized as mercenary warriors. The shields of the crew were generally hung along the sides of the ship to afford protection from attack and to signal that the crew was prepared to defend itself. In v. 11, the metaphor shifts to the portrayal of Tyre as a walled city defended by men from Arvad, i.e., Phoenicia, as above, and Gammad, uncertain but identified as Cappodocia by the Aramaic Targum Jonathan on the Pentateuch (a Targum is an Aramaic translation of the Bible used by Jews in antiquity). As the sailors hung their shields on the ship, so the defenders of Tyre hang their quivers on the wall to indicate that the city is defended. The portrayals of armed sailors and defenders complete the portrayal of Tyre's beauty.

The third major section in vv. 12-25a portrays Tyre's trading partners in an effort to emphasize the extent of its power and wealth. Tarshish refers to the city of Tartessos in southwestern Spain. Javan refers to the Greeks, and Tubal and Meshech are locations in Asia Minor (Gen 10:2). Beth Togarmah is Armenia (Gen 10:3). Dedan refers to an Arabian people south of Israel in the central regions of the Arabian Peninsula (Gen 10:6-7; 25:1-3; Isa 21:13; Jer 25:23; 49:8). Aram is Syria. Judah and Israel are of course the two central kingdoms of the Bible. Minnith is located in Ammonite territory (Judg 11:33). The medieval Jewish commentator, Radak (Rabbi David Kimhi), considers Pannag to be a place name, but its location is unknown. Damascus is the capital of Aram/Syria, and Helbon is located about thirteen miles north of Damascus. Uzal is the city of Sana in Yemen (Gen 10:27). Kedar is located in Arabia (Gen 25:13). Sheba is located either in Ethiopia or Arabia (Gen 10:7), and Raamah is believed to be located by the Persian Gulf. Haran, Canneh, and Eden are all cities in Aram (Gen 12:4; 10:10; Isa 10:9; 2 Kings 19:12; Isa 37:12; Amos 1:5). Assyria is the ancient Assyrian empire in northern Iraq, and Chilmad is Media, located in Iran.

The fourth major section of the dirge in vv. 25b-27 metaphorically portrays the sinking of the ship as a means to illustrate Tyre's impending downfall. Shipwreck as a result of high winds and seas was a common fate among ancient ships. Here, the wind is described as the east wind, which often functioned as YHWH's natural weapon against enemies, such as the Egyptian army at the Red Sea (Exod 14:21). Iron-Age ships were relatively small, usually less than 100 feet, with sails and oars. They typically sailed close to the coast and beached at night because they were not large or stable enough to sail on the high seas. Our knowledge of ancient ships is enhanced by the many shipwrecks that have been excavated just off the eastern Mediterranean coast.

The fifth and final major section appears in vv. 28-36, which portrays mourning for the wrecked Tyre by the various peoples and nations with which she had interacted. A crowd gathered to watch a ship wrecked at sea would have been an all-too-common event in the ancient world, as little could be done to render assistance. Casting dust and ashes on the head, pulling out hair, and wearing sackcloth were typical acts of mourning in antiquity. The horrendous sight of a wrecked ship elicits pity. The hissing mentioned in v. 36 is not an expression of contempt, but an expression of empathy and concern to avoid the same fate (see Jer 18:16; 49:17; Job 27:23; Lam 2:15).

Oracular Account: Concerning the Prince of Tyre (28:1-10)

Ezekiel 28:1-10 begins with a typical example of the prophetic word formula in v. 1. The oracular account in vv. 2-10 is formulated as YHWH's instruction to Ezekiel to speak an oracle concerning the prince of Tyre. YHWH addresses Ezekiel in typical form as "son of Adam" to acknowledge his status as a Zadokite priest of the Jerusalem Temple even though he is in Babylonian exile. YHWH employs the Hebrew term *nagid*, generally translated as "prince," to refer to the king of Tyre (cf. Ezek 28:12 below). The term *nagid* often functions as a synonym for *melek*, "king," in biblical Hebrew (e.g., 1 Sam 9:16; 2 Sam 6:21; 1 Kings 1:35; 2 Kings 20:5). Formulated as a passive participial form of the verb root *ngd*, "to be conspicuous, to tell or declare" (see BDB, 616–18), it probably means "designated one" or the like. The prophetic messenger formula follows immediately upon YHWH's instruction to speak to the prince of Tyre in v. $2a\alpha^{1-9}$. The prophetic messenger formula identifies the following material as an oracle of YHWH.

The oracle to be spoken by Ezekiel to the prince of Tyre appears in vv. $2a\alpha^{10}$-$10b\alpha$. It is formulated as a prophetic judgment speech in which YHWH accuses the prince of Tyre of arrogantly claiming to be the equal of a god and then announces that the prince of Tyre will be brought down to the underworld for his claim. The accusation or grounds for judgment appears in vv. $2a\alpha^{10}$-5. It begins with the stereotypical particle *ya'an*, "because," followed by the basic statement of the accusation in v. $2a\alpha^{11}$-b. The basis for YHWH's charge of arrogance is the purported claim by the prince of Tyre that he considers himself to be a god, enthroned in the heart of the sea. But YHWH's statement counters that the prince is not a god, but a human being who considers his mind to be the equal of a god. The charge has some analogies with Eve's eating from the fruit of the Tree of Knowledge in the Garden of Eden, prompting the expulsion of Adam and Eve because they had attained knowledge like that of G-d (Gen 3). Indeed, the judgment of death against the prince of Tyre recalls the mortality that Adam and Eve must suffer when they are expelled from the Garden of Eden. YHWH elaborates on the intelligence of the prince of Tyre in vv. 3-6 by comparing him to Daniel. Although readers of the Bible might think of the biblical sage Daniel, Ezekiel refers to the well-known Canaanite sage Dan-El, who appears in the Ugaritic Aqhat Epic as the wise father of Aqhat, who saves his dead son from the netherworld. Although the latter portions of the Aqhat tablets have been destroyed, parallels to the myth suggest that Aqhat's sister, Paqhat, goes down to the netherworld to bring him back from the dead. Her descent to the netherworld thereby inaugurates the rainy fall season that symbolizes fertility and new growth in the world. Of course, the onset of the dry summer season marks the return of Aqhat to the netherworld until he is rescued once again by his sister (for the Aqhat Epic, see *ANET*, 149–55). YHWH characterizes the wisdom of the prince of Tyre in relation to his commercial expertise. Such a characterization differs from that of Dan-El, who was known for his knowledge of divine matters, but it is entirely appropriate for Tyre, which attained considerable commercial success and great wealth by sending out its ships to engage in trade with other nations. Indeed, King Hiram of Tyre counseled Solomon in commercial matters and played an important role in making Solomon—and Israel/Judah—rich (1 Kings 4–5; 9-10).

The announcement of judgment appears in vv. 6-10, introduced in typical form by the particle *laken*, "therefore," and followed by the prophetic messenger formula to certify the following as an oracle from YHWH. The oracle actually appears as a miniature version of the prophetic judgment speech insofar as it begins with a brief accusation, introduced by *ya'an*, "because," in v. 6b. The accusation reiterates the charges of vv. 2aα^{10}-5 above that the prince of Tyre arrogantly considers his mind to be equal to that of G-d. The announcement of punishment per se appears in vv. 7-10bα, once again introduced by *laken*, "therefore." The announcement plays upon the motifs of death and the underworld in the Aqhat Epic. But instead of envisioning the Tyrian prince's rise from the netherworld like that of Aqhat, the announcement condemns the prince of Tyre to death in the netherworld, here identified as the "pit" in v. 8. The means of the prince's death is realized by YHWH bringing foreign nations to carry out the sentence by unsheathing their swords against him. The irony of the death sentence is made clear in vv. 9-10bα when YHWH rhetorically asks the Tyrian prince if he is indeed a god when he is struck down by his enemies, thereby proving that he is a human being and not a god. Insofar as the Phoenicians are believed to have been circumcised like Israel/Judah and other nations in the region, the reference to "the deaths of the uncircumcised" apparently means death at the hands of the uncircumcised, apparently a reference to the Babylonians who will carry out the divine death sentence.

The oracle concludes with the oracular formula "utterance of YHWH" in v. 10bβ.

Oracular Account: Dirge for the King of Tyre (28:11-19)

Ezekiel 28:11-19 begins with the stereotypical prophetic word formula in v. 11, which introduces the oracle in vv. 12-19. The oracle is formulated as YHWH's instruction speech to Ezekiel, addressed in the usual manner as "son of Adam" to signify his status as a Zadokite priest. YHWH instructs Ezekiel to chant a dirge (Heb., *ainah*) over the king of Tyre in keeping with the death sentence imposed upon him in Ezekiel 28:1-10. The prophetic messenger formula identifies the following material as an oracle by YHWH.

The dirge per se appears in vv. 11bβ-19. The dirge is a funeral chant that is typically set in burial rituals in the ancient world. It is typically formulated in a 3/2 metrical pattern to accompany a slow march in which the body is carried to the grave, first with three steps and then with only two, to facilitate a halting and reluctant procession to the burial site (for study of the dirge, see Jahnow). The portrayal of the king of Tyre labels him as "the seal of perfection" (*hotem toknit*, lit., "sealing of the pattern"), thereby building upon ancient Near Eastern, particularly Mesopotamian, traditions that posited the king as the ideal representation of the human being sent by the gods to earth. The purpose of the ideal human king was to raise the level of human life to that of the gods. Assyrian monarchs were often portrayed as trees, growing upside down from heaven and embodying ideal qualities of wisdom, perfect form, sweet smell, etc., as a means to express the human ideal expected by the gods. In biblical literature, the ideal human is identified with Adam and Eve in the Garden of Eden. Although Christian theology tends to identify Eve and Adam as the founders of original sin, Eve gains the knowledge of good and evil identified with G-d when she eats of the Tree of Knowledge. She nevertheless fails to eat from the Tree of Life and thereby fails to gain immortality for human beings. The imagery of the ideal is expressed through precious stones in v. 13. The nine stones that appear here correspond to nine of the twelve stones that appear in the Ephod or breast piece of the high priest of the temple (see Exod 28:15-21). The reason for the absence of three of the stones is not made clear, although it is possible that Ezekiel chooses to identify the king of Tyre with the lost tribes of northern Israel (n.b., three tribes survived the destruction of northern Israel: Judah, Benjamin, and Levi). Such identification might be explained by the fact that King Hiram of Tyre was Solomon's principle architect and supplier in building the Jerusalem Temple, and Solomon was forced to cede twenty Israelite cities to him to pay his debt (see 1 Kings 5; 9). Ezekiel apparently sees the Tyrian king as a corrupting influence on Israel insofar as he put Israel into trading relations with foreign nations that eventually brought about Israel's downfall.

Another element of the idealization of the Tyrian king is his portrayal as a cherub in vv. 14-16. Cherubs were composite human and animal figures, often with a human head, a bovine body, eagles' wings, and lions' feet, which stood guard over thrones, gates to cities, and even over the Ark of the Covenant in the Jerusalem Temple. The dirge appears to presuppose Tyre's role as guardian of Jerusalem, especially since the Tyrian "cherub" is placed on G-d's holy mountain. But when Tyre allied with Egypt against Babylon in the late seventh and early sixth centuries, Tyre ceased to be a protector of Jerusalem and instead became an agent in instigating revolt against Babylon, thereby bringing about Jerusalem's desecration and destruction. The dirge pinpoints Tyre's extensive commerce with foreign nations as the cause of the problem, viz., because Tyre played a role in introducing Jerusalem to foreign nations, such as Egypt, Tyre bore responsibility for Jerusalem's demise. Indeed, the alliance of King Jehoiakim of Judah with Egypt played an important role in prompting Judah to revolt against Babylon in 598, 588, and again in 582 BCE. For that, Ezekiel posits that Tyre is to be destroyed like Jerusalem. The dirge concludes with a portrayal of the demise of the king of Tyre as fire issues from him and passersby are appalled by the king's downfall.

Oracular Account: Concerning Sidon and Israel (28:20-26)

The final segment of the oracles concerning Tyre in Ezekiel 26–28 appears in Ezekiel 28:20-26, which present oracles concerning Sidon and Israel. The segment is introduced with the prophetic word formula in v. 20, and it is formulated as an instruction speech to Ezekiel to speak the following oracle to Sidon. YHWH addresses Ezekiel as "son of Adam" in typical form to signal his status as a Zadokite priest. The oracle begins with the prophetic messenger formula to indicate its divine origin.

The oracle appears in three parts, Ezekiel 28:20aα^2-23, 24, and 25–26, each concluding with an example of the divine recognition formula to identity the realization of each event named as a revelation of YHWH.

The first segment of the oracle appears in Ezekiel 28:20aα^2-23, which is formulated simply as an announcement of punishment against Sidon. Sidon was a close ally of Tyre throughout much of the Iron Age, although Sidon was sometimes the dominant partner. It is likely included here as an ally of Tyre. Because Sidon was located on the mainland, unlike the island fortress of Tyre, the Babylonians conquered it far more easily. The oracle portrays the downfall of Tyre as an occasion to reveal YHWH's glory. Indeed, the recognition formula appears twice in this oracle to emphasize that the downfall of Tyre is an act that reveals YHWH to all witnesses. The portrayal of pestilence, bloodshed, and the slain in the streets is typical of a city in the ancient world that suffers through a siege before finally succumbing to be overrun by invading forces.

The second segment of the oracle appears in Ezekiel 28:24, which announces that the house of Israel shall no longer be afflicted as a result of the downfall of Sidon. The imagery of briars and thorns recalls imagery employed in the book of Isaiah for Israel's afflictions (e.g., Isa 5:6, although the terminology is different). Israel's restoration comes in the aftermath of the downfall of her enemies, and thereby constitutes a revelation of YHWH's sovereignty. In Ezekiel's view, Tyre and Sidon apparently bear responsibility for Israel's demise.

The third and final segment of the oracle appears in Ezekiel 28:25-26, which once again focuses on the restoration of Israel. The subunit begins with an example of the prophetic messenger formula to identify the following as an oracle from YHWH. The oracle anticipates the gathering of Israel from the nations to which it had been exiled and its restoration to the land of Israel given to Jacob. Again, such images of restoration recall those of Isaiah (Isa 11:10-16; 27:12-13; 35:1-10). The identification of Jacob as the ancestor to whom the land was promised (Gen 28:13-15; 35:10-12) is noteworthy in that it focuses on the ancestor identified with the northern kingdom of Israel. Perhaps this oracle recalls the early years of Josiah's reform when the Judean king sought to restore Davidic rule over the territory and people of the former northern kingdom of Israel. Of course, Josiah's early death disrupted these plans. But Ezekiel appears to have viewed the death of Josiah and the Babylonian exile as a delay in the implementation of Josiah's plans until Jerusalem was fully purged and restored to its holy state. Only then could Josiah's plans reach their full realization and thereby reveal YHWH to the world.

The First Oracular Account: Concerning Egypt

Ezekiel 29:1-16

Ezekiel 29:1-16 is the first of six dated oracular accounts concerning Egypt and the Egyptian Pharaoh (see also Ezek 29:17-30:19; 30:20-26; 31:1-18; 32:1-16; 32:17–33:20). With the exception of Ezekiel 29:17–30:19 (see discussion of this oracle below), all are dated to the tenth through twelfth years of Jehoiachin's exile, which would place them in the years 587/585 BCE, i.e., the years when Nebuchadnezzar conquered Jerusalem and commenced his siege of Tyre. Insofar as Nebuchadnezzar's ultimate goal was the conquest of Egypt, the campaigns against Judah and Tyre must be viewed as preliminary campaigns designed to subdue Egypt's primary allies in the region before continuing on to the ultimate prize. Although the Assyrians conquered Egypt under Esarhaddon in 671 BCE, as did the Persians under Cambyses in 525 BCE, Babylonia was never able to conquer Egypt. Ezekiel's oracles against Egypt reveal his belief that YHWH was identified with the Babylonians, much as Isaiah and Jeremiah identify YHWH with the Persian Empire in their respective books, and that Babylonia's conquest of Judah, Tyre, Egypt, and other nations must be viewed as acts of YHWH. Nebuchadnezzar's failure to conquer Egypt, however, left Ezekiel's Egyptian oracles largely unfulfilled, much like the later vision of the restored temple in Ezekiel 40–48. Ezekiel's unfulfilled oracles prompt many interpreters to view Ezekiel as a proto-apocalyptic prophet whose visions are yet to be realized. In both Judaism and Christianity, Ezekiel becomes an important model for those who would posit visionary ascents to heaven to appear before the throne of G-d. Such examples appear in the Merkavah (Chariot) Heikhalot (Palaces) literature of Talmudic Judaism and the book of Revelation in the New Testament. Nevertheless, Ezekiel's Egyptian oracles have a historical dimension, viz., as a priest born at the outset of King Josiah's reign, Ezekiel would have viewed Egypt as a major enemy of Judah, both because Egypt was an ally of Assyria and because Egypt played such an important role in Judah's foundational narratives in early forms of the Pentateuchal literature.

With the death of Josiah and the collapse of Judah, anticipation of the downfall of Egypt would be attributed to YHWH working through Babylonia. Given the concentration of oracles concerning Egypt dated to the tenth through twelfth years, it may be that these oracles formed an early collection that was later incorporated into the book of Ezekiel and its chronological framework.

Ezekiel 29:1-16 appears as a chronologically formulated oracular account of YHWH's instruction speech to the prophet. It begins with a chronological formula in v. 1a, which dates the account to the tenth year, the twelfth day of the tenth month, which would correspond to 12 Tevet (December–January) 587 BCE. At this time, the siege of Jerusalem would have been underway, and the Egyptian attempt by Pharaoh Hophra (a.k.a., Apries, r. 589–570 BCE; see Redford, 286–87) to relieve Jerusalem would have been repulsed by the Babylonians (Jer 37:5-11; cf. 44:30). Ezekiel's oracle is likely set in relation to the Babylonian defeat of Hophra's army. Following the chronological formula, the prophetic word formula in v. 1b identifies the following material as YHWH's oracle to Ezekiel. No other examples of the prophetic word formula appear within Ezekiel 29:1-16.

Verses 2-16 are formulated as YHWH's instruction speech to Ezekiel to deliver the Egyptian oracle. YHWH addresses Ezekiel in typical form at the outset of v. 2 as "son of Adam" to indicate his status as a Zadokite priest. The rest of v. 2 and the first two words of v. 3 include YHWH's instruction to prophesy against the Pharaoh. The prophetic messenger formula in v. 3aα$^{3-6}$ identifies the following material as an oracle from YHWH.

The oracle per se in vv. 3aβ-16 is formulated as a prophetic judgment speech, but it deviates from the usual form due to its poetic and metaphorical character. Overall, the oracle employs the metaphor of the Nile River, which forms the backbone and natural foundation of Egypt in both ancient and modern times, to portray the king of Egypt as a fish that has been caught and pulled out from the Nile. Such a portrayal is deliberate insofar as the Nile is the chief means to sustain Egyptian life, but here, even the Nile cannot protect the Egyptian Pharaoh from YHWH's efforts to trap him. An analogous fishing metaphor appears in Habakkuk 1:12-17, which portrays the Chaldean (Babylonian) king as a fisherman who traps his prey. The gist of the oracle appears in v. 3aβ-b in which YHWH announces the intention to strike against Pharaoh and identifies the reason for the judgment. In this case, the Pharaoh's statement, "The Nile is mine, and I made it for myself," is tacitly understood as a direct challenge to YHWH's role as creator and sovereign of the universe. Indeed, the identification of the Pharaoh with "the great serpent who crouches in the midst of the Nile" recalls the combat imagery of creation in which YHWH defeats a chaos monster, such as Leviathan, Behemoth, or the Serpent, to bring order and stability to the created world (see Isa 11:10-16; 27:1; Ps 74; Job 40:15-32).

After announcing the grounds for judgment in v. 3aβ-b, vv. 4-16 concentrate on the announcement of judgment per se. The segment in vv. 4-7 employs the fishing metaphor to depict YHWH's efforts to place hooks into the Pharaoh monster and haul it in from the channels of the Nile. The carcass is hauled in with fish still clinging to its scales. In an ironic twist on the exodus motif, YHWH will toss the carcass into the wilderness where it will serve as food for wild animals and birds. The recognition formula in v. 6 indicates that the Egyptians will then know that YHWH is the cause for the Pharaoh's demise. The reference to Egypt as a reed staff that splinters and wounds the hand when one leans upon it draws upon an image that is also known in Isaiah 36:6 and 2 Kings 18:21, where it is used by the Assyrian delegation to Hezekiah to portray the futility of reliance on Egypt for support.

Two further segments in vv. 8-9 and 10-16, each introduced by *laken*, "therefore," then apply the metaphor to the realities of the day. Verses 8-9 make it clear that YHWH will bring the sword against Egypt to destroy it. The brief oracle employs the prophetic messenger formula to identify the statement as YHWH's, and it also includes a recognition formula to indicate that they will know YHWH. The oracle concludes with the reason for the punishment, i.e., a reiteration of Pharaoh's claim, "The Nile is mine, and I made it."

Verses 10-16 are somewhat more complicated. The first part of the oracle in vv. 10-12 focuses on judgment against Egypt to depict the complete ruin of the nation "from Migdol to Syene, all the way to the border of Cush." The exact site of Migdol is unknown, but it lies in the eastern delta region so that it functioned as a northern gateway to Egypt (Lott, 822). Syene is identified with the modern site of Aswan, located in the southern part of the country near the border with Cush (Ethiopia or Nubia; see Betz, 250). The statement that the judgment will last for forty years as the people of Egypt are scattered among the nations is a deliberate association with the forty years of wandering by Israel following the exodus. The point is to demonstrate that Egypt will suffer much as Israel did as a result of its Egyptian captivity. But vv. 13-16 complete the analogy with Israel's wilderness period. Just as Israel entered the land of Israel after forty years of wandering, so the exiled Egyptians will return home after their forty years of punishment. Unlike Israel, however, Ezekiel projects Egypt's reduced status. The oracle identifies Patros, the "upper" portion of Egypt located in the southern highlands on the way to Cush, as the birthplace of the people of Egypt. But lofty Patros will become a "lowly" or "fallen" (Heb., *shefelah*) kingdom as a result of YHWH's judgment. Egypt will never again dominate other nations as it had in the past.

The Second Oracular Account: Concerning Egypt

Ezekiel 29:17–30:19

Ezekiel 29:17–30:19 is unusual for two basic reasons. First, it employs a chronological formula that dates the section to the twenty-seventh year, the first day of the first month of Jehoiachin's captivity. This date corresponds to 1 Nisan (March–April) 570 BCE. Insofar as Ezekiel's fiftieth year corresponds to the twenty-fifth year of Jehoiachin's exile (see Ezek 40:1), the date stands outside of the twenty-year chronological framework in Ezekiel that extends from Ezekiel's thirtieth through his fiftieth years, viz., the expected years of his service at the Jerusalem altar. Second, although Ezekiel 29:17 employs the prophetic word formula to introduce YHWH's oracle to Ezekiel, the oracle is not formulated as an instruction speech; rather, it is formulated simply as YHWH's communication to Ezekiel of an oracle concerning Nebuchadnezzar's futile expenditure of effort in the siege of Tyre and YHWH's intention to give him the land of Egypt to compensate for his efforts. The prophetic word formula in Ezekiel 30:1 then introduces the next segment of the unit, viz., an oracle concerning the Day of YHWH against Egypt in Ezekiel 30:1-19.

Because of its differences, Ezekiel 29:17-21 constitutes an anomaly among Ezekiel's oracles concerning Egypt. But interpreters have noted that the date for the oracle falls after the conclusion of Nebuchadnezzar's thirteen-year siege of Tyre, which lasted from 585 through 572 BCE. Consequently, interpreters have concluded that the present form of the oracle was updated to account for the unusually long duration of the siege (e.g., Greenberg 1997, 616–18; Joyce 2007, 182; Tuell, 206). The oracle should have been dated to the eleventh year, i.e., 586 BCE, when Jerusalem fell and immediately prior to the commencement of the siege of Tyre in 585 BCE. Ezekiel could easily have written this oracle himself at the age of fifty-two after his presumed "retirement" as a Zadokite priest and visionary prophet of YHWH. In part because Tyre held out for so long before submitting to Babylonia, Nebuchadnezzar was never able to complete his conquest of Egypt, Tyre's major ally. Nevertheless, the oracle anticipates that one day Egypt would fall to Babylon—which it never did—and that Israel would be relieved by the downfall of Egypt—which it never was. Nebuchadnezzar did invade Egypt in 668 BCE, but the campaign failed. Although Tyre submitted to Nebuchadnezzar by 572 BCE, there is no evidence that Nebuchadnezzar stormed the city, which meant that his army never got to take booty from the site. Ezekiel would have opened his mouth at this time—and there is no evidence that he ever spoke after this date—so that the world would know that YHWH was the ultimate cause of these events.

Ezekiel 30:1-19 constitutes the second subunit of Ezekiel 29:17–30:19. It appears in a much more conventional form with its introductory prophetic word formula in v. 1 and its formulation as YHWH's instruction to Ezekiel, here addressed as "son of Adam" to recognize his status as a Zadokite priest, to speak an oracle concerning Egypt in vv. 2-19. Following the instruction to prophesy in v. 2aα, the oracle per se appears as an announcement of judgment against Egypt on the Day of YHWH. The Day of YHWH tradition is well known in the prophetic literature, where it is understood as a day of judgment against YHWH's enemies, whether Israel (Isa 2:6-21; Amos 5:18-21; Zeph 1:2-18; 2:1-3) or foreign nations (Isa 13; 34; Joel; Obadiah). Although the Day of YHWH is frequently understood as an eschatological day of judgment, the concerns of the traditions are with events of the present and the historical future. The supposed eschatological character of the tradition derives from its cultic setting in the Jerusalem Temple, where heaven and earth meet. Consequently, the mythological dimensions of the revelation of YHWH's presence in the temple—and thus in the world and creation at large—are commonly misunderstood as an indication of the end of time. But revelation of YHWH's presence at the temple is hardly an eschatological event; rather it points to the manifestation of YHWH's presence at times of worship, such as the major holidays and observances that take place on a regular, fixed schedule each and every year. YHWH's revelation in the temple at Rosh ha-Shanah, Yom Kippur, Sukkot, Passover, Shavuot, and every Shabbat is a liturgical event in the temple calendar, not an indication of the end of time. YHWH's revelation at a given event presumes YHWH's action in the world to restore the holy order of creation by defeating the forces of chaos that threaten it, whether such forces might be the enemies of Israel that threaten the temple or those among Israel who do not observe YHWH's expectations (Levenson 1988). Consequently, the language employed to designate the future, "and it shall come to pass in that day," and the like simply designates the future when the consequences of YHWH's revelation and action in the world are to be accomplished

(Munch; De Vries 1975 and 1995). In the present instance, the Day of YHWH against Egypt is identified with Nebuchadnezzar's efforts to conquer Egypt that would follow his campaigns against Judah and Tyre. As it happens, Nebuchadnezzar never succeeded in conquering Egypt, which leaves the present oracle unfulfilled.

The oracle includes three major portions, each of which is introduced by the prophetic messenger formula. The first is an announcement of the Day of YHWH against Egypt in vv. 2aβ-5 and three oracles in vv. 6-9, 10-12, and 13-19 concerned with various aspects of Egypt's impending demise.

The first oracle in vv. 2aβ-5 announces the Day of YHWH against Egypt. It begins in v. 2aβ with a call to wail for the impending Day of YHWH, followed by an extended statement of the reason for the wailing in vv. 3-5 introduced by the particle *ki*, "because." The initial statement of cause in v. 3a corresponds closely with other statements of the Day of YHWH by emphasizing that "near is the day, and near is the day of YHWH" (cf. Isa 13:6; Joel 1:15; 2:1; 4:14; Ob 15; Zeph 1:14). Verse 3b combines theophanic elements by describing the Day of YHWH as a day of cloud combined with warring elements that describe the day as a time of invading nations. The cloud motif of course recalls the smoke and cloud typically associated with divine theophanies, which in turn derive from the use of incense smoke in the temple to symbolize the presence of YHWH. The motif of the invading nations is a common motif for those Day of YHWH texts concerned with threats to Jerusalem (e.g., Isa 13; 34; Joel; Obadiah). Verses 4-5 then turn to the specific condemnation of Egypt and Cush (Ethiopia). Ancient Egypt was a combined kingdom of the northern delta regions and the southern highlands of Ethiopia. Other allies, Put, Lud, and Cub, are also included in the projected slaughter. Put is Libya, Lud is Lydia, and Cub is unknown.

The second oracle in vv. 6-9 generally describes the devastation that will overtake Egypt at YHWH's hand. The segment is introduced by the prophetic messenger formula to indicate it as an oracle of YHWH. It focuses on the downfall of the exalted might of Egypt and her allies in a manner that recalls Isaiah 2:6-21. As noted above, the reference to Migdol and Syene indicates the totality of Egypt from Migdol in the north to Syene (Aswan) in the south. The oracular formula at the end of v. 6 further defines YHWH as the author of the statement, and the recognition formula at the end of v. 7 indicates that the downfall of Egypt will reveal YHWH's presence and action in the world. The final statement in v. 9, introduced by the formula *bayyom hahu'*, "in that day," anticipates the future downfall of Cush, which had been the dominant partner in the Egyptian coalition during the late eighth and early seventh centuries BCE.

The third oracle in vv. 10-12, again introduced with the prophetic messenger formula, identifies Nebuchadnezzar of Babylon as YHWH's agent for punishing Egypt. Such a claim is in keeping with earlier Isaian tradition that identifies the Assyrians as YHWH's agents of punishment against Israel and Judah. Ezekiel's pro-Babylonian political alignment is clear in this instance. Such an alignment is consistent with King Josiah's foreign policy and with that of his great-grandfather Hezekiah before him. Insofar as Ezekiel was born at the outset of Josiah's reform, it would seem that Josiah's alignment with Babylon against Assyria and Egypt continues to play a role in Ezekiel's thinking.

The fourth oracle in vv. 13-19, again introduced by the prophetic messenger formula, delineates YHWH's judgment among the various provinces and cities of Egypt. Noph is Memphis, the early capital of Egypt south of present-day Cairo. Pathros is the name for upper Egypt, the southern portion of Egypt north of Cush. Zoan, also known as Rameses, Tanis, and Avaris, is a delta city identified with the site of Hebrew slavery in the exodus tradition (Ps 78:12, 43; Exod 1:11; Num 13:22). No is Thebes, Egypt's capital throughout much of Israel's history. Sin is Pelusium in the northeastern delta near Zoan. Aven is On or Heliopolis, about six miles northeast of modern Cairo. Pi-Beseth is Bubastis in the eastern delta. Tehaphnehes is located by the north shore of the Gulf of Suez (Jer 2:16; 43:7-13). The motif of covering Egypt with cloud recalls YHWH's theophany in the exodus and Sinai tradition (Exod 19; 40), and the recognition formula concludes the unit with a statement that the downfall of Egypt will reveal YHWH once again.

The First Oracular Account: Concerning Pharaoh

Ezekiel 30:20-26

This brief unit in the chronological framework of the book of Ezekiel dates to the seventh day of the first month of the eleventh year of Jehoiachin's exile, which corresponds to 7 Nisan (March–April 586 BCE), about four months prior to the fall of Jerusalem. It appears in typical form with the prophetic word formula in v. 20 and an address to Ezekiel as "son of Adam" at the outset of the oracle in v. 21. The oracle is not formulated as an instruction speech to the prophet, but only as an oracle, delivered directly to Ezekiel, concerning the downfall of Pharaoh, the king of Egypt. The content of the oracle indicates that it addresses Nebuchadnezzar's defeat of Pharaoh Hophra of Egypt, who sent an army north in an attempt to relieve Jerusalem from Nebuchadnezzar's siege (2 Kings 24:7; Jer 37:5). The oracle makes it clear once again that Babylon is the agent of YHWH's defeat of the Pharaoh. But it also employs a characteristic motif of the exodus tradition of YHWH's earlier defeat of Pharaoh, i.e., the outstretched arm of Moses/YHWH that initiated the plagues, the parting of the Red Sea, and other elements of YHWH's punishment against Pharaoh and Egypt. Interpreters note that the arm of Pharaoh is an important element in the iconography of Pharaoh's defeat of enemies (see the depiction of Pharaoh Nar-Mer striking a kneeling prisoner in *ANEP*, 296). Once again, the recognition formula identifies the demise of the Pharaoh as a revelation of YHWH's presence and power.

The Second Oracular Account: Concerning Pharaoh

Ezekiel 31:1-18

The chronological formula in v. 1a followed by the prophetic word formula in v. 1b introduces the second oracular account concerning Pharaoh in Ezekiel 32:2-18. Although only one oracular account appears within this passage, it constitutes the ninth major unit of the book of Ezekiel. The date ascribed to the oracle, the first day of the third month of the eleventh year, would be 1 Sivan 586 BCE, some six days prior to the festival of Shavuot and about two months prior to the destruction of the temple and the city of Jerusalem. Insofar as the earlier oracle in Ezekiel 30:20-26 presumed Nebuchadnezzar's defeat of Pharaoh Hophra's attempt to relieve Jerusalem, the present oracular account follows up with the threats made against him. As the siege of Jerusalem was progressing, it was obvious that Egypt was going to be among the next targets of the Babylonian empire. Again, Nebuchadnezzar never succeeded in taking Egypt, and so the present oracle would have been delivered in the expectation of an Egyptian defeat, not the realization of such an outcome.

The oracle is formulated as YHWH's instruction to Ezekiel to speak to the Pharaoh of Egypt and his minions. The instruction formula in v. 2a introduces an oracle in vv. 2b-18 that is formulated as an allegory that portrays Assyria as a high and mighty tree in the Garden of Eden that was felled by YHWH due to its arrogance. Insofar as the oracle begins and ends with rhetorical questions in vv. 2b and 18 concerning to whom the Pharaoh might be compared, the oracle threatens the Pharaoh with downfall and defeat based upon the prior experience of Assyria. The reason for the comparison between Pharaoh and Assyria is not difficult to fathom. Egypt had been a close ally of Assyria from 667 BCE when the Assyrian king Assurbanipal invaded Egypt and set up the twenty-sixth Saite dynasty as a vassal to control Egypt on Assyria's behalf (Grayson, 143–45). Throughout the seventh century BCE, the Saite Pharaohs supported their Assyrian overlords by attempting to control western Asia on behalf of Assyria and by sending armies to Mesopotamia to support Assyrian interests. Indeed, when the Saite Pharaoh Necho II killed King Josiah of Judah at Megiddo in 609 BCE, he was attempting to move his army northward to support the Assyrians in their final battle against Babylonia at Haran in 609 BCE. Josiah succeeded in delaying Necho long enough so that the Assyrians were already defeated and the Assyrian Empire ceased to exist. Egypt then became the primary enemy of Babylon in the west and succeeded in holding off the Babylonians until 605 BCE, when they were defeated at Carchemesh and forced to withdraw from western Asia back into the Egyptian homeland. Even then, the Egyptians played a major role in instigating revolt against the Babylonians, including the ill-fated Judean revolt of 588 BCE and those of its allies, such as Tyre and the other small nations in the vicinity.

Following the initial rhetorical question in v. 2b, "to whom do you compare in greatness?" vv. 3-9 present an allegorical portrayal of Assyria as a great tree that had no peer in the Garden of Eden. Many interpreters have attempted to emend the initial statement of v. 3, "Behold, Assyria was a cedar in Lebanon," because it was not clear to them why Assyria should be the focal point of an oracle against Egypt. But the lack of demonstrable text-critical alternatives and the above-noted relationship between Assyria and Egypt during the seventh century BCE demonstrate that Assyria is indeed the correct reading in this text. Just as Assyria was brought down by Babylon in 609 BCE, so Egypt would be brought down by Babylon in 586 BCE. By depicting Assyria as a cedar of Lebanon, Ezekiel's oracle employs the imagery of the tallest and most majestic trees known in western Asia at the time. In addition, the oracle borrows intertextually from Isaian oracles that portray the Assyrian monarch as a great tree that is about to be chopped down by YHWH for its arrogance. With the downfall of the Assyrian king portrayed as a tree, a new Davidic king could then grow from the stump of Jesse, according to Isaiah 10:5–11:16 (Sweeney 1996, 196–211). The portrayal of the tree in the oracle also draws on biblical traditions concerning the trees of the Garden of Eden, including the Tree of Life and the Tree of the Knowledge of Good and Evil (Gen 2:4–3:24, esp. 2:8-9).

The use of such tree imagery for Assyria also makes eminent sense from the standpoint of Assyrian mythology. Assyrian mythology portrayed the Assyrian king as the ideal human being who was sent from heaven to earth by the gods to rule Assyria and the world on their behalf. The ideal king was typically portrayed as a tree growing upside down from heaven to earth, and its branches embodied the various qualities, wisdom, strength, integrity, etc., that would be necessary to govern on behalf of the gods (Widengren,

42–58). The downfall of the tree that symbolizes the Assyrian king entails the downfall of Assyria itself.

Overall, vv. 3-9 portray the tree in grandiose terms as a lofty, mighty, and luxuriant tree fed by the waters of the divine garden in which it is planted. Its capacity to rule is signaled by its towering height over the other trees of the garden (cf. Jotham's fable in Judg 9:7-21 in which he employed the allegory of a vine that wished to rule over the other trees as a means to undermine Abimelech's attempt to install himself as king over Israel). All of the birds and the animals of the field take shelter in the tree, and the allegory is made explicit when the oracle notes that all of the great nations lived in its shadows as well. By v. 8, the allegory states that even the great cedars in the garden of G-d could not compare with the tree. Further, in v. 9, YHWH speaks in the first person to claim, "I made it beautiful in the multitude of its branches, and all the trees of Eden envied it, which was in the garden of G-d." Clearly, the oracle envisions the tree as the centerpiece of the Garden of Eden, just as the Assyrian king was conceived as the centerpiece of the human world and creation in Assyrian mythology.

Verses 10-17 then shift from the idyllic portrayal of the tree in the garden to the downfall of the tree at YHWH's command. The section begins with the particle *laken*, "therefore," which normally introduces the announcement of judgment in the prophetic judgment speeches. Here, *laken* signals the shift from might to devastation. Two oracles, each introduced by the prophetic messenger formula, then lay out the judgment against the "Assyrian" tree respectively in vv. $10a\alpha^2$-14 and 15-17. Verses $10a\alpha^2$-14 are formulated as prophetic judgment speech. Following the messenger formula in v. $10a\alpha^{2-5}$, they lay out the grounds for judgment in v. $10a\beta$-b introduced by the particle *ya'an*, "because." The tree is charged with arrogance and attempting to dominate other nations, charges not unlike those made against the Assyrian king in Isaiah 10:5-34. Indeed, the theme of arrogance against YHWH is a major motif in Isaiah 2:6-21, which announces the Day of YHWH to bring down all who are arrogant and lift themselves up against others. Verses 11-14 then lay out YHWH's actions against the tree. YHWH gives it over to the mightiest of the nations, presumably Babylon, so that foreigners will be able to chop it down, strip it of its branches, and scatter its pieces throughout creation (cf. Isa 6:12-13; 10:5-34). Such actions will of course prompt the birds, animals, and nations who took shelter in the tree to abandon it as they now find themselves consigned to death in the underworld.

The second oracle in vv. 15-17 takes up where the first leaves off. It, too, begins with the prophetic messenger formula in v. $15a\alpha^{1-4}$, which introduces the following announcement of judgment in vv. 15aα^5-17. Although the announcement continues the tree imagery of the earlier segments of the passage, it also shifts to imagery pertaining to the reversal of creation, as the downfall of the tree now portends its submersion into the ocean deeps in a bid to demonstrate that chaos will now overtake order (contra Gen 1:1–2:3). Such a portrayal of mythological chaos frequently expresses the downfall of political order in the Bible and the ancient Near East (Levenson 1988). The mourning trees of Lebanon and the quaking nations frequently accompany such scenarios as the tree descends into the Pit or the Underworld (e.g., Isa 24–27). Once again, this portrayal draws on the oracles of Isaiah, particularly Isaiah 14:3-23, which depicts the downfall of the Babylonian king who now descends into the netherworld. Scholars note that although this oracle portrays the downfall of the Babylonian king in its present context in Isaiah 13:1–14:23, Isaiah 14:3-23 originally portrayed the death of the Assyrian king Sargon II in 705 BCE (see Erlandsson; Sweeney 1996, 218–39).

The final segment of the oracle appears in v. 18, which reprises the rhetorical question that began this oracle, "To whom do you compare yourself in honor and greatness among the trees of the Garden?" Such a repetition takes the reader back to the initial premise of the oracle, but it also takes the reader forward to the conclusion that—like Assyria—the Pharaoh of Egypt is doomed. Verse 18b first notes that "you" (i.e., the Pharaoh to whom the oracle is addressed) will be brought down to the underworld with the trees of Eden and that "you" will lie among the uncircumcised (n.b., Egyptian priests and perhaps others were circumcised) and those killed by the sword. The final statement in v. 18 makes the issue clear, viz., "that is Pharaoh and all his minions." The oracular formula concludes the oracle and certifies it as an oracle from YHWH.

The Third Oracular Account: Concerning Pharaoh and Egypt

Ezekiel 32:1-16

The chronological formula in Ezekiel 32:1a dates the unit to the first day of the twelfth month in the twelfth year of Jehoiachin's exile. That date would correspond to 1 Adar (February–March) 585 BCE, about fifteen months following the destruction of the temple. The prophetic word transmission formula in v. 1b identifies the following material in vv. 2-16 as an account of YHWH's oracle to Ezekiel. There is no second instance of the prophetic word formula in this unit.

The oracular account is formulated as an instruction speech by YHWH to Ezekiel. YHWH addresses Ezekiel in typical form as "son of Adam" to acknowledge his status as a Zadokite priest, and instructs him to intone a dirge (Heb., *qinah*) over the Pharaoh, king of Egypt in v. 2aαβ. The typical 3/2 dirge metrical beat appears only sporadically throughout the following material, but the contents of the dirge anticipate the downfall of the Pharaoh and Egypt.

The oracle begins with an initial address to Pharaoh in v. 2aγ-b that states the essential premise of the dirge: the Pharaoh is doomed. Such a threat apparently expresses the expectations of many that the Babylonian army would move against Egypt in the aftermath of the downfall of Jerusalem and the anticipated downfall of Tyre. In fact, Nebuchadnezzar was never able successfully to invade Egypt. The initial address metaphorically portrays the Pharaoh first as a lion (Heb., *kefir*) among the nations and then as a dragon or serpent (Heb., *tannim*) in the seas. The first instance uses a metaphor commonly employed by the kings of Egypt to depict themselves, i.e., the young lion who terrorizes enemies and rules over its dominion. But here, the lion is doomed. The second instance uses the common metaphor of mythology, i.e., the dragon or serpent of the sea that so frequently represents the forces of chaos in the world that are conquered by the creator god acting on behalf of a human monarch. In this case, the image of the serpent speaks to the central role that the Nile River plays in Egyptian life and thought, i.e., the Pharaoh acts as a threat to order in the world rather than as its protector. The Pharaoh/dragon is portrayed as a monster that disturbs the waters of the Nile and stirs up mud as it moves about. Such an image must have been common along the banks of the Nile as the various crocodiles and other threatening life forms moved about in the water in search of prey.

Two oracle complexes then follow in vv. 3-8 and 9-16. The first focuses on YHWH's actions to bring down the Pharaoh, and the second focuses on YHWH's actions to stir up the nations, here led by Babylonia, against Egypt.

Ezekiel 32:3-8 begins in v. 3aα with a prophetic messenger formula that certifies the following material as an oracle by YHWH, and it concludes in v. 8bβ with the oracular formula that serves the same function. It builds on the imagery of v. 2aγ-b by continuing to portray the Pharaoh as a lion and as a dragon trapped by YHWH and cast out dead for the nations, the birds of the heavens, and the beasts of the field to witness and to devour. The net cast over the lionized Pharaoh is a typical device used for hunting lions; it immobilizes them and makes them easier to kill or to take alive for anyone brave and skilled enough to do it. Hauling the dragon up in toils portrays a great beast caught in water and then thrown out on the ground to die. The portrayal of the birds and animals feasting on the carcass of the dragon reverses the normal imagery of such a beast as hunter, but it also points to YHWH's role as creator, who tames the chaos monster and feeds its carcass to the creatures of creation itself. The depiction of the blood of the dead beast covering the hills and filling the streams portrays a land befouled. In this case, Egypt is defiled by the rotting carcass of its own monarch. As a result of the demise of Pharaoh, YHWH proposes to block all the lights of the heavens and darken the land of Egypt. Such a statement reprises the plagues of the exodus as YHWH demonstrates to Pharaoh and Egypt who the true G-d of creation really is.

Ezekiel 32:9-16 appears somewhat parallel to Ezekiel 32:2aγ-b, 3-8. Verses 9-10 state the premises of the following oracular material, viz., that YHWH will display the fallen Pharaoh/beast to the nations at large in an effort to raise the nations against Egypt. Again, such a statement recalls the exodus narratives insofar as the plagues unleashed against Egypt were intended as a sign to both the Egyptians and the nations that YHWH is G-d. Verses 11-14 comprise an oracle parallel to vv. 3-8. Again, the oracle is introduced by the prophetic messenger formula (plus the particle *ki*, "therefore") in v. 11 and closed by the oracular formula in v. 14b to certify the oracle as YHWH's. YHWH here announces the intention to raise Babylon against Egypt. Not only will Egypt's armies be destroyed, but the feet of its cattle will no longer muddy the waters of the rivers as they have in past times of tranquility. The settling of the waters that then flow like oil recalls the natural cycle of the Nile when it rises and then recedes in the spring, but this time, the rise and fall of the Nile will empty the land of its inhabitants and animals. This theme appears in an additional subunit in vv. 15-16 that follows with a portrayal of the land of Egypt bereft of all life after the waters have fallen. The recognition formula indicates that the disaster inflicted upon Egypt will reveal YHWH as the true G-d. The summary statement in v. 16 reiterates that the preceding material is a dirge over Egypt and its minions to be intoned by the women of the nations. The concluding oracular formula certifies YHWH as the source.

Final Oracles concerning the Nations and Ezekiel's Role as Watchman

Ezekiel 32:17–33:20

Ezekiel 32:17–33:20 begins with the chronological statement in Ezekiel 32:17a that dates the unit to the fifteenth day of an unspecified month in the twelfth year of Jehoiachin's exile. The lack of specification for the month suggests that the present formula follows upon that of Ezekiel 32:1. The month would then be the twelfth month, and the date would be 15 Adar (February–March) 585 BCE, about two weeks following the oracle of Ezekiel 32:1-16 and some fifteen months following the destruction of the temple. Again, expectations for a Babylonian invasion of Egypt would have been high in the aftermath of the destruction of Jerusalem and the anticipated fall of Tyre. The unit contains two examples of the prophetic word formula. The first in Ezekiel 32:17b introduces the oracular account in Ezekiel 32:18-32 that announces YHWH's intentions to bring down Egypt and other nations. The second in Ezekiel 33:1 introduces the oracular account in Ezekiel 33:2-20 that reflects upon Ezekiel's role as watchman and his responsibility to warn Israel of approaching calamity, particularly punishment from YHWH for wrongdoing by Israel. The two major components of this unit were not likely written to function as a single unit, but in the current chronological structure of the book of Ezekiel they have been grouped together to make a point. Just as the impending destruction of the nations, particularly Tyre and Egypt in the preceding units, demonstrate that YHWH is G-d, so Israel must be prepared to recognize impending world events as evidence that YHWH is G-d of all creation. Ezekiel's appointment as watchman for Israel entails that he bears responsibility for preparing the people for what is to come, not only the destruction of Jerusalem and Judah, but the restoration of Jerusalem and Israel as well.

The formal structure of the unit may be presented as follows:

VI. Final oracles concerning the nations and Ezekiel's role as watchman (Ezek 32:17–33:20)

A. Oracular Account concerning the Impending Downfall of Egypt (32:17-32)
B. Oracular Account concerning Ezekiel's Role as Israel's Watchman (33:1-20)

Oracular Account concerning the Impending Downfall of Egypt (32:17-32)

Following the chronological formula and the prophetic word formula in v. 17, Ezekiel 32:18-32 announces once again the impending downfall of Egypt. The passage is formulated as an instruction speech in which YHWH initially addresses Ezekiel as "son of Adam" and then instructs him to join the women of the nations in lamenting (Heb., *neheh*) the descent of Egypt into the netherworld. Verses 19-32 are formulated as YHWH's address to the prophet, but they include instances in which YHWH addresses Egypt in second-person form. Verse 19 echoes the question addressed to Pharaoh in Ezekiel 31:2, 18, i.e., "to whom do you compare in greatness?" but this time it is expressed in terms of beauty and vitality, i.e., "from whom are you more comely?" The purpose of such a question is to signal the rotting state of a corpse as it lies in the netherworld. The instruction speech focuses on the lowered state of the dead among whom Egypt will lie, viz., they are uncircumcised, unlike the priests of Egypt, and they were all killed by sword—which would do little to enhance their appearance—and now Egypt will join them. Verses 21-30 give an accounting of the various nations that Egypt will join in the depths of Sheol. First among them is Assyria, Egypt's erstwhile ally before it was destroyed by the Babylonian Empire in 609 BCE. Assyria had once ruled the world, but now it lies among the dead—as Egypt will lie. Second is Elam, which was located in the southern regions of modern Iran to the east of Babylonia. Elam was once a powerful country like Assyria, but it was subjugated by the Assyrians and now lies dead. Meshech and Tubal are also identified. Although interpreters believe that they were located in Asia Minor, their specific identities and locations remain unknown. Nevertheless, they are portrayed as once-powerful contenders on the world scene who now lie among the dead in the netherworld. Verse 28 interrupts the accounting of the dead with a second-person statement directed to Egypt, "And you will be buried among the uncircumcised, and you will lie with those slain by the sword," to underscore the point of the passage that Egypt, too, will die and go to Sheol. Nations near to Israel are also included, such as Edom, Israel's neighbor, which began to disappear after the Babylonian invasion, and the princes of the north, apparently a reference to the Phoenicians, as indicated by the explicit mention of the Sidonians, who suffered invasion like Judah.

Verses 31-32 close the unit with pointed statements that the Pharaoh of Egypt will see all of these nations as his own minions die by the sword. Following the oracular formula that closes v. 31, v. 32 presents YHWH's statement, "I strike terror in the land of the living, and Pharaoh and all his minions are lain with the uncircumcised and those slain by the sword," to emphasize Egypt's fate. Again, the oracular formula closes the unit and identifies it as an oracle by YHWH.

Oracular Account concerning Ezekiel's Role as Israel's Watchman (33:1-20)

The prophetic word formula in Ezekiel 33:1 introduces the oracular account of Ezekiel's appointment as Israel's watchman in Ezekiel 33:2-20. In typical form for Ezekiel, YHWH addresses the prophet as "son of Adam" to acknowledge his role as a Zadokite priest. The instruction formula in v. 2aα introduces the oracle per se in vv. 2aβ-20.

YHWH's oracle is formulated as a commissioning speech in which Ezekiel is appointed as watchman for the nation, and it is combined with a disputation speech that defines Ezekiel's obligations to warn the people concerning their potential guilt before YHWH. Ezekiel's role as watchman for Israel and his obligations as such appear earlier in Ezekiel 3:16-21. The role is a metaphorical portrayal of Ezekiel's role as priest, viz., just as the watchman for a city must warn its residents of impending danger, i.e., attack by an enemy, so must Ezekiel, the priest and prophet, warn the people concerning their conduct before YHWH. As a Zadokite priest, Ezekiel is responsible for teaching the people holy conduct. Leviticus 10:10-11, Deuteronomy 33:10, and Ezekiel 44:23 make it clear that the priests' role is to instruct the people in the difference between what is holy and profane and what is clean and unclean. Because he is a priest, Ezekiel is to be held accountable; i.e., if the people suffer punishment for failing to observe YHWH's expectations, Ezekiel will be held accountable if he failed to teach or warn them properly concerning the matter at hand. If the people suffer and Ezekiel warned them, however, he is not to be held accountable.

Disputation speeches normally express disagreement with a premise, state a counterthesis, and lay out the grounds for the disagreement in argumentative form (Murray; cf. Graffy). Although the premise to be disputed normally appears at the outset of the speech, the present text does not disclose the premise to be disputed until vv. 10-11 and 17-20. From the statements in vv. 10-11, it appears that the people believe that they are doomed. The reason for their belief would be recognition that YHWH's/Ezekiel's announcements of judgment against Jerusalem, Israel, the nations, and all creation are in fact about to be realized. In the face of impending judgment, the audience maintains that it has no chance to survive. Ezekiel will challenge this statement by claiming that there is still room for repentance before YHWH. The secondary premise accepted by Ezekiel's audience is that "the way of YHWH is not fair" (v. 17). From the preceding argumentation of the passage, it appears that the audience's premise would entail that a guilty person deserves punishment unconditionally and that a righteous person is innocent, again, unconditionally. In other words, Ezekiel's audience accepts the contention that it is guilty and therefore subject unconditionally to punishment. The counterargument presented in the preceding verses, however, holds that a guilty person may be considered innocent following repentance and that an innocent person who then commits a transgression must be considered guilty. The purpose of the counterargument is to build up to Ezekiel's assertion that repentance can save the people's lives.

The argumentation proceeds in four stages, beginning with an initial presentation of the premise in vv. 2aβ-6 and followed by three instructions by YHWH to Ezekiel in vv. 7-9, 10-11, and 12-20, each introduced by the address "and you, son of Adam," which present the parameters of the discussion. The first section in vv. 2aβ-6 describes the basic premises of the case, viz., that the watchman for a city is responsible to warn the city when YHWH brings the sword against it. If the watchman warns the city and people ignore him, the people are responsible for their own deaths, but if the watchman fails to warn them, the watchman is responsible. Verses 7-9 follow with YHWH's statement to Ezekiel that Ezekiel is appointed as watchman over the house of Israel. The terms of the appointment are laid out, viz., Ezekiel is responsible for warning those who are guilty and therefore subject to judgment by YHWH. If he warns them properly, he is not responsible, but if he fails to warn them, Ezekiel is responsible. Verses 10-11 challenge the people's contention that they are doomed. As noted above, Ezekiel contends that the time for repentance has arrived, viz., if the people repent, they will save their lives. Finally, vv. 12-20 provide the counterargumentation to the people's premise, i.e., if a guilty person repents and does what is right, that person's life is saved. Likewise, if an innocent person turns to wicked behavior and does what is wrong, that person's life is forfeit. This argument countermands the people's contention that YHWH's ways are not fair. The argument concludes with the contention that YHWH will judge each person according to his or her own ways.

The placement of this account immediately following the last oracle against Egypt in Ezekiel 32:17-32 provides a clue to its interpretation. Ezekiel's role as watchman has already been defined in the context of the account of his commissioning as a prophet in Ezekiel 3:16–5:17, but Ezekiel 33:1-20 appears at the conclusion of the various oracles warning Israel about the impending judgment to be executed against Israel and the various nations named in the book of Ezekiel. Throughout, these oracles have employed the recognition formula as an announcement that YHWH will be recognized as the G-d who brought about these judgments at the time when they are realized. Insofar as Ezekiel 33:1-20 appears at the conclusion of these announcements of judgment and immediately prior to the announcement of Jerusalem's downfall in Ezekiel 33:21-33, it would appear that the present text is intended as a means to reiterate and summarize Ezekiel's roles. He is both watchman and priest for the people of Israel and has a responsibility as such to warn Israel concerning the dangers of their alleged failure to observe YHWH's will. To a degree, the passage asserts that Ezekiel has done his job, and the string of oracles in which YHWH has instructed Ezekiel to speak oracles to the people concerning YHWH's intentions stands as testimony to the fact that Ezekiel has performed as YHWH expected. Such a contention is particularly important because once the judgment against Jerusalem, Israel, the nations, and all creation has been realized, the time for restoration will be at hand. In this respect, the present oracular account surreptitiously functions as a means to signal that the time for repentance on the part of the people is at hand as a prelude to restoration. YHWH instructs Ezekiel in v. 11 to tell the people that they must now repent: "Say to them, as I live, declares YHWH, it is not my desire that the wicked shall die, but that the wicked shall turn from his ways and live. Return, return from your evil ways; and why shall you die, O house of Israel?"

Oracles concerning the Impending Restoration of Israel

Ezekiel 33:21–39:29

The chronological formula in Ezekiel 33:21 marks Ezekiel 33:21–39:29 as a major unit of the book of Ezekiel concerned with the impending restoration of Israel. The date noted in Ezekiel 33:21, the fifth day of the tenth month of the twelfth year (5 Sivan 585 BCE), follows from previous dates noted in Ezekiel 32:1 and 32:16, and indicates a date after the destruction of the city of Jerusalem. Insofar as the initial premise of the unit is Ezekiel's receipt of a fugitive's announcement in Ezekiel 33:21-22 that Jerusalem has fallen, the unit shifts its focus to preparations for the restoration of Israel. Following the initial announcement of Jerusalem's downfall in Ezekiel 33:21-22, six instances of the prophetic word formula mark the subunits of this segment (Sweeney 2005b, 156–72). Ezekiel 33:23-33 presents an oracular account concerning Ezekiel's role as a prophet of YHWH who will announce the purging of the land. Ezekiel 34:1-31 presents an oracular account concerning the downfall of Israel's leadership. Ezekiel 35:1-36:15 presents an oracular account concerning the contrasting fates of Edom and Israel. Ezekiel 36:16–37:14 presents an oracular account concerning the purification and restoration of Israel. Ezekiel 37:15-28 presents an oracular account concerning the reunification and restoration of Israel. Ezekiel 38:1–39:29 presents an oracular account concerning the purification of the land from the corpses of the army of Gog from Magog as a preparation for the reestablishment of the Jerusalem Temple at the center of creation.

The formal structure of the unit appears as follows:

VII. Oracles concerning the Impending Restoration of Israel (Ezek 33:21–39:29)
   A. Introduction: Ezekiel resumes speaking following the downfall of Jerusalem (33:21-22)
   B. Oracular account concerning Ezekiel's role as a prophet of YHWH who will announce the purging of the land (33:23-33)

C. Oracular account concerning the downfall of Israel's leadership (34:1-31)
D. Oracular account concerning the contrasting fates of Edom and Israel (35:1–36:15)
E. Oracular account concerning the purification and restoration of Israel (36:16–37:14)
F. Oracular account concerning the reunification and restoration of Israel (37:15-28)
G. Oracular account concerning the purification of the land from the corpses of the army of Gog from Magog (38:1–39:29)

Introduction: Ezekiel Resumes Speaking following the Downfall of Jerusalem (33:21-22)

As noted above, this brief unit begins with the chronological formula that introduces Ezekiel 33:21–39:29. The date noted, the fifth day of the tenth month of the twelfth year (5 Sivan 585 BCE), follows earlier chronological references in Ezekiel 32:1 and 16 to date the block to the aftermath of the capture of Jerusalem in the eleventh year of the reign of Zedekiah (586 BCE; see 2 Kings 25:2). Second Kings 25:8 dates Nebuchadnezzar's coming to Jerusalem to the seventh day of the fifth month of the eleventh year of Zedekiah and notes that the destruction of the city and the temple occur thereafter. Jeremiah 52:12-13 dates the burning of the temple and the city to the tenth day of the fifth month, but does not identify the year, which suggests that the year is the eleventh year of Zedekiah (see Jer 52:5). That dating would place Ezekiel's reception of the news exactly one year to the day following the destruction of the temple.

The introduction makes two essential points. The first is Ezekiel's reception of the news that the city of Jerusalem has fallen. The news comes from a refugee who apparently fled the doomed city at the time of its conquest by Nebuchadnezzar. Whereas earlier portions of the book anticipate the downfall of Jerusalem, Israel, the nations, etc., Ezekiel 33:21-22 notes that Jerusalem has actually fallen. Now is the time for the book to begin to shift its focus from the anticipated downfall of Jerusalem to the anticipated restoration of Jerusalem. The second point is that Ezekiel began to speak once again on the evening prior to the arrival of the fugitive. Ezekiel had apparently been struck dumb at some point following the death of his wife in Ezekiel 24:15-27. As noted in Ezekiel 24:25-27, Ezekiel would speak once again upon hearing the news of Jerusalem's downfall from a fugitive.

Oracular Account concerning Ezekiel's Role as a Prophet of YHWH (33:23-33)

The introductory prophetic word formula in Ezekiel 33:23 introduces the first oracular account concerning Ezekiel's role as a prophet of YHWH in Ezekiel 33:21-33. The oracle is formulated as YHWH's instruction speech to Ezekiel, identified as "son of Adam" to acknowledge his priestly status, concerning his role as YHWH's prophet to Israel. YHWH's instruction speech employs elements of the disputation speech form, which is designed to challenge the people's contention that they will take possession of the land of Israel. By contrast, Ezekiel will announce that the people will not possess the land because of the contention that they have failed to observe YHWH's expectations.

The oracle includes three basic subunits. The first appears in vv. 24-26 in which YHWH instructs Ezekiel to challenge the contention of the people that they will possess the land of Israel. YHWH begins by pointing out the argument of the people that Ezekiel is to challenge, viz., "Abraham was only one man, and he possessed the land; but we are many, and the land is given to us as a possession." YHWH instructs Ezekiel to challenge this premise by pointing out the alleged wrongdoing of the people, viz., they do not follow YHWH's instructions concerning holy conduct (see Ezek 18; Lev 17–26). He charges that they eat meat with blood in violation of kosher dietary laws (see Lev 19:26; cf. Lev 11); that they worship idols (Heb., *gillulim*, "turds"; Lev 19:4); and that they shed blood (Lev 17). He further charges that the people have relied on their swords to shed blood (Lev 17); that they have committed abominations (Lev 18:22, 26, 27, 29); and that they have defiled other men's wives (Lev 18; 20). Given such conduct, Ezekiel claims that it is impossible for the people to possess the land of Israel.

The second subunit appears in vv. 27-29. This subunit begins with an instruction formula "thus you shall say to them" followed by the prophetic messenger formula to identify the following as an oracle from YHWH. The oracle promises that those left in the ruins and environs of Jerusalem will perish in the aftermath of the destruction of the city. As noted in Ezekiel 11, those who were exiled would form the basis of those who would return to the land of Israel to rebuild Jerusalem and the temple. This subunit concludes with the recognition formula, i.e., the people would know YHWH when the land of Israel was left desolate.

The third subunit appears in vv. 30-33. The subunit begins with a direct address to Ezekiel, "and you, son of Adam." Here YHWH informs Ezekiel that the people will come to hear Ezekiel's prophesies but they will not obey them. Insofar as they view Ezekiel as a mere entertainer, a singer of base songs who sings and plays well, they will not take him seriously. Only when the disasters announced by the prophet take place will they recognize that a prophet has been in their midst.

Oracular Account concerning Israel's Leaders (34:1-31)

The prophetic word formula in Ezekiel 34:1 identifies Ezekiel 34:1-31 as an oracular account within the larger structure of Ezekiel 33:21–39:29. The unit is formulated as an instruction speech by YHWH to Ezekiel. YHWH addresses Ezekiel in v. 2a-bα$^{1-3}$ as "son of Adam" to acknowledge his status as a Zadokite priest, and instructs him to prophesy, first to "my shepherds" in vv. 2bα^{4}-16 and then to "my flock," concerning "the rams" and "the bucks" in vv. 17-31. Both portions of the oracular account employ the prophetic judgment speech form, although they also employ the allegorical representation of Israel's leadership, first as shepherds and later as sheep, including rams and bucks that abuse their place within the larger flock. The two portions of the oracle announce the removal of Israel's leadership, here portrayed as shepherds and later as rams and bucks that have charge of the flock. A number of scholars maintain that the announcement in vv. 23-31 concerning the establishment of the Davidic ruler as shepherd over the people is a secondary expansion of the text (e.g., Zimmerli 1983, 203–23; Hals, 245–54), but the following discussion of this material demonstrates that such a contention is mistaken. Indeed, the establishment of the one Davidic ruler over the flock in place of the earlier shepherds or rams and bucks is the essential point of this unit.

The first portion of the oracular account directed to the shepherds in vv. 2bα^{4}-16 begins with the notation of the addressees, "to the shepherds" (Heb., *laroʿim*), followed by the prophetic messenger formula "thus says my L-rd, G-d" in v. 2bα$^{4-8}$ to certify the following material as an oracle from YHWH. The shepherd metaphor involves a common image to refer to monarchs or leaders in the ancient Israelite and Near Eastern world (see Odell, 426). Shepherds have overall charge of a flock and are tasked with defending the flock from threats, guiding it in search of food, water, and other means of sustenance, and returning it safely to its home. The portrayal of David as a shepherd boy in 1 Samuel 16, for example, signals his capacity to serve as king of Israel. The oracle per se employs the "woe!" (Heb., *hoy*) form to introduce the grounds for judgment against the shepherd in vv. 2bα^{5}-6 within the larger prophetic judgment speech form. Woe oracles are typically employed to warn the addressees of impending danger (Sweeney

1996, 543); in this case, the woe address signals the impending downfall of the shepherds. A rhetorical question addressed to the shepherds immediately following the woe exclamation makes this purpose clear, i.e., "Woe, O Shepherds of Israel, who were tending them; is it not the flock that shepherds tend?" The question essentially charges that the shepherds in fact are not meeting their responsibilities with regard to their flock. Verses 4-5 make a series of charges against the shepherds indicating that they have deliberately abused their positions by serving their own needs rather than by tending to the needs of the flock. Pressing the metaphor, vv. 5-6 portray YHWH's flock scattered across the mountains and the land, where they are threatened by wild beasts.

The announcement of judgment then follows in vv. 7-16, introduced by the particle *laken*, "therefore," and the call-to-attention formula directed to the shepherds (Sweeney 1996, 544), "therefore, O Shepherds, hear the word of YHWH." YHWH's oath formula (Sweeney 1996, 546) in v. 8 then introduces a reiteration of the charges of neglect and self-interest against the shepherds that affirms YHWH's decision to see to it that the punishment will indeed be carried out. Verses 9-10 then repeat the particle *laken*, "therefore," and the call-to-attention formula together with another instance of the prophetic messenger formula to accentuate and dramatize the announcement of judgment per se, i.e., YHWH will hold the shepherds accountable for the condition of the flock and dismiss them from their roles as shepherds over Israel. Verses 11-16 then present YHWH's contentions that YHWH will take over the responsibility of serving as shepherd for the flock of Israel, seeking out the lost sheep, gathering them from the places where they have been scattered, feeding them in good grazing areas in the land of Israel, healing the injured sheep, etc. The portrayal of YHWH's actions in v. 12 on a day of cloud and deep darkness (Heb., *beyom 'ananwey 'arafel*) has suggested to many that this is an eschatological event, but such imagery pertains to theophany insofar as it employs the imagery of clouds of incense smoke in the temple to portray YHWH's presence. The imagery simply indicates YHWH's divine presence in the world when YHWH takes action against the shepherds.

A particular problem arises in v. 16 in which YHWH states, "and the fat and the strong I will destroy (Heb., *'ashmid*); I will shepherd them in justice." Many interpreters follow the LXX text in reading *'ashmid*, "I will destroy," as *'eshmor*, "I will watch"; the emendation presumes the similar appearance of the Hebrew letters *dalet* (d) and *resh* (r), which are sometimes confused, as well as the similar forms of the vowel letters *yod* (y, here representing i) and *waw* (w, here representing o) in ancient Hebrew manuscripts from the Judean wilderness. Such an emendation, however, misses the point; the following material in vv. 17-31 makes it clear that YHWH intends to eliminate "the fat and strong sheep" from the flock, i.e., those leaders who led Israel astray, and replace them with the Davidic monarch mentioned in vv. 23-30.

The second major portion of the oracular account in vv. 17-31 addresses the flock. It begins with the address form and statement in v. 17abα "and you, my flock, thus says my L-rd, G-d, behold I am judging between one sheep and another," and it concludes with a similar address in v. 31. The address form signals the shift to the second part of the oracular account, and the prophetic messenger formula certifies this material as an oracle from YHWH. The primary contention of this portion of the oracle is to signal to the flock that YHWH will judge among the sheep. This statement builds upon the final statement of v. 16 in which YHWH stated the intention to destroy the fat and the strong sheep, i.e., those who had abused their power by taking advantage of the weak. Verse 17bβ then directs the following oracle to the strong, here metaphorically defined as rams and bucks, i.e., "to the rams and to the bucks (Heb., *l'elimwey 'attudim*)," which parallels the initial reference to the shepherds "to the shepherds" in v. 2bα[4]. Again, the oracle takes the form of the prophetic judgment speech. The accusations of wrongdoing are expressed once again in the form of three rhetorical questions in vv. 18-19. These questions assert charges of abuse against the powerful rams and bucks in terms that express the typical behavior of sheep in the pasture and at the pond. The powerful sheep graze and trample what is left to the weaker sheep; they drink water and muddy the pond with their feet; the rest of the flock is left with what has been spoiled by those who partook first. Such actions are typical of flocks, but here they are highlighted to accentuate the charges of abuse against Israel's leaders.

The announcement of judgment then follows in vv. 20-30, introduced by the particle *laken*, "therefore," and the prophetic messenger formula in v. 20a. The first part of the oracle in vv. 20b-22 announces the basic principles of YHWH's judgment against the powerful sheep, viz., because the powerful and fat sheep pushed the weaker and leaner sheep aside, YHWH will deliver the weaker sheep and pass judgment upon the stronger sheep. Although vv. 23-31 are often judged to be secondary to the oracle, they are absolutely essential because they specify how YHWH will remove the abusive leaders and replace them with a true Davidic monarch. Insofar as the block of material in Ezekiel 33:21-39:29 dates to the aftermath of the fall of Jerusalem, it presupposes the period in which Zedekiah ben Josiah, the last Davidic monarch to sit on the throne of Judah, had been removed and exiled by the Babylonians and the administration of conquered Judah had been handed over to Gedaliah ben Ahikam ben Shaphan (see Jer 39–41). Although little is known of Gedaliah's administration, the account in Jeremiah makes it clear that he was assassinated in 582 BCE in an attempted coup led by Ishmael ben Nethaniah ben Elishama, a member of the Davidic House (Jer 41:1). Ishmael himself was killed and the coup was put down by native Judeans before the Babylonian army arrived, but the coup nevertheless signals Judean dissatisfaction with a ruler who was serving as a Babylonian puppet ruler. Ezekiel's oracle predates the assassination of Gedaliah, but it would seem that it has Gedaliah's appointment by the Babylonians in mind and that it views such a move as anathema. Instead, Ezekiel 34:23-30 calls for the restoration of a Davidic monarch, here identified not as *melek*, "king," but as *nasi'*, "prince; elevated one," a term that is used to signal the ruler's subservient status, usually to YHWH, but here perhaps to the Babylonians as well. YHWH's validation of the monarch is expressed through his identification as "my servant, David," a term elsewhere applied to David as YHWH's chosen monarch (2 Sam 3:18; 7:5, 8, 20) and to Moses as YHWH's chosen leader (Exod 14:31; Josh 18:7) as well as to other worthy figures in biblical literature. The covenant of peace (Heb., *berit shalom*) granted to the new Davidic monarch employs an expression used elsewhere in Ezekiel (Ezek 37:26) and other biblical works (Num 25:12; Isa 54:10; Mal 2:5) as a term that functions much like *berit 'olam*, "eternal covenant." The purpose here is to replace Judean leadership, viewed as unqualified by Ezekiel, with a Davidic monarch who will serve under YHWH and perhaps also under the Babylonians whom YHWH brought against Judah. With the new Davidic ruler established, YHWH promises to serve as a good shepherd, protecting the people from threats, bringing the rains and fruit in the land, and ensuring in v. 29 that they will become "a planting for a name" (Heb., *matta' leshem*), a term that indicates Israel's permanent residence in the land. When all of this is accomplished, the recognition formula in v. 30 indicates that the people will know that "I YHWH, their G-d, am with them, and they, the house of Israel, are my people." This phrase is a variation of the covenant formulary that binds Israel and YHWH together in covenant (see Rendtorff).

The final address appears in v. 31, once again directed to the sheep, "and you, my sheep." This final statement explains that the oracles concerning the shepherds and the sheep were in fact metaphorical and that the sheep tended by YHWH are in fact human beings. YHWH's final statement, "You are human, and I am your G-d," reiterates the covenant formulary of v. 30. The oracular formula that closes the verse certifies the statement as an oracle of YHWH.

Oracular Account concerning the Contrasting Fates of Edom and Israel (35:1–36:15)

The prophetic word formula in Ezekiel 35:1 opens the unit in typical fashion to identify the following material as YHWH's oracle to Ezekiel. The extent of the oracle introduced, however, has been a subject of contention. Ezekiel 35:2-15 presents YHWH's oracle concerning the downfall of Edom for its hostility against Israel, and Ezekiel 36:1-15 presents a second oracle concerning YHWH's efforts to restore the land of Israel following its devastation. Many interpreters consider the two oracles to be separate because they are concerned with different topics. Others (Zimmerli 1983, 224–40; Greenberg 1997, 710–25; Hals, 254–61), however, have noted that an editor, either an anonymous editor or even Ezekiel himself, has deliberately placed them together to address the different fates of Edom and Israel in the aftermath of the Babylonian invasion of the land of Israel. Indeed, both oracles are formulated as YHWH's direct address to Ezekiel, identified in typical manner as "son of Adam" to acknowledge his status as a Zadokite priest, instructing him to deliver the following oracle to the hill country of Seir/Edom and the hill country of Israel, respectively. The basis for the association of Edom and Israel in the same unit is the well-known Pentateuchal tradition presented in Genesis 25–35, which identifies Esau and Jacob, the fraternal twin sons of Isaac and Rebekah, as the eponymous ancestors of Edom and Israel. The narrative posits considerable tension between the two brothers/nations and eventually traces the sequence of events throughout their lifetimes that resulted in the fact that the two could not live together. Although Esau/Edom is the older brother, Jacob/Israel obtains his father's blessing and the right of the firstborn over Esau/Edom. But Esau gains a blessing from his father that envisions his eventual break from Jacob's control, so that by the end of the narrative the two brothers live separately in their respective territories.

Indeed, such a scenario represents the historical realities of the relations between the two nations (Bartlett, 287–95). Edom is a small country located to the east and south of the Dead Sea (Gen 36:8; Num 24:18; cf. Gen 33:16); it is separated from Israel by the Aravah, the dry, barren depression that extends from the southern tip of the Dead Sea to the Red Sea. The hill country to the east of the Aravah is called Seir, derived from the Hebrew term for "hairy" because it is covered with brush. Archeological investigation indicates little evidence of settlement in Edom until the eighth century BCE (MacDonald, 295–301). The Amarna Letters indicate a potential source for the origins of Israel and Edom as seminomadic groups identified as the Habiru/Apiru, an Akkadian term that means barbarian, who migrated into the region from the Arabian Desert to the East. Egyptian records speak of a seminomadic group known as the Shasu in the region of Edom as well. Edom is presumably the older of the two nations because of its position to the east and its seminomadic history in its early years in contrast to the agriculturally based Israelite population of the land of Israel. Hymnic texts in the Bible likewise emphasize that YHWH is revealed each morning from Seir (Deut 33:2; Judg 5:4).

The biblical record is filled with instances of conflict between Edom and Israel (Dicou). Second Samuel 8:13-14 notes that David forced Edom to submit to him during his reign, although 1 Kings 11:14-22 relates the revolt of Hadad of Edom against Solomon. Second Kings 3 indicates that Edom remained a vassal of Israel when the Edomite king accompanied King Jehoram of Israel and King Jehoshaphat of Judah on a campaign against Moab, but 2 Kings 8:8:20-22 indicates that Edom revolted against Judah during the reign of King Jehoram of Judah. The most serious issue between Edom and Israel/Judah is the charge in a number of biblical texts that Edom somehow participated in the destruction of Jerusalem, and especially in the destruction of the Jerusalem Temple (Ob 11–14; Ps 137:7-9). Others stress judgment for Edom as a result of its actions and enmity against Israel (Isa 34; 63:1-6; Jer 49:7-22; cf. Obadiah). Although interpreters remain uncertain as to Edom's role in the destruction of Jerusalem, it is clear that the Edomites disappear during the later sixth and fifth centuries as Edom is overrun once again by seminomadic Arab groups who eventually form the Nabatean kingdom.

The tradition of Edom's enmity against Israel certainly comes to expression in the present passage, and it would explain the deliberate effort to contrast the fate of Edom with that of Israel. The passage need not presuppose Edom's actual destruction, but it presupposes the very bad relationship between Israel and Edom. Although certainty remains elusive, there is little reason to deny that Ezekiel could well be the editor who put these two oracles together. The purpose of the passage is to contrast Edom's demise with Israel's restoration in the aftermath of destruction. Both events then combine to serve as demonstrations that YHWH is the G-d of creation and of human events.

The first instruction speech concerning the fate of Edom appears in Ezekiel 35:2-15. Ezekiel 35:2-3aα^2 presents YHWH's instruction statement to the prophet, including the address to Ezekiel as "son of Adam" and the instruction to prophesy against the hill country of Seir. Two oracles follow in vv. 3aα³-13 and 14-15, each of which is introduced by the prophetic messenger formula to certify the following material as a statement by YHWH.

The formulation of the first oracle in vv. 3aα³-13 is based on the prophetic judgment speech genre, although it exercises great freedom in the specific formulation of the passage. The oracle begins in vv. 3aα³-4 with YHWH's announcement of punishment against Edom beginning with the formulaic statement "behold, I am against you, Mt. Seir," followed by specifications of what YHWH intends to do to Edom. The scenario is one familiar to readers of the exodus plague narratives (Exod 7–12) or Isaiah's oracles of judgment (Isa 9.7–10:4) in which YHWH (or Moses) extends a hand to punish those opposed to divine purpose. This particular segment concludes with the divine proof formula, which characterizes the projected punishment of Edom as an act that reveals YHWH.

The following two subunits in vv. 5-9 and 10-13 then specify the very general announcement of vv. 3aα³-4. Each is formulated as a brief example of the prophetic judgment speech with all of its basic elements. The first in vv. 5-9 begins with a statement of the grounds for punishment introduced by the particle *ya'an*, "because," followed by the charge in v. 5. In this case, the charge is Edom's eternal hatred (Heb., *'eybat 'olam*) against Israel and its belligerent actions against Israel at a time of crisis, apparently a reference to Edom's participation in Babylonian actions against Jerusalem and Judah. The formal announcement of YHWH's punishment against Edom then appears in vv. 6-9, introduced in typical form by the particle *laken* "therefore," followed by YHWH's oath formula "as I live" (Heb., *hay 'ani*) and the oracular formula "utterance of my L-rd G-d" (Heb., *ne'um 'adonay 'elohim*). The scenario of instruction includes threats to lay waste to Mt. Seir with blood revenge. Such an act presumes that Edom had or would shed Israelite blood and that it would be repaid in kind as a matter of justice, leaving the land of Edom and its towns strewn with the dead and virtually uninhabited. The oracle concludes with an instance of the proof formula to indicate that the realization of such an event would reveal YHWH.

The second prophetic judgment speech in vv. 10-13 again begins in typical fashion with a statement of the grounds for punishment in v. 10 introduced by *ya'an*, "because." In this case, the charge is that Edom apparently sought to rule over Israel in the aftermath of Israel's collapse, presumably to Babylon. The statement notes that Edom's plans for hegemony were conceived despite the fact that "YHWH was there," i.e., YHWH was identified with the land of Israel and would presumably protect it from Edom's—but not Babylon's—incursions. The statement "YHWH is there" also concludes Ezekiel's vision of the new temple and restored land of Israel in Ezekiel 48:35. The announcement of punishment in vv. 11-13 again begins typically with the particle *laken*, "therefore," the oath formula *hay 'ani*, "as I live," and the oracular formula *ne'um 'adonay 'elohim*, "utterance of my L-rd G-d." The announcement emphasizes retribution in kind for the Edomites' anger and hatred expressed against Israel. Again, the punishment is portrayed as a revelatory act as indicated by the proof formula in v. 12. The latter portions of the announcement focus on the arrogant taunts made against the hill country of Israel (cf. Zeph 2:8, which mentions taunts made by Moab and Ammon). The announcement concludes with YHWH's statement "I heard" (Heb., *'ani shama'ti*).

A second oracle then follows in vv. 14-15, again introduced by the prophetic messenger formula. It is formulated as a simple announcement of punishment, but its premise is Edom's rejoicing at the downfall of the Jerusalem Temple. The initial statement, "When all the earth rejoices," presumes the worldwide rejoicing that Ezekiel imagines will take place when the temple is restored (cf. Isa 60–62; Hag 2:6-9). In contrast to the rejoicing of the world at the restoration of the temple, the hill country of Seir and all of Edom will be laid waste (cf. Isa 63:1-6). Again, the proof formula at the conclusion of the oracle indicates that the downfall of Edom will become a revelatory event.

The second instruction speech concerning the restoration of Israel appears in Ezekiel 36:1-15. The oracular account is formulated in typical fashion as YHWH's instruction speech to Ezekiel. YHWH addresses Ezekiel as "son of Adam" and instructs him to speak to the hill country of Israel in v. 2a-bα, much as YHWH instructed Ezekiel to speak to the hill county of Seir in Ezekiel 35:1-15.

Ezekiel's speech to the hills of Israel comprises two oracular accounts in vv. 1bβ-12 and 13-15. Both are formulated according to the patterns of a prophetic judgment speech, but ultimately both are concerned with the restoration of Israel in the aftermath of Israel's punishment.

The first oracle in vv. 1bβ-12 must be considered as a prophecy of restoration even though it is so heavily influenced by the prophetic judgment speech form. It includes two basic components in vv. 1b -7 and 8-12, each introduced by a direct address to the mountains of Israel.

The first component in vv. 1bβ-7 begins with an example of the call-to-attention formula in v. 1bβ, which introduces the address to the hills of Israel. Following the formulation of the prophetic judgment speech, the account begins with a statement of enemy taunts against Israel in v. 2. This segment begins with a prophetic messenger formula that identifies the following as a speech by YHWH, and it continues with the retrospective portrayal of enemy taunts against Israel introduced by the particle *ya'an*, "because," a typical element of the prophetic judgment speech. Whereas the prophetic judgment speech would normally begin with a statement of the grounds for judgment, v. 2 actually provides the grounds for YHWH to punish Israel's enemies and to restore Israel itself. Verses 3-7 then continue with a series of subunits, each introduced by the particle *laken*, again a typical element to introduce the announcement of judgment in the prophetic judgment speech form. But here there are five such statements in vv. 3, 4, 5, 6, and 7, each of which builds the case for the restoration of Israel by pointing to the wrong done to Israel by its enemies. Verse 3 employs *laken*, YHWH's instruction to prophesy against the enemies, a prophetic messenger formula, and the emphatic particle combination *ya'an beya'an*, "indeed because," to introduce a statement that charges the enemies of Israel with having eagerly anticipated that Israel would become their possession. Verse 4 employs the particle *laken*, an address formula to the mountains of Israel, and the prophetic messenger formula to address the desolate and depopulated land of Israel concerning the abuse that has been leveled against it. Verse 5 employs the particle *laken* and the prophetic messenger formula to introduce YHWH's speech concerning YHWH's speaking against the nations, particularly Edom, that have so abused Israel. Verse 6 employs the particle *laken*, an address formula to the land of Israel, a prophetic messenger formula, and the particle *ya'an* to announce YHWH's blazing wrath due to the abuse leveled against Israel by the enemy nations. Finally, v. 7 employs the particle *laken* and the prophetic messenger formula to announce YHWH's oath of punishment against the nation, viz., that they will suffer disgrace much like Israel for their actions against Israel. Verses 8-12 then follow with an address to the mountains of Israel in which YHWH outlines the various elements of the restoration of the land of Israel, including a portrayal of fertility in the land, a statement of YHWH's care for the land, the resettlement of the land employing a variation of the priestly formula to be fruitful and multiply (Gen 1:22, 28; 9:7), a recognition formula indicating that the mountains of Israel shall know YHWH, and YHWH's promise that the people of Israel will be restored to possess the land once again.

The second component in vv. 13-15 employs a similar pattern to portray YHWH's protection of the land from the insults of the nations. The unit begins in v. 13aα with the prophetic messenger formula to demonstrate that the following is a speech by YHWH. It follows in v. 13aβ-b with a statement introduced by the particle *ya'an*, "because," that rehearses Israel's reputation as a land that consumes its own people. Verses 14-15, introduced by the particle *laken*, "therefore," then lay out YHWH's promise that the land of Israel will no longer consume its own people nor will it suffer the insults of the nations. The oracular formula closes the subunit.

Oracular Account concerning the Purification of the Land of Israel (36:16–37:14)

Ezekiel 36:16–37:14 constitutes a unit that addresses the impending purification of the land of Israel as a prelude to its restoration. It begins in typical fashion with the prophetic word formula in Ezekiel 36:1, which introduces the entire unit. Although some interpreters have viewed the formulaic statement in Ezekiel 37:1 "and the hand of YHWH came upon me" as an introduction to a discrete unit, it must be subsumed under the prophetic word formula in Ezekiel 36:1 that serves as the basic structuring formula within the major units that comprise the book of Ezekiel. Insofar as Ezekiel 37:1-14 portrays the coming to life of the dead bones in the valley, it illustrates the process by which the land of Israel will be purified, and in this instance, the land is purified from the desecration of death when the dead bones are brought back to life. Consequently, Ezekiel 36:16–37:14 comprises two major subunits: Ezekiel 36:16-38 presents YHWH's oracular instruction to Ezekiel in which YHWH focuses on the purification of the land as a means to sanctify the divine name, and Ezekiel 37:1-14 employs the vision of the dead bones as an illustration of that purification.

The first unit of this text in Ezekiel 36:16-38 begins with the prophetic word formula, which introduces the entire unit as a statement of YHWH's word to Ezekiel. Verses 17-38 are formulated as YHWH's statement to Ezekiel. Although it is not evident at the outset, the instruction statement in v. 22, "therefore say to the house of Israel," indicates that the whole must be considered as YHWH's instruction statement to Ezekiel. It comprises two major portions. Verses 17-21 are an explanatory statement in which YHWH establishes the context for the concern with the holiness of the divine name throughout the unit. Verses 22-38 present the three oracles that Ezekiel is to speak to Israel concerning the means by which YHWH will purify Israel to protect the sanctity of the divine name.

Ezekiel 36:17-21 begins with YHWH's address to Ezekiel as "son of Adam" to acknowledge his status as a Zadokite priest. YHWH employs the metaphor of a monstrous woman to charge that Israel defiled its land. In priestly thought, blood, whether shed due to bodily injury or due to natural bodily function, is a defiling substance. Although it is a source of life in the body, once blood is emitted from the body, it can no longer survive on its own. Blood therefore defiles because it is dead, and death is the ultimate source of defilement in priestly thought. Consequently, Leviticus 15:19-30 portrays menstrual blood as a defiling element that requires a woman to cleanse herself with clean water once her menstrual period is over (n.b., men must also purify themselves with water when they are defiled; see e.g., Lev 11). YHWH employs the menstrual metaphor to justify punishment against Israel, charging that Israel had defiled the land with its actions, and therefore YHWH had been compelled to exile the people among the nations. The exile of the people in and of itself desecrates the divine name in this passage because the exile points to the failure of the relationship between YHWH and Israel. Because Israel is exiled, they must have violated their relationship with their G-d, YHWH, thereby compromising the sanctity of the divine name. Insofar as the divine name represents YHWH in the world, such a charge essentially claims that YHWH has become defiled.

As a result of the defilement of the divine name, YHWH instructs Ezekiel to speak three oracles to the people of Israel in Ezekiel 36:22-38. YHWH's instruction statement appears in v. 22aα$^{1-4}$, introduced by the particle *laken*, "therefore." The three oracles, each introduced by the prophetic messenger formula "thus says my L-d, G-d," appear respectively in vv. 22bα^5-32, 33-36, and 37-38.

The first and longest oracle in Ezekiel 36:22bα^5-32 states that YHWH will act to restore the people of Israel to their land, not for the sake of the people of Israel per se, but for the sake of YHWH's divine name. Although at various points Ezekiel holds out the possibility of human repentance (e.g., Ezek 18; 33:1-20), the portrayal of the restored Israel in this passage appears to presuppose an absence of human volition as YHWH replaces the purported heart and spirit (i.e., mind) with a living heart or a heart of flesh that prompts the people to observe YHWH's expectations. YHWH will gather the people from the nations to which they have been exiled, cleanse them with clean water much as a woman immerses in clean water at the conclusion of her menstrual period, and then give the people a new heart and a new spirit that will replace the heart of stone with a heart of flesh (cf. Ezek 11:19; 18:31; Jer 31:31-34). Once YHWH places a new "spirit" within the people, they will observe YHWH's expectations. Although some view this as a means to eliminate moral choice from the people, interpreters must recall that the Hebrew terms "heart" (Heb., *leb*) and "spirit" (Heb., *ruah*, lit., "wind") refer to the intellect. The heart is the seat of the intellect (as opposed to the brain in modern Western cultures) and the spirit refers to the intellect itself, including the capacity for choice. In short, YHWH replaces a flawed intellect, here expressed as a heart of stone, with a new intellect that enables the people to make the proper choice to observe the divine will and thereby to assert the sanctity of the divine name. Once this choice is made, the people will be able to reside in the land and the relationship between YHWH and Israel will be restored, here expressed by means of the covenant formula "will be my people and I will be your G-d" (Rendtorff). Once the relationship is restored, several actions follow, i.e., YHWH will restore fertility to the land and protect Israel from further humiliation, and Israel will reflect upon its past evil and be disgusted with itself for what it allegedly has done. YHWH restates the guiding principle of this, "not for your sake do I do this, utterance of YHWH," and then reiterates the need for Israel to reflect upon its past actions and feel shame. The purpose of such shame is not an inherent goal of YHWH's action; it is intended to ensure that the people continue to make the right choices in the future.

The second oracle in Ezekiel 36:33-36 reflects upon the repopulation of the land. Again, the oracle begins with an example of the prophetic messenger formula to certify the following as an oracle from YHWH. YHWH promises to repopulate the land with the people of Israel. The purpose of this act is so that passersby will see the repopulated land, observe that it is like the Garden of Eden, and as a result recognize YHWH as the one who rebuilds, who speaks, and who acts. In short, the restoration of the land restores YHWH's credibility.

The third oracle in Ezekiel 36:37-38 again begins with the prophetic messenger formula to certify the following as an oracle from YHWH. Here, YHWH promises to act for the sake of the people by multiplying their numbers like sheep, much like Jerusalem is filled with sheep for the offerings at the temple during the festivals. When this restoration is seen, then the people will recognize YHWH.

Ezekiel 37:1-14 then illustrates the process by which the land of Israel will be purified with a vision account of the restoration of the dry bones in the valley. Because the dry bones are the remains of dead bodies, they contaminate the land with the impurity of death. The restoration of the dead bones to life removes the corpse contamination that has affected the land and thereby constitutes the restoration of the land to its pure and holy status. The passage provides no clue as to the identities of the dead bones or their location other than the reference to the valley (Heb., *habbiqʻah*) in v. 1. Insofar as Ezekiel 38–39 portray the purification of the land from the corpses of the invading army of Gog from Magog, the dead bones in Ezekiel

37 may well represent the bodies of the dead Judeans who fell in defense of the land against this foreign invader. Gog from Magog is never identified with a specific invader, but a few scenarios suggest themselves. Perhaps Gog from Magog represents the Babylonian army, leaving the dead bones of Ezekiel 37:1-14 to represent the bodies of Judean soldiers who died resisting the Babylonians. Yet interpreters know little of the Babylonian campaigns against Judah other than the details of the siege of Jerusalem provided in 2 Kings 25, 2 Chronicles 36, and Jeremiah 25. In any case, there is no indication of a battle in a valley. Alternatively, Gog from Magog may represent the Egyptian army of Pharaoh Necho II, who killed King Josiah of Judah at Megiddo (2 Kings 23:29-30; 2 Chr 35:20-25). Insofar as 2 Chronicles 35:20-25 portrays a battle between Necho and Josiah at Megiddo, it appears to be the more historically accurate account of Josiah's death. Josiah's forces would have met Necho's army in the valley before the city of Megiddo, which would account for the location described in Ezekiel 37:1. The following oracle in Ezekiel 37:15-28, with its portrayal of the reunification of Israel and Judah under a Davidic king, does represent the ideology of Josiah's reform. Ezekiel would have been eighteen years old when Josiah was killed in 609 BCE. As indicated in Ezekiel 37:15-28, Ezekiel's use of purging imagery to portray the destruction of Jerusalem in Ezekiel 8–11 and the vision of the restored temple in Ezekiel 40–48 indicate that Josiah's reform had considerable impact on the theological world view of the prophet.

Ezekiel 37:1-14 appears as a combination of vision account and instruction speech by YHWH to the prophet. Verses 1-2 establish the context of the vision report in which YHWH conveys Ezekiel to the valley filled with dry bones. The passage begins with the formula "the hand of YHWH was upon me," which is typically employed to portray visionary experience in Ezekiel (Ezek 1:3; 3:14, 21; 8:1; 33:22; 40:1) and other prophets as well (2 Kings 3:15; see Hals, 360–61). Likewise, Ezekiel's conveyance by YHWH's "spirit" (Heb., *ruah*, lit., "wind") also appears in the context of prophetic vision reports (e.g., Ezek 8:3; 1 Sam 10:6; 19:23-24; 2 Kings 2:16, cf. 2 Kings 2:1, 11). Upon being placed by YHWH in the midst of the valley, Ezekiel sees that it is full of dry bones. Insofar as Ezekiel is a priest, he is defiled by contact with a corpse (Lev 21:11). Yet YHWH intentionally places him in the midst of a valley filled with corpses to illustrate the impurity of the land in the aftermath of battle.

Ezekiel 37:3-14 presents a dialogue between YHWH and Ezekiel in which YHWH instructs Ezekiel to prophesy to the bones so that they might live again. The first element of the dialogue appears in vv. 3-6 in which YHWH gives the initial instruction to Ezekiel. The passage employs a disputation form in which YHWH asks Ezekiel if these bones may live, to which Ezekiel replies, "My L-rd, G-d, you know." Ezekiel's rhetorical answer functions as an affirmation of YHWH's instruction, which then follows in detail. YHWH employs the proof saying in v. 6 to make it clear that the restoration of the dry bones will be a revelatory event.

The second element of the dialogue between YHWH and Ezekiel appears in vv. 7-9. Ezekiel relates his compliance with YHWH's instruction and the results of his compliance. Having prophesied to the bones, they were now covered with sinews and flesh, but had no breath within them. This prompts YHWH's second instruction to Ezekiel to prophesy once again, so that the four winds of creation might breathe new breath into the bodies.

The third element of the dialogue appears in vv. 10-14 in which YHWH instructs Ezekiel to prophesy a third time and explains the meaning of the vision to the prophet. The passage begins with Ezekiel's report of his compliance in v. 10. YHWH's speech to Ezekiel then follows in vv. 11-14. Again, YHWH employs the form of a disputation speech by beginning in v. 11 with a statement by the dead bones that they cannot possibly live again. To counter this premise, YHWH instructs Ezekiel to prophesy a third time to declare that YHWH will open their graves, lift them out of the graves, and bring them to the land of Israel. Verses 13-14 employ two instances of the proof formula to assert that such a restoration of the dead will reveal YHWH to YHWH's people. An oracular formula *ne'um yhwh*, "utterance of YHWH," closes the unit with a certification of YHWH's oracle.

Oracular Account concerning the Restoration of the People of Israel (37:15-28)

Ezekiel 37:15-28 begins in typical fashion with the prophetic word formula in v. 1, which introduces the unit. Verses 16-28 are formulated as YHWH's instruction speech to perform a symbolic action that symbolizes the restoration and reunification of the nation of Israel. YHWH addresses Ezekiel in typical form as "son of Adam" to acknowledge his status as a Zadokite priest.

The instruction proceeds in five stages, each of which is marked by verbs indicating YHWH's direct address to Ezekiel.

The first appears in v. 16a in which YHWH instructs Ezekiel to "take" a stick or piece of wood and to "write" on it, "for Judah and for the Sons of Israel his colleagues." Although the Hebrew word *'ets* usually means "tree" or "stick," it appears to designate a piece of wood on which Ezekiel can write. The inscription, of course, indicates an address to the southern kingdom of Judah and other Israelite tribes associated with it, such as Benjamin, Levi, and perhaps remnants of other tribes.

The second instruction appears in v. 16b in which YHWH instructs Ezekiel to "take" a second piece of wood and "write . . . for Joseph, the staff of Ephraim, and all the house of Israel, his colleagues." Joseph was the father of Ephraim and Manasseh, the two principal tribes that constituted the northern kingdom of Israel. Insofar as Ephraim was the dominant tribe of the north, the reference to the house of Israel refers to the other tribes that constituted the northern kingdom together with Ephraim.

The third instruction appears in v. 17 in which YHWH instructs Ezekiel to "bring near" or to "join" the two wooden tablets to symbolize the reunification of Judah and Joseph/Ephraim/Israel. Such a symbolic action would illustrate the goals of King Josiah's program of national restoration and religious reform to reunify southern Judah and northern Israel.

The fourth instruction appears in vv. 18-19 in which YHWH instructs Ezekiel to "speak" or to "respond" to the people who ask the meaning of the symbolic action. The response in v. 19 begins with a prophetic messenger formula to certify it as a message from YHWH. At this point in the explanation of the symbolic action, Ezekiel's response simply states that the act symbolizes the reunification of Ephraim and Judah as one stick, i.e., one nation.

The fifth instruction in vv. 20-28 is the culmination of the entire passage insofar as YHWH instructs Ezekiel, with the two pieces of wood in his hands so the people can see them, to provide a full explanation of the meaning of the symbolic action. Again, YHWH's statements begin with the prophetic messenger formula to certify them as a message from YHWH. The message itself begins in v. 21 with YHWH's promise to gather the people of Israel from the lands to which they have been exiled and return them to the land of Israel, thereby ending the exiles of both the northern kingdom of Israel and the southern kingdom of Judah. A series of further promises then follow in v. 22, viz., YHWH will make them a single nation in the land or hill country of Israel, there will be one king over all of them, and the people will never again be divided into two kingdoms. It is noteworthy that this statement refers to the Davidic monarch as "king" (Heb., *melek*) rather than the usual "prince" (Heb., *nasi'*) employed throughout Ezekiel. Such usage suggests a reflection of Ezekiel's early years under King Josiah when the nation was ruled by a strong king. Again, the reunification of northern Israel and southern Judah was a major goal of Josiah's reform (2 Kings 22–23; see Sweeney 2001). A second series of promises follows in v. 23, viz., the people will no longer be defiled by their idols, here portrayed as "their turds" and "their craps," YHWH will deliver the people in their settlements where they sinned, and YHWH will purify them so that they will become YHWH's people and YHWH will become their G-d. The use of the covenant formula "they will be my people, and I will be their G-d" is a typical expression for constituting the covenant between YHWH and Israel (Rendtorff). The religious purification of the people of Israel was also a goal of Josiah's program of religious reform.

YHWH's speech continues in vv. 24-28, which reiterate and develop the promises made in vv. 22-23. YHWH begins in v. 24 with the assertion that "my servant David will be king over them; there will be one shepherd for all of them" (cf. Ezek 34). Again, the term *melek*, "king," appears rather than the usual *nasi'*, "prince," indicating Josiah's independent reign. YHWH promises that the people will observe YHWH's laws and walk in YHWH's statutes in keeping with Josiah's goals of promoting religious observance in Israel. Although some would see this statement as an indication that Ezekiel does not envision free will among the people, interpreters must recognized that the changed circumstances of the restored nation will prompt religious observance once YHWH is revealed as the source of the restoration. YHWH further promises in v. 25 that the people will remain in the land promised to Jacob, a very telling reference insofar as Jacob was the eponymous ancestor of northern Israel in particular and all Israel in general (see Gen 28; 35). This promise is followed by a reference to the Davidic "prince" (Heb., *nasi'*) to indicate the king's subservience to YHWH. The shift in terminology may indicate that Ezekiel's earlier Josianic oracle may have been updated for the circumstances of the Babylonian exile. YHWH promises in v. 26 to make a covenant with the people, here described both as "a covenant of peace" (Heb., *berit shalom*) and "an eternal covenant" (Heb., *berit 'olam*). These phrases signal both the eternal covenant granted to the house of David (2 Sam 7; Ps 89; 132) and the eternal priestly covenant and covenant of peace granted to Phineas ben Eleazer ben Aaron, the ancestor of the Zadokite priestly line that served in the Jerusalem Temple. Indeed, YHWH follows with a promise to place "my sanctuary" (Heb., *miqdashi*) in the midst of the people forever. Verse 27 then reiterates the significance of this move, i.e., YHWH's divine presence (Heb., *mishkani*, lit., "my tabernacle") will be upon them as YHWH serves as their G-d and the people serve as YHWH's people in a repetition of the covenant formula. The passage concludes in v. 28 with a statement that the nations will know that YHWH sanctifies Israel when YHWH's sanctuary stands in their midst. Once again, YHWH's holy sanctuary, placed in the middle of a unified Israel under a single Davidic king, expresses the ideals of the Josian program of national restoration and religious reform. In this case, the Josian ideal has been updated for the projected end of the Babylonian exile (Sweeney 2006, 239–53).

The Purification of the Land of Israel from the Army of Gog from Magog (38:1–39:29)

Many interpreters view Ezekiel 38–39 as a later apocalyptic or proto-apocalyptic text that was inserted into the book of Ezekiel. Hitzig in his 1847 commentary (pp. xiv–v) was the first to point to the apocalyptic character of these chapters, although he attributed the entire book to Ezekiel. Herrmann (1908; 1924) began to experiment with redaction-critical theories for the book's composition, although he argued that Ezekiel edited much of his own work, including Ezekiel 38–39. Hölscher (1924) denied major sections to Ezekiel, including Ezekiel 38–39, and Cooke standardized the view that Ezekiel 38–39 was a later composition in English-language scholarship (1936, xxv). But Zimmerli began to reconsider Ezekiel's authorship of at least an early core of these chapters (1983, 302–304; cf. Allen 1990, 202–204; Hals, 282–85), and many scholars now follow Greenberg in reading Ezekiel holistically as a book that derives largely from the prophet even if his work has been edited. As a result, many recognize Ezekiel 38–39 as an integral part of the book—and perhaps also of Ezekiel's prophecies—despite its apocalyptic features (e.g., Klein 1988, 157–58; Block, 426–27; Odell, 463–66; Joyce 2007, 208–18; but cf. Darr, 1512–14; Tuell, 3).

A major issue is the portrayal of Gog from Magog as the enemy brought by YHWH for the punishment of Israel and then punished in turn and left for dead. Gog from the land of Magog is identified as the chief prince of Meshech and Tubal who leads an army that includes Persia, Nubia, Put, Gomer, and Beth-Togarmah against the land of Israel. Gog is a known name in the Hebrew Bible; 1 Chronicles 5:4 identifies a Gog as a descendant of Reuben, but Gog in Ezekiel 38–39 remains unknown. Magog is identified in Genesis 10:2 and 1 Chronicles 1:5 as a son of Japhet, together with Gomer, Tubal, Meshech, Madai, Javan, and Tiras. The names listed here are generally identified with lands in southeastern Europe and northwestern Asia, i.e., Gomer refers to the Cimmerians of central Asia Minor, Beth-Togarmah refers to Armenia, Javan refers to Greece, and Madai refers to the Medeans, who ultimately allied with Persia. Meschech, Tubal, and Tiras are less certain, although they appear to represent non-Semitic peoples in Asia Minor. Insofar as Japheth represents the non-Semitic peoples of Europe and western Asia, interpreters have attempted to identify Gog of Magog with the Gagu people who lived north of Assyria or with the seventh-century King Gyges of Lydia in Asia Minor. The fact of the matter is that we do not know who Gog of Magog is, although he seems to be identified with non-Semitic peoples of Asia Minor. Insofar as the Babylonian army would have included many units from Asia Minor, Gog from Magog may be a cryptic reference to Nebuchadnezzar and the Babylonian army. The notion that YHWH would bring an army to punish Israel and then punish that army in turn is well known from Isaiah and Nahum in which YHWH brings the Assyrians and then punishes the Assyrians and their king in turn (see Isa 5–12; 13–14; Nahum 1–3). Ezekiel 38–39 draws on imagery from Isaiah and Nahum in depicting Gog from Magog as the enemy of Israel. But insofar as Ezekiel was a Judean exile in Babylonia, he may not have had the capability to portray the impending downfall of the Babylonian Empire once the punishment of Israel was complete.

Indeed, Ezekiel 38–39 is an integral part of Ezekiel, and it plays an important role in Ezekiel 33:20–39:29. Ezekiel 38–39 represents the culmination of the restoration and purification of the land of Israel portrayed in Ezekiel 33:20–39:29. Whereas Ezekiel 36:16–37:14 portrays the purification and restoration of Israel, including the purification of the land from the dead bones of fallen Judean soldiers, and Ezekiel 37:15-28 portrays the reunification of Judah and Joseph/Ephraim, Ezekiel 38–39 portrays both the invasion of the land of Israel by foreign soldiers and the purification of the land from their fallen corpses. Such purging of the land from defilement caused by the corpses of both Judean and enemy soldiers of Gog from Magog is requisite to the restoration of the holy temple and the sanctity of Israel and all creation in Ezekiel 40–48.

Ezekiel 38:1–39:29 begins in typical fashion with the prophetic word transmission formula in Ezekiel 38:1. The entire unit is formulated as an instruction speech by YHWH to Ezekiel in which YHWH instructs Ezekiel to deliver a series of oracles to Gog of Magog and to the birds and wild animals of all creation. The unit includes three basic addresses by YHWH to the prophet, viz., Ezekiel 38:2-23, a two-part address which takes up YHWH's decision to bring Gog from Magog against Israel and then defeat it; Ezekiel 39:1-16, which takes up YHWH's plans to destroy Gog from Magog; and Ezekiel 39:17-29, which takes up YHWH's plans to call upon the birds and wild animals of all creation to devour the corpses of the army of Gog from Magog and thereby purify the land and facilitate the restoration of Israel.

The first address appears in Ezekiel 38:2-23, which is formulated as an account of YHWH's first instruction speech to Ezekiel. The address begins in Ezekiel 38:2-3aα[1] in which YHWH addresses Ezekiel in typical form as "son of Adam" to acknowledge his status as a Zadokite speech and then instructs him to turn his face to Gog from Magog and prophesy to him. Gog from Magog is identified here as the chief prince (Heb., *nasi' rosh*, lit., "head prince") of Meshech and Tubal. As noted above, the identities of Magog, Meshech, and Tubal are all uncertain, although the genealogies in Genesis 10:2 and 1 Chronicles 1:5 identify all three as sons of Japheth, which means that they represent non-Semitic nations or peoples from Europe or Western Asia, most likely from Asia Minor. Ezekiel 38:2-3aα^1 introduces the first portion of the address in Ezekiel 38:2-3aα^2 3 and 38:3aα^3-13. A second and much shorter address formula, linked to the preceding material by the conjunctive particle *laken*, "therefore," appears in Ezekiel 38:14aαβ, introducing the second portion of the address in Ezekiel 38:14aγ-23. This formula again addresses Ezekiel as "son of Adam" and instructs him to prophesy once again to Gog.

Ezekiel 38:3aα^2-13 constitutes the first portion of the first oracle that Ezekiel is to speak to Gog from Magog. The oracle outlines YHWH's plans to rouse Gog to attack the land of Israel as part of a larger purpose to reveal YHWH to the nations at large. The oracle comprises two basic parts in vv. 3aα^2-9 and 10-13, each of which begins with the prophetic messenger formula to certify the following as a message from YHWH.

The first portion of the oracle in vv. 3aα^2-9 begins with the challenge formula (Hals, 359), "Behold, I am against you, Gog, chief prince of Meshech and Tubal," which functions as a means to announce YHWH's intention to bring down Gog. The scenario by which YHWH will accomplish this end then follows Verse 4 announces that YHWH will put hooks in Gog's jaws and drag him and his army away. Such language draws upon Isaiah 37:29 (cf. 2 Kings 19:28), which portrays YHWH's actions against the Assyrian king Sennacherib for his assault against the land of Israel and his siege of Jerusalem. The description of Gog's army includes an array of arms and equipment as well as a number of nations that comprise his host, including Persia, Cush (Ethiopia), Put (Libya), Gomer (the Cimmerians), and Beth-Togarmah (Armenia). Beth-Togarmah is described in v. 6 as coming from "the farthest reaches of the north," which suggests some interdependence on Jeremiah's oracles concerning the "foe from the north" in Jer 2–6. These nations here named represent an array of nations surrounding Mesopotamia and the land of Israel, but they do not include Babylon, Assyria, or Aram. Nevertheless, they represent nations from the farthest edges of the known world of Ezekiel's day and suggest that the oracle envisions all the nations of creation. Furthermore, the attack is envisioned for the distant future, i.e., in later years, Hebrew *be'aharit hashanim*, a term that is often interpreted eschatologically, but that simply refers to distant years (DeVries 1995, 89–93). The nations are directed against Israel, here described as "a land restored from the sword, gathered from many peoples upon the hills of Israel and dwelling in safety" (v. 8), which indicates that a time after the scenario of purging and restoration outlined throughout the book has already taken place but prior to the final revelation of YHWH's divine presence in the world. At the conclusion of this subunit, Gog is commanded to attack Israel like a cloud covering the earth.

The second portion of the oracle in vv. 10-13 again begins with a prophetic messenger formula to introduce a section concerned with Gog's own intentions in attacking Israel. Again, the passage draws on earlier prophetic tradition, particularly Isaiah, who is very well known for the "in that day" (Heb., *bayyom hahu*) formula with which this subunit begins. The references to Gog's evil thoughts indicate an intertextual relationship with Nahum 1:2-14, which envisions the downfall of Assyria at YHWH's hands and chides the reader for the evil thought of believing that YHWH was powerless to stop Assyria from ravaging Judah (see esp. Nah 1:9, 11). The subunit goes on to depict Gog's plans to plunder and despoil Israel. The questions of Sheba (identified either as Ethiopia or Yemen), Dedan (central Arabia or Rhodes), and Tarshish (Tartessos, a Phoenician trading partner in Spain), who ask Gog if it is his intention to plunder the land, signal this intention.

As noted above, Ezekiel 38:14-23 is joined to Ezekiel 38:2-13 by the particle *laken*, "therefore," and an address formula to Ezekiel that instructs him to prophesy to Gog. Such a formulation allows the oracle to begin to shift its focus from Gog's intentions to plunder Israel to YHWH's intentions to destroy Gog and thereby reveal YHWH to all the nations of the earth. Again, this unit contains two portions in vv. 14aγ-16 and 17-23, each of which begins with a prophetic messenger formula.

Ezekiel 38:14aγ-16 again draws on the Isaian "in that day" and the Jeremian "enemy from the north" traditions to depict the advance of Gog against a secure Israel. The oracle envisions such an event in "later days" (Heb., *be'aharit hayyamim*), a term that has also been interpreted eschatologically, although it simply refers to the future (DeVries 1995, 89–93). The notion that YHWH will bring Gog "to my land" recalls Isaiah 14:24-27, which announces YHWH's intentions to destroy Assyria "in my land" after having brought Assyria to punish Israel. By reprising the Isaian scenario, the present passage intends that YHWH be revealed as holy to all the nations of the world through YHWH's actions against Gog.

Ezekiel 38:17-23, again introduced by the messenger formula, makes the interest in revitalizing earlier prophetic scenarios in relation to the present interest in Gog from Magog. The passage begins with a statement that identifies Gog with the enemy spoken of in earlier times by YHWH's prophets, viz., Assyria in Isaiah and Nahum and the enemy from the north in Jeremiah. The passage portrays the downfall of Gog in relation to a raging earthquake that will affect the entire land of Israel (cf. Amos 1:1) and all creation. Drawing on creation as portrayed in Genesis 1, the passage maintains that the fish, birds, animals, creeping things, and humans will all be affected by the quake. YHWH will then summon the sword and the various elements of creation (cf. the destruction of Sodom and Gomorrah in Gen 18–19) to bring down Gog. In the end, the nations will know YHWH's holiness and greatness. The passage concludes with the proof formula "and they shall know that I am YHWH."

YHWH's second major instruction address to Ezekiel appears in Ezekiel 39:1-16, which builds upon the earlier address to describe in detail the cleansing of the land of Israel from the corpses of the army of Gog from Magog. The passage begins with YHWH's instruction formula addressed in v. 1aαβ. The statement addresses Ezekiel as "son of Adam" to acknowledge his status as a Zadokite priest and instructs him to prophesy against Gog once again.

The oracular material that Ezekiel is to speak to Gog then follows in vv. 1aγ-16. It begins in v. 1aγ with the prophetic messenger formula to identify it as a message from YHWH. The oracle comprises a series of subunits in vv. 1b-5, concluded by the YHWH speech formula and the oracular formula; in vv. 6-8, concluded by the oracular formula and a YHWH speech formula; in vv. 9-10, concluded by the oracular formula; and the culminating section in vv. 11-16, introduced by the *wehayah bayyom hahu*, "and it shall come to pass in that day," formula, and includes the oracular formula in v. 13.

The first subunit in vv. 1b-5 addresses Gog directly with YHWH's threat to strike Gog down on the mountains of Israel. It begins with the challenge formula "behold, I am against you," and it continues with a scenario in which YHWH promises to turn Gog and his army around from the farthest reaches of the north and bring them to the mountains of Israel where YHWH will strike them down, leaving their carcasses for the birds and wild animals to consume. The imagery here derives from several earlier prophetic texts, including Jeremiah's prophesies concerning the enemy from the north in Jeremiah 4–6, Isaiah's oracle concerning the destruction of Assyria on the mountains of Israel in Isaiah 14:24-27, and Isaiah's oracle in Isaiah 14:1-23 against the king of Babylon, identified as Helel ben Shahar, who was to be killed in battle with his body left unburied on the battlefield.

The second subunit in vv. 6-8 constitutes a proof saying designed to announce that the nations will know YHWH once the actions against Gog from Magog are taken. But this passage specifies that the recognition of

YHWH also entails the recognition of YHWH's holy name among the people of Israel. Such a contention, coupled with the promise that YHWH's holy name will never be profaned again, holds that Israel will recognize YHWH's holiness and act upon it to serve as a holy nation in the midst of creation and the nations of the world. The subunit concludes with a statement that the time for such recognition is now at hand, just as YHWH decreed. In this respect, the earlier prophetic passages noted above have now come to realization.

The third subunit in vv. 9-10 portrays the burning of the weapons and equipment of the army of Gog from Magog by the people of Israel. The amount of equipment—and therefore also the size of the army of Gog from Magog—is so great that the burning will continue for seven years until it is all consumed. The seven-year duration also corresponds to the seven-year sabbatical periods that sanctify the agricultural cycle of the land of Israel and its various economic activities in Leviticus 25:1-7, Exodus 23:10-11 (cf. Exod 21:1-6), and Deuteronomy 15:1-18. In this respect, the seven-year period of burning functions as a means to sanctify the land from the defiling presence of the army of Gog from Magog.

The fourth and culminating subunit appears in vv. 11-16, which employs the formula *wehayah bayyom hahu,* "and it shall come to pass in that day," to project the cleansing of the land of Israel by means of the burial of the corpses of the bodies of the army of Gog from Magog. The burial site will be in the Valley of Those Who Pass By (Heb., *ge' ha'obrim*) located to the east of the sea. The exact location of this valley is uncertain, although a likely candidate is the Jezreel Valley, located in northern Israel to the east of Megiddo and to the west of Beth Shean, insofar as the Jezreel is the major passageway that allows access to the land of Israel from the north. Others identify it with the Valley of Abarim east of the Dead Sea, but it is not clear that this region is included in the land of Israel or the hill country of Israel. The valley is described as clogged with the bodies of the army of Gog from Magog, which impedes travelers through the region. The burial will take some seven months, after which the valley will be known as the Valley of the Multitude of Gog (Heb., *ge' hamon gog*), perhaps indicating an intertextual reference to Isaiah 15:12-14, which describes the multitude (Heb., *hamon*) of invaders that will be repulsed from the land of Israel. Such an act will reveal YHWH's glory (v. 13b). The oracle envisions roving bands of Israelites to locate and bury the bones of any invaders that might remain, thereby ensuring the cleansing of the land of Israel from the dead bodies of the army of Gog from Magog. In addition to the Valley of the Multitude of Gog, the oracle envisions a city called Multitude (Heb., *hamonah*). The identity of this city remains unknown, although it might be either Megiddo or Beth Shean.

YHWH's third and final address to Ezekiel appears in Ezekiel 39:17-29, which provides the culminating scenario for the restoration of the land of Israel. The passage begins with YHWH's address formula to Ezekiel combined with a prophetic messenger formula in v. 17aα^{1-14}. YHWH instructs Ezekiel, identified as "son of Adam" as usual, to acknowledge his status as a Zadokite priest and to speak to the bird and animals of creation. The subsequent oracle begins with the oracle that Ezekiel is to speak to the birds and animals in vv. 17aα^{15}-21 followed by YHWH's culminating reflections on the restoration of Israel in vv. 22-29.

The oracle to the birds and animals in vv. 17aα^{15}-21 calls upon them to assemble and feast on the flesh and blood of the corpses of the army of Gog from Magog. Such an act facilitates the purification of the land by removing the dead flesh that pollutes the land. The feasting on the dead bodies is portrayed as an analogy to a sacrificial feast at the temple to accentuate the degree to which the consumption of the dead flesh by the birds and animals of creation represents an act of purification that aids in restoring the sanctity of the land. Such an act likewise manifests YHWH's glory by pointing to YHWH as the source of judgment against the army of Gog from Magog, much as YHWH punished the Assyrians in the books of Isaiah and Nahum.

The final portion of the oracle in vv. 22-29 is addressed specifically to Ezekiel once again and takes up YHWH's culminating announcement concerning the restoration of Israel. The oracle begins in vv. 22-24 with an announcement that Israel will recognize YHWH in the future, specifically from that day on, i.e., from the day that the land is purified from the corpses of the army of Gog from Magog. The passage is an example of theodicy insofar as it attempts to justify YHWH's actions against Israel by claiming that Israel was judged and exiled for its iniquity against YHWH. The statement by YHWH in v. 23 (see also v. 24) that "I hid My face from them and delivered them into the hands of their enemies" takes up the motif of the hidden face of YHWH from Isaiah 8:16 (see also the psalms; Balentine). Verse 24 maintains that Israel's iniquity rendered it unclean and thereby justified the hidden face of G-d. Modern discussion of the theological impact of the Shoah has called into question attempts at justifying calamities such as the Shoah and the destruction of the temple. These attempts justify genocide insofar as they blame victims for their own victimization (see Berkovits; Sweeney 2008). The second segment of this oracle appears in vv. 25-29. It is introduced by the particle *laken*, "therefore," which links this segment to the preceding material, and the prophetic messenger formula, which identifies the following as a message from YHWH. This portion of the oracle is formulated as an oracle of salvation that projects the restoration of Israel following its period of punishment. It employs the formula for restoring the fortunes of Jacob/Israel, which some read as restoring the captivity of Jacob/Israel. The issue turns on the interpretation of the Hebrew term *shebut* (Qere), which may be derived either from the root *shbh*, "to capture," or the root *shub*, "to return, restore." The passage envisions full restoration for Israel and YHWH's zeal for the holy name. Such zeal indicates YHWH's own commitment to maintain the sanctity of both the land and the people Israel as a means of self-revelation to Israel and the nations at large. The passage concludes with a rendition of the covenant formula in v. 28, i.e., that Israel will know that YHWH is their G-d (Rendtorff), and a promise in v. 29 that YHWH will never again hide the divine face from Israel. The reference to pouring out the divine spirit on Israel is a metaphor for YHWH's ensuring the holiness of the people. The oracular formula closes the unit and certifies it as an oracle from YHWH.

Ezekiel's Vision of the New Temple

Ezekiel 40:1–48:35

The chronological formula in Ezekiel 40:1 marks the beginning of the next major unit of the book of Ezekiel in Ezekiel 40:1–48:35. Insofar as this is the last chronological formula, the unit comprises the entirety of Ezekiel's temple vision account and stands as the final and culminating segment of the book. The chronological formula dates the vision account to "the twenty-fifth year of our exile," at the beginning of the year (*berosh hashanah*), on the tenth of the month, in the fourteenth year after the fall of the city of Jerusalem. This would place the date as the tenth day of Tishri, 573 BCE, which would be Yom Kippur, the Day of Atonement, in the Jewish calendar. This date also marks Ezekiel's fiftieth year, twenty years after his initial vision of YHWH's divine presence in Ezekiel 1:1-28, and the year that Ezekiel would have retired from his priestly position had he remained in Jerusalem to serve in the temple. Yom Kippur, the Day of Atonement, marks the fast in which Israel atones for its sins before YHWH. As part of the Yom Kippur ritual, the high priest performs the scapegoat ritual, in which one goat is presented as a sin offering (*hatta't*) to YHWH and another is released into the wilderness symbolically to carry away the sin of the people (Lev 16). But Leviticus 16 also makes it clear that the priest may enter the holy of holies of the temple once per year with a sin offering to make atonement for the people. Insofar as Leviticus 16:2 states that YHWH appears in the cloud over the cover of the Ark of the Covenant, it would appear that Ezekiel's vision account is constructed as a vision of the priest at Yom Kippur. Because the narrative progression of the book of Ezekiel centers on the purging of the temple and its restoration, Ezekiel 40–48, with its vision of the restored temple, constitutes the culmination of the book. Interpreters have noted that Ezekiel's vision of the temple corresponds neither to Solomon's temple (1 Kings 6–7; 2 Chr 3–4) nor to the portrayal of the Second Temple in Rabbinic literature (*m. Middot* 5), Josephus, or elsewhere. Consequently, the rabbinic historical work *Seder Olam Rabbah* 26:51-52 identified it as "the future Temple," and subsequent medieval Jewish commentators, including Rashi and R. David Kimhi, understood it to refer to the third temple of future times.

A series of guidance verbs forms the linguistic structure of the temple vision account. These verbs present the basic action of the narrative as Ezekiel is guided from place to place throughout the narratives. The first instance of such a verb appears in Ezekiel 40:1, "on that same day, the hand of YHWH was upon me, and he brought me (*wayyabe'*) there." Further examples of guidance verbs, such as variations of *wayyabe'*, *wayyotsi'eni wayyasheb*, etc., appear in 40:2, 40:3, 40:17, 40:28, 41:1, 42:15, 43:1, 43:5, 44:1, 44:4, 46:19, 46:21, 47:1, 47:2, and 47:6b to define Ezekiel's movement as the basic linguistic structure of the unit. But these verbs do not define the macro-structure of the unit. The macro-structure of Ezekiel 40–48 comprises three major sections, including the introduction in Ezekiel 40:1, which presents the chronological setting of the unit, a first vision account in which Ezekiel is shown the new temple in Ezekiel 40:2–42:20, and a second vision account in Ezekiel 43:1–48:35 in which the presence of YHWH appears to instruct Ezekiel concerning the *halakhot* or laws to be observed at the new temple. The guidance formulas then signal the constituent subunits of each of these blocks. Although earlier interpreters, such as Gese (1957), Zimmerli (1983, 325–553), and Hals (285–347), view the temple vision account as the product of long tradition-historical growth, more recent interpreters, such as Greenberg (1987, 215–36), Levenson (1976), Joyce (2007, 219–41), and Tuell (276–344), emphasize the literary coherence of the account.

The formal structure of this unit appears as follows:

VIII. Vision Account: Ezekiel's vision of the temple (Ezek 40–48)
    A. Introduction: chronological Setting: twenty-fifth year; tenth day of the month (Yom Kippur); city destroyed (40:1)
    B. The first vision account: tour of the new temple (40:2–42:20)
        1. Vision account introduction; set in land of Israel on a high mountain with the city on the south side of the hill (40:2)
        2. First stage ("and he brought me in"): outer walls and gates (40:3-16)
        3. Second stage ("and he brought me in"): outer court and gates (40:17-27)
        4. Third stage ("and he brought me in"): inner court; south gate (40:28-31)
        5. Fourth stage ("and he brought me in"): inner court; east gate (40:32-34)

6. Fifth stage ("and he brought me in"): inner court; north gate (40:35-47)
   7. Sixth stage ("and he brought me in"): Ulam (40:48-49)
   8. Seventh stage ("and he brought me in"): Heikhal and holy of holies (41:1-26)
   9. Eighth stage ("and he brought me out and in") to the priestly chambers of outer court (42:1-14)
   10. Summation: measurements of the entire temple complex (42:15-20)
C. The second vision account: Halakhot pertaining to the temple (43:1–48:35)
   1. First stage ("and he led me"): east gate; entry of divine presence (43:1-4)
   2. Second stage ("and the wind lifted me up and brought me"): inner court (43:5-27)
   3. Third stage ("and he returned me"): outer court; gate closed; prince eats (44:1-3)
   4. Fourth stage ("and he brought me"): north gate before the temple; Halakhot/instruction concerning the priests and Levites (44:4–46:18)
      a.) Introduction: guidance to the north gate and presence of YHWH (44:4)
      b.) Account of YHWH's instruction speech (44:5–46:18)
   5. Fifth stage: northern chambers of the priests: kitchens (46:19-20)
   6. Sixth stage: outer court: corner structures and kitchens for the preparation of the offerings by the people (46:21-24)
   7. Seventh stage: return to the east gate of the temple with water flowing eastward (47:1)
   8. Eighth stage: out the north gate to outer eastern gate with water flowing eastward (47:2-6a)
   9. Ninth stage: return to bank of *wadi*: portrayal of new creation (47:6b–48:35)

Introduction: Chronological Setting (40:1)

As noted above, Ezekiel 40:1 defines the chronological setting of the vision account as "the twenty-fifth year of our exile, on the tenth day of the month at the beginning of the year," fourteen years following the fall of Jerusalem. The date would therefore be on the tenth day of Tishri in 573 BCE, which marks both the fast of Yom Kippur, the Day of Atonement, and Ezekiel's fiftieth year, when he would be expected to retire from his duties as a priest. The reference to the hand of YHWH that has come upon the prophet signals a visionary trance state as Ezekiel is about to be guided through the new temple by a heavenly figure (see Ezek 40:3).

The First Vision Account: Tour of the New Temple (40:2–42:20)

Ezekiel 40:2–42:20 constitutes the first vision account in which Ezekiel serves as narrator as he is guided about the new temple by an angelic figure described as "a man whose appearance was like that of copper" with measuring implements in hand.

Vision Account Introduction (40:2)

The basic sequence of guidance formulas begins at the outset of the subunit in Ezekiel 40:2, which reads, "In visions of G-d he brought me to the land of Israel and he set me down on a very high mountain, and upon it was the appearance of a city to the south." This statement defines the setting of the account in the land of Israel, on a high mountain, with a city to the south. The location proves to be an idealized understanding of the temple mount in Jerusalem. This statement introduces the sequence of ten subunits and defines the location of the vision as the city, viz., Jerusalem, set on a hill in the midst of the land of Israel. The following subunits in Ezekiel 40:3-16, 40:17-27, 40:28-31, 40:32-34, 40:35-47, 40:48-49, 41:1-26, 42:1-14, and 42:15-20 each begin with a guidance verb as Ezekiel is taken around to the various areas of the temple structure.

First Stage: Outer Walls and Gates (40:3-16)

Ezekiel 40:3-16 focuses on the outer walls and gates as Ezekiel is brought to the temple, enters the complex, and moves progressively to its inner areas. In vv. 3-5 he meets the man whose appearance was like bronze with measuring tools in his hand by the south gate where the people of Israel would have entered from the city of David to the south. The copper-like appearance of the man recalls the bronze appearance of the four creatures that bore the throne of YHWH through the heavens in Ezekiel 1–3. The bronze-like appearance is reflective and thereby signifies the appearance of another world, much like a mirror would reflect a parallel reality. In this case, it apparently signifies the heavenly reality of the realm of G-d. Later times understood the bronze-like appearance of the heavenly beings to refer to their fiery presence, much like the seraphim or fiery figures in Isaiah 6. The cord of linen is a measuring device apparently analogous to our modern measuring tapes and tape measures. The measuring rod is a device analogous to modern measuring rods. The man instructs Ezekiel to look closely and listen, as his task is to report what he has seen to the house of Israel. Ezekiel will thereby show Israel what is possible in the future once the process of purging the temple and the world of creation is complete.

The man's measuring device is described as six cubits and one handbreadth in length. A regular cubit was the standard measure of the ancient Near East, equivalent to an adult man's forearm or five handbreadths, which equals 20.68 inches or 518 millimeters. The extra handbreadth would add approximately another four inches, and indicates that the measure is the longer royal cubit that was employed in state building projects. The outer walls of the temple complex are one rod high and one rod deep, i.e., approximately 144 inches (= twelve feet) high and 144 inches (= twelve inches) deep.

Verses 6-16 take up the eastern gate through which the king would walk in temple processions. It is also the gate from which YHWH would symbolically enter the temple insofar as YHWH's entrance would coincide with the rising of the sun in the east (see Deut 33:2; Judg 5:4). The morning service at sunrise would signal the beginning of the liturgical day, and symbolically reenact creation as light would shine into the temple structure and illumine its insides, bringing order into the world. The various elements of the gate structure are measured. The gate was built in typical fashion with outer and inner gates and three chambers with doors included within. The purpose of such structures was to protect the gate, the weakest point in the wall. By building a structure with three chambers and a total of four doors, the gate structure was designed to trap enemy soldiers within the inner chambers after they had forced an outer gate, leaving them exposed to attack from the ramparts of the gate structure. Windows were built into the various chambers to allow air to circulate within and to provide ports for observation and firing arrows.

Second Stage: Outer Courts and Gates (40:17-27)

Ezekiel 40:17-27 focuses on the outer courts and gates. Verses 17-19a focus on the outer court, which was identified as the women's court in later times (*m. Middot* 2:5), insofar as women were permitted to enter this court. These verses also take up the east gates of the outer court, but the text does not make this clear until v. 19a. The passage notes the pavement of the outer court and the thirty chambers that line the outer court. The functions of these chambers are undefined.

Verses 19b-23 focus on the north gate. Again, the text presents a detailed account of the architectural features and measures of the north gate. The north gate was a particularly important location in the monarchic period, as the north wall of the court would have formed the northern defensive perimeter of the city of Jerusalem. The north side of the city and temple mount was the only side of the city not defended by a natural valley, making it especially vulnerable to attack.

Verses 24-27 focus on the south wall of the outer court. The text presents the architectural details together with the relevant measurements. The south wall is particularly important because it faces the city of Jerusalem situated to the south.

Third Stage: Inner Court and South Gate (40:28-31)
Ezekiel 40:28-31 focuses on the inner court and the south gate. The inner court was known as the Israelite's Court in the Second Temple period (*m. Middot* 2:6) insofar as Jewish men who were not priests were permitted to enter. The south gate is particularly important because it allows access to the temple complex from the city of David located to the south. Again, architectural details and measurements are provided.

Fourth Stage: Inner Court and East Gate (40:32-34)
Ezekiel 40:32-34 focuses on the inner court and the east gate. Details of architecture and measurements are referred to the previous description of the south gate. Again, the east gate is the processional entrance to the temple court, which follows the path by which YHWH would be conceived to enter the temple each morning.

Fifth Stage: Inner Court and North Gate (40:35-47)
Ezekiel 40:35-47 focuses on the inner court and the north gate. The passage begins in vv. 35-37 with a description of the measurements and architectural features of the north gate, which are identical to those of the prior two gates. Verses 38-43 then turn to a description of the facilities for washing the whole burnt offering (Heb., *ha'olah*; see Lev 1) and for slaughtering the whole burnt offering, the sin offering (Heb., *hahatta't*; see Lev 4), and the guilt offering (Heb., *ha'asham*; see Lev 5). These facilities are placed on the north side of the temple court so that they might not interfere with the entry of people from the city to the south. The passage indicates that four tables flanked both sides of the gate for a total of eight tables with their equipment for slaughter placed upon them. Ledges were built around the stone tables to facilitate the work of the priests. Verses 44-46 focus on the chambers reserved for the temple singers on the north wall of the inner court facing south and for the Zadokite priests on the south wall facing north. The reason

for the distinction is that the singers would be priests who perform the duties of the temple whereas the Zadokites were the line of priests assigned to perform the duties of the altar. Verse 47 then provides the dimensions of the inner court, viz., 100 cubits square, and notes the placement of the altar directly before the temple.

Sixth Stage: The Ulam (Portico) (40:48-49)

Having completed the measurements of the temple courts, the text now turns to the temple structure. Ezekiel's temple is built according to a standard three-room model, like that of Solomon's temple and temples from throughout the ancient Phoenician/Canaanite and Syrian/Aramean world. The structure was based on that of a royal palace (Halpern), and included the Ulam (Heb., *'ulam*) or portico at the entrance of the temple structure; the Heikhal (Heb., *heykal*), "palace" or "great hall"; and the Devir (Heb., *devir*) or holy of holies, which functions as YHWH's throne room where the Ark of the Covenant resided in Solomon's temple. Ezekiel 40:48-49 focuses on the Ulam. The dimensions of the Ulam differ from those of Solomon's temple. Solomon's temple had an Ulam that was twenty cubits wide and twenty cubits deep (see 1 Kings 6:3) whereas Ezekiel's Ulam is twenty cubits wide and eleven cubits deep (in the LXX, the measure is given as twelve cubits). No explanation for the difference is given, although it is possible that the extra cubit accounts for the steps that allow entry to the Ulam. The dimensions of its gate, fourteen cubits, and its flanks, three cubits each, are also given.

Seventh Stage: Heikhal and Holy of Holies (41:1-26)

Ezekiel 41:1-26 constitutes the seventh stage of Ezekiel's tour of the future temple. This section focuses on the Heikhal or central hall of the temple and the holy of holies where the Ark of the Covenant, symbolizing the presence of YHWH, resided in Solomon's temple. In Ezekiel's temple and in the later Second Temple, the holy of holies remains empty to symbolize the amorphous presence of YHWH.

Verses 1-4 begin with the measurements of the Heikhal and the holy of holies. The Heikhal or great hall of the temple serves as the major reception or audience area. In Solomon's temple, the Heikhal was filled with ten incense altars, ten menorot or candelabra, and the table of the presence where the bread of the presence was placed before YHWH. Ezekiel's temple vision does not account for these features, but we do not know if they were deliberately excluded from the vision or simply not mentioned. In any case, the Second Temple included these features for the Heikhal. Ezekiel is able to enter the Heikhal with his guide because he is a Zadokite priest and is therefore permitted access. The first measure is of the jambs (Heb., *'elim*, lit., "rams"), which were placed on either side of the entrance to the Heikhal to secure the doors that permitted entry. Each of the jambs measures six cubits in width. The door (Heb., *petaḥ* itself measures ten cubits in width, and the flanking walls (Heb., *kitpot hapetah*, lit., "wings of the door") on either side of the door measure five cubits each. The length of the Heikhal measures forty cubits and its width measures twenty cubits.

The guide then enters the inner room, i.e., the Devir or holy of holies of the temple. Ezekiel does not accompany his guide into the Devir because only the high priest was permitted entry into the Devir and only on Yom Kippur. Even though the vision takes place on Yom Kippur, it is not clear that Ezekiel is the high priest. The Devir or holy of holies is the place where YHWH's presence is manifested in the temple. Although the Ark of the Covenant resided in this location in Solomon's temple, no ark is mentioned here. The reason is that either the furnishings of the temple are not included in the description of Ezekiel's temple or that the Ark of the Covenant had disappeared, perhaps destroyed in the destruction of the temple, carried off as a trophy of war by the Babylonians, or hidden or carried off by the priests at the time of the conquest of Jerusalem. The jambs at the entrance of the Devir measure two cubits wide, the door at the entrance measures six cubits wide, and the flanking walls of the entrance each measure seven cubits. The length of the Devir is twenty cubits and the width of the Devir is also twenty cubits. Ezekiel's guide never refers to the Devir as such; instead, he calls it the holy of holies (Heb., *qodesh haqqodashim*).

Verses 5-15a then turn to the measurements of the temple wall, the side chambers, and the walkway, and vv. 15b-26 provide the details for the wall decorations and the interior furnishings.

Verses 5-12 provide a detailed account of the measurements of the major structural components of the temple.

This section begins in vv. 5-7 with the measurements of the wall of the temple structure, which is six cubits thick on each side of the temple. Side chambers surround the outer wall, which each measure four cubits across. The side chambers are placed along the two sidewalls and the rear wall of the temple in three stories totaling some thirty-three chambers. Thus, each story would include five chambers along each of the sidewalls and one chamber along the rear wall. The side chambers are supported by projections (Heb., *tsela'ot*, lit., "ribs") built against the side of the temple so that they do not compromise the temple walls. The projections serve as points to fasten the side chambers against the wall of the temple. The "encompassing structure"

(Heb., *musab*, read by the Targum as "the winding structure"; cf. *m. Tamid* 1:1) of the temple widens for each of the three stories; apparently the chambers at the bottom of the structure are built widest at the bottom and progressively more narrow at the top to provide greater structural stability. This results in a smaller platform for the lower story of the encompassing structure and progressively larger platforms for the two upper stories. The encompassing structure provides access for each story of the chambers built along the sides of the temple.

Verses 8-12 describe the open walkway that surrounds the temple structure and its side chambers. It is described as "a raised pavement/platform" (Heb., *gobah*, lit., "height") that apparently served as the foundation for the side chambers of the temple structure. Its elevation is defined as a rod's length or six cubits along the side of the chambers. The outer wall of the side chambers is five cubits thick, and the walkway around the chambers is twenty cubits wide between the side chambers of the temple structure and the facing chambers built along the wall of the inner court (see Ezek 42:1-14). There were two entrances into the side chambers from the surrounding walkway, one on the north side of the temple side chambers and one on the south side of the temple side chambers. The parapet (Heb., *munnah*, "open resting space") around the side structure was five cubits wide. A structure (Heb., *banyan*, "building") is built along the western wall of the temple building. The function of the structure is uncertain, although it does provide a backing and thus architectural protection for the rear wall of the holy of holies. It measures seventy cubits deep; its walls are five cubits wide, and the width of the entire structure is ninety cubits.

Verses 13-15a then provide a summation of measurements for the entire structure. The length of the temple structure is 100 cubits and the length of the building built to the west of the temple is also 100 cubits. The front side of the temple is 100 cubits wide, and the width of the structure built to the west of the temple is also 100 cubits. Both the temple and the structure behind it each form a perfect square.

Ezekiel 41:15b-26 provides details about the construction of the wall decorations and interior furnishings of the temple. Verses 15b-16 focus on the paneling and the windows of the Heikhal or great hall of the temple and the Ulam or portico of the inner court. The thresholds (Heb., *sippim*) of the temple doors, the framed windows (Heb., *hahallonim ha'atumot*) of the temple, and the doorframes (Heb., *ha'atiqim*) of the thresholds are all overlaid with wood.

Verses 17- 20a indicate that wainscoting was built along the interior walls from the floor to the windows of the temple including the window frames and the doors of the temple structure for both the interior and exterior surfaces. The decoration of the interior walls included engravings of cherubim and palm trees with a palm tree between every two cherubs. Such imagery is intended to evoke the imagery of the Garden of Eden that included cherubs and palm trees (Levenson 1985, 111–37). Each of the cherubim had two faces, as compared to the four faces in Ezekiel's inaugural vision (Ezek 1). One was a human face, representing divine wisdom, turned to the palm tree on one side, and the other was a lion's face, representing divine sovereignty, turned to the palm tree on the other side. These engravings appear on the interior temple walls throughout from the floor to a point above the doors.

Verses 20b-26 then focus on the paneling of the holy of holies, the altar table, and the wall decorations. The passage begins with a stance in the Heikhal or the great hall as one faces the entrance to the Devir or the holy of holies. The Heikhal had a squared doorpost (Heb., *mezzuzat rebu'ah*, "quartered doorpost") at its entrance (cf. 1 Kings 6:33). A quartered doorpost refers to a doorpost with four surfaces, i.e., a squared doorpost at the entrance to the holy of holies. The doorposts for Solomon's holy of holies had five sides (1 Kings 6:31), but it is not clear that Ezekiel's temple shared the same feature. The wooden altar before the door to the holy of holies measures three cubits high and two cubits long with a rim (Heb., *miqtso'ot*, lit., "corner buttresses," which indicates an inner angle and hence a rim) and walls of wood. Ezekiel's guide informs him that this structure is "the Table that stands before YHWH." In Solomon's temple, this table held the two loaves of the Bread of the Presence (1 Kings 7:48). The doors for the Heikhal and the holy of holies each included two paired doors that would pivot on their own doorposts. The doors were carved like the walls with engraved cherubim and palm trees to represent the Garden of Eden. A carved lattice (Heb., *'ab 'ets*, lit., "cloud/thicket [?] of wood") was also placed before the Ulam or portico at the entrance to the temple structure. Windows with frames and palm trees were carved into the flanking walls of the Ulam as well as on the temple side chambers and the lattices.

Eighth Stage: The Chambers of the Outer Court (42:1-14)
Ezekiel 42:1-14 focuses on the priestly chambers of the outer court. The visionary guidance formula in v. 1 indicates that Ezekiel was led out through the northern gate into the outer court. Here, he will view the priestly chambers built along the northern side of the outer court alongside the temple building and to the east of the structure that stands to the west of the temple building. This area would be reserved as living and dining quarters for the

priests who served at the temple altar. It stands alongside the area to the east where animals were kept, prepared, and slaughtered for the offerings at the temple altar. Ezekiel 42:10-12 indicates that a second complex will stand along the southern side of the temple complex.

Ezekiel 42:2-9 presents the discussion of the northern complex of chambers. The length of the structure is 100 cubits from the north side where one would enter the complex. The width of the structure was fifty cubits. The length of the structure corresponds to the five chambers of twenty cubits each that are built alongside the northern wall of the temple. The structure is also built against the pavement of the outer court. Again, the structure is built with three stories. This structure was separated from the inner court by a passageway measuring ten cubits wide with a path one cubit wide running along the inner court wall. Although the Greek Septuagint reads 100 cubits instead of one cubit, such an area would be entirely too large. A one-cubit path might well be a walkway or a ledge meant to mark the boundary of the inner court wall. Entrances to this walkway are arrayed along the north from the chambers that form the structure. The three stories of this structure were progressively smaller as the stories were stacked upon each other with the larger stories on the bottom and the smaller stories on top. This would allow a small walkway for each story that would allow entrance into the two stories of upper chambers as well. The reason for this structural feature is that the building lacked columns for support and therefore had to rely on the larger size of the lower stories to support the upper stories. A wall fifty cubits long was built in the outer court from the chamber complex to the outer courtyard wall to enclose the area to the north of the chamber complex. The result was a 100-cubit-square area set alongside the 100-cubit-square temple structure.

Ezekiel 42:10-12 describes a parallel structure to that depicted in vv. 2-9 built along the south side of the temple complex to the east of the area occupied by the structure west of the temple. The Septuagint locates this complex to the south of the structure, but it confuses the western structure with the temple building itself. The measurements, layout, and exits and entrances of the southern structure were identical to the northern structure. The entrance to the complex was on the eastern side, apparently parallel to the northern structure described in vv. 2-9.

Ezekiel 42:13-14 describes the purpose of the two chamber complexes. They are to serve as places for the priests of the temple to eat the holy offerings that they receive from the people. These offerings include the meal offering (Heb., *minhah*; see Lev 2), the sin offering (Heb., *hatta't*; see Lev 4), and the guilt offering (Heb., *'asham*; see Lev 5). Because the priests eat the most holy offerings of the people in these chambers, the chambers are considered as a sacred area. The priests enter these chambers from the inner courtyard of the temple where the altar is located and the offerings presented to YHWH. When the priests leave these chambers to enter the outer court, they must remove their sacred garments worn when officiating at the altar in the temple court. When leaving these chambers for the sacred area before the temple in the inner court, the priests must once again don their holy garments.

Summation: Measurements of the Entire Temple Complex (42:15-20)
Ezekiel 42:15-20 provides the summation of measurements for the entire temple complex. The text indicates that Ezekiel's guide leads him out through the eastern gate and then proceeds to measure the outer measurements of the entire temple complex. The guide measures each wall. The east wall measures 500 cubits. The north wall measures 500 cubits. The south wall measures 500 cubits. Finally, the west wall measures 500 cubits. The whole complex therefore measures a perfect 500 cubits square.

The Second Vision Account: Halakhot pertaining to the Temple (43:1–48:35)

Ezekiel 43:1–48:35 constitutes a second vision account within the larger structure of Ezekiel 40–48. Whereas the first vision account in Ezekiel 40:2–42:20 focused on the temple structure per se, the second vision account in Ezekiel 43:1–48:35 focuses on the halakhot or divine laws that pertain to the new temple. In the first vision account, an angelic figure guided Ezekiel through the new temple structure and instructed him on the measurements and significance of each of the features that he saw. In the second vision account, YHWH's divine presence enters the new temple structure, and YHWH then proceeds to instruct Ezekiel in all of the laws concerning the temple. The second vision account culminates in a portrayal of all Israel restored around the new temple and all creation renewed by the waters that flow from underneath the new temple. The establishment of the new temple thereby inaugurates a new stage in creation.

The various guidance formulas that indicate Ezekiel's movement throughout the new temple together with the instructions given to him by YHWH as he moves about demarcate the formal structure of the second vision. Nine stages, each introduced by a conveyance formula, appear within this unit. The first in Ezekiel 43:1-4 places Ezekiel at the east gate where he witnesses the entry of the divine presence of YHWH into the new temple complex. The second in Ezekiel 43:5-27 places Ezekiel in the inner court of the temple where he receives instruction concerning the sanctity of the new temple and the functioning of the altar in the inner court. The third stage in Ezekiel 44:1-3 places Ezekiel in the outer court where he receives instruction concerning the gate and the place where the prince eats. The fourth stage in Ezekiel 44:4–46:18 places Ezekiel at the north gate before the new temple where he receives instruction concerning the priests and Levites. The fifth stage in Ezekiel 46:19-20 places Ezekiel in the northern chambers of the priests where he receives instructions concerning their kitchens. The sixth stage in Ezekiel 46:21-24 places Ezekiel in the outer court by the corner structures and the kitchens where he receives instruction concerning the preparation of the offerings presented by the people. The seventh stage in Ezekiel 47:1 places Ezekiel once again at the east gate where he witnesses water flowing from beneath the new temple toward the east. The eighth stage in Ezekiel 47:2-6a moves Ezekiel out the north gate to the outer eastern gate where the water flows eastward. The ninth stage in Ezekiel 47:6b–48:35 returns Ezekiel to the bank of the *wadi* (dry streambed) where he witnesses a portrayal of the new creation that will result from the establishment of the new temple.

First Stage: East Gate; Entry of Divine Presence (43:1-4)
Ezekiel 43:1-4 constitutes the first stage in the second vision account. It takes place at the eastern gate of the temple complex where Ezekiel witnesses the entry of the divine presence (Heb., *kabod yhwh*, lit., "the glory of YHWH"). The unit begins with a conveyance formula in v. 1 in which the angel guiding the prophet leads him to the east gate. The east gate is the processional entryway into the temple complex that follows YHWH's metaphorical entrance into the temple at the time of morning worship each day. YHWH is metaphorically portrayed analogous to the sun rising in the east over Seir or Edom in what is now modern Jordan (Deut 33:2; Judg 5:4) and travelling across the heavens in a divine chariot to enter the temple (Hab 3; Ps 1–4). The roar of mighty waters, a theophanic element that often accompanies appearances of the divine presence (e.g., Isa 17:12-14), is designed to evoke YHWH's defeat of enemy nations that threaten Israel as in the defeat of Egypt by the Red Sea (Exod 14–15). Similar imagery appeared in Ezekiel's inaugural vision in Ezekiel 1:24. The Hebrew text includes a statement by Ezekiel, "The vision was like the vision that I saw when I came to destroy the city, and the visions were like the vision that I saw by the Chebar Canal." The reading "when I came" (Heb., *bebo'i*) is likely a scribal slip for Hebrew *bebo'o*, "when He [i.e., YHWH] came." The letters *yod* and *waw* look very similar in Hebrew script. Nevertheless, the present reading

suggests that the prophet identifies with YHWH and acts on YHWH's behalf. As in the inaugural vision, Ezekiel falls upon his face in the presence of YHWH, just as he would at a time of worship. YHWH enters the temple complex by the east gate in order to reside in the Devir or holy of holies of the temple where the Ark of the Covenant resided during the time of Solomon's temple.

The Second Stage: The Inner Court (43:5-27)
Ezekiel 43:5-27 constitutes the second stage of Ezekiel's second vision account in which he is conveyed by a wind or spirit, presumably from YHWH, to the inner court of the temple. Verse 5 presents Ezekiel's conveyance to the inner court where he witnesses YHWH's presence filling the temple. Such a vision presupposes the notion that YHWH appears from the Devir or holy of holies in the temple to fill the entire temple structure. Such an image would have been facilitated by the use of the ten incense burners placed in the Heikhal or palace of the temple. The smoke released by the incense burners would metaphorically represent the amorphous presence of YHWH to the people assembled before the temple.

Verses 6-27 present Ezekiel's account of YHWH's speeches from the temple. Verse 6 presents Ezekiel's narrative statement of the setting of the speeches that he said he heard from the temple. Ezekiel acknowledges that his angelic guide remains beside him as YHWH speaks. The guide appears to be necessary to Ezekiel's hearing of YHWH's speech. Some translations indicate that YHWH spoke to Ezekiel through the man, but the Hebrew simply states, "I heard speaking to me from the temple, and the man was standing beside me." Verses 7-17 present YHWH's first speech, and verses 18-27 present YHWH's second speech.

The account of YHWH's first speech appears in vv. 7-17. The speech formula in v. 7aα^{1-2} indicates that "he" spoke to me, as though it referred to Ezekiel's angelic guide standing beside him, but the speech employs the first person as though YHWH were speaking. YHWH's speech takes up three major topics concerning the sanctity of the temple and the altar.

The first topic appears in vv. 7aα^3-9 when YHWH instructs Ezekiel concerning the sanctity of the temple. YHWH addresses Ezekiel as "son of Adam" to acknowledge his role as a Zadokite priest of the temple. YHWH begins with a statement that the temple is the place of YHWH's throne and the place for the soles of YHWH's feet where YHWH will dwell in the midst of Israel forever. YHWH's statement addresses the role of the Devir or holy of holies as the throne room of YHWH where YHWH's presence is manifested to the people. Whereas Solomon's temple housed the Ark of the

Covenant, which functioned as YHWH's throne, Ezekiel's temple includes no Ark of the Covenant. YHWH's throne chariot, the imagery of which is based on the imagery of the Ark of the Covenant, will serve as YHWH's throne instead. It appears only at times when YHWH's presence is manifested in the temple. Consequently, the holy of holies will remain empty in Ezekiel's temple, just as it did in the Second Temple. YHWH complains that the people of Israel and their kings have defiled the temple by their apostasy (Heb., *zenut*, "harlotry") and the corpses of their kings. Because the relationship between YHWH and Israel was metaphorically portrayed as a marriage between the husband YHWH and the bride Israel or daughter Zion (see Hos 1–3; Jer 2; Ezek 16; Isa 54; Zeph 3:14-20), the term "harlotry" is employed to describe Israel's apostasy as the abandonment of her husband for other gods. The reference to the corpses of the kings refers to the burials of the Davidic kings in the city of David (e.g., 1 Kings 2:10). The burial of dead bodies in the city of David defiles the temple. The practice was discontinued with the burial of Manasseh, who was buried in his palace in the Garden of Uzza (2 Kings 21:18), although his palace may well have been in the city as well. YHWH indicates that this defilement was a cause for the destruction of Jerusalem and the temple (see Ezek 8–11). YHWH proposes that the apostasy and the bodies of the kings be placed far away from the temple, and YHWH will remain among the people forever.

YHWH's second topic appears in vv. 10-12. YHWH addresses Ezekiel as "son of Adam" once again and instructs him to teach the people the pattern (Heb., *toknit*) for the temple so they might measure it and implement its laws. YHWH is careful to state that Ezekiel will teach them the plan of the temple only after the people have become ashamed of what they have done. Ezekiel is to write the plan for the temple before their eyes so that the people might follow the plan and its laws. This portion of YHWH's speech concludes with a summary statement, "Behold, this is the instruction of the Temple."

YHWH's third topic appears in vv. 13-17, which presents the measurements of the altar. The altar is a particularly important feature of the temple complex as it is the place where the various offerings are presented to YHWH. It begins with its own introductory statement, "And these are the measurements of the altar." It employs the larger royal cubit, which includes a cubit and a handbreadth. The trench dug about the altar is intended to catch any blood that might drain away from the offering and thereby keep blood, the seat of life (cg. Gen 9:1-6), separate from the rest of the temple complex so that it might enter the ground below the temple and thereby avoid defiling the temple's sanctity. The lower ledge of the altar is two cubits from the trench on the ground, and the height of the altar hearth is four cubits with the four horns of the altar projecting upward from the hearth. The hearth is twelve cubits square. The base of the altar is fourteen cubits square. The rim around the altar is a half cubit, and the trench measures one cubit wide. The ramp for the altar faces east. Exodus 20:22-23 stipulates that the altar is to be built of unhewn stones with no steps. Ezekiel's altar gives no indication that the altar stones are hewn, but its ramp (Heb., *ma'alotehu*) employs the same term that appears in Exodus 20:23 as "steps." The pattern of Ezekiel's altar appears to contrast with that employed in the Torah in Exodus 20:22-23. This would have been one of the discrepancies that R. Hanina ben Hezekiah would have addressed (*b. Shabbat* 13b; *b. Hagigah* 13a; *b. Menahot* 45a; see Sweeney 2011, 11–23).

The account of YHWH's second speech appears in vv. 18-27. Again, it is introduced by a speech formula "and he said" in v. 18aα$^{1-2}$, which indicates that YHWH speaks to Ezekiel through the guide. YHWH's speech is an instruction speech concerning the *halakhot* pertaining to the altar. It begins with an address to Ezekiel as "son of Adam" and a prophetic messenger formula in v. 18aα$^{3-7}$ that certifies the following oracle as a message from YHWH. The oracle takes up four topics. The first appears in vv. 18aβ-b, which introduces YHWH's instruction speech by defining its fundamental purpose, viz., "these are the statutes of the altar on the day that it is built to send up upon it whole burnt offerings and to sprinkle upon it blood." The whole burnt offering (Lev 1) is the daily offering presented to YHWH. The second topic appears in vv. 19-21. These verses take up the bull that is presented as a sin offering (Heb., *hatta'at*; Lev 4) at the time of the eight-day ordination of the priests who will serve at the altar (Exod 29; Lev 8; Num 8). YHWH's instruction specifies that the Zadokite priests who serve at the altar will offer the bull of the sin offering on the first day only. Earlier references to this offering refer only to the priests and Levites without specifying the Zadokites, so this instruction appears to be innovative in Ezekiel. The altar is also consecrated at the time of the priests' ordination. As in the other texts, the blood of the bull of the sin offering is employed to consecrate the horns of the altar. The blood is also applied to the rim and base of the altar to complete its consecration. Once the consecration of the priests and the altar is complete, the remains of the bull are burned in a designated area outside of the sanctuary. Verses 22-26 take up the consecration offerings of the remaining seven days of the ordination period. For each of the seven days, the priests are to offer a goat as a sin offering for the altar together with a bull and a ram as a whole burnt offering to YHWH. All animals are to be unblemished, which is a standard stipulation for offerings at the temple. Ezekiel's stipulations differ from the Torah, which calls for a bull and two rams each day (Exod 29) or a bull and one ram each day (Lev 8). Numbers 8 refers to the ordination of the Levites. Finally, v. 27 summarizes the results of the ritual. From the eighth day on the priests will be able to present the offerings to YHWH at the altar and YHWH will grant favor to the people. The passage concludes with the oracular formula "utterance of YHWH" (*ne'um yhwh*) to certify the preceding as an oracle of YHWH.

The Third Stage: East Gate, Outer Court (44:1-3)

Ezekiel 44:1-3 treats the east gate of the outer court. The angel who guides Ezekiel returns him to this location so that YHWH may instruct him in its exclusive use by YHWH and the prince. Once Ezekiel has returned to the gate, YHWH speaks to him and states that the gate must remain closed. No one may enter the gate other than YHWH, who symbolically enters the temple from the east as an analogy with the daily rising of the sun. Indeed, the eastern gate of the outer court on the present-day temple mount is walled up in keeping with the instructions presented in this passage. The eastern gate will remain closed until such time as the temple is rebuilt and YHWH reenters its premises. The prince is allowed to eat his sacrificial offerings in this location before YHWH. He may enter and exit the temple complex from the east, i.e., from the direction in which the Ulam or portico faces.

The Fourth Stage: North Gate before the Temple: Halakhot/Laws concerning the Priests and Levites (44:4–46:18)

Ezekiel 44:4–46:18 constitutes the fourth stage in Ezekiel's second vision account, which places him by the north gate before the temple structure. This is the area where the priests would prepare the sacrificial offerings of the temple, and the passage treats issues of access to the sacred precincts of the temple by the priests and Levites. The text begins in Ezekiel 44:4 with an introduction that indicates that Ezekiel is guided to the north gate together with a depiction of YHWH's divine presence. The account of YHWH's instruction speech to Ezekiel then follows in Ezekiel 44:5–46:18.

Introduction: Guidance to the North Gate and Presence of YHWH (44:4). Ezekiel 44:4 presents a brief introduction to the account of YHWH's instruction speech in Ezekiel 44:5–46:18. The passage notes that Ezekiel is guided to the north gate of the temple complex before the temple structure. This area is set aside for the preparation by the priests and Levites of the sacrificial offerings presented at the temple altar. The passage also includes a brief visionary account in which Ezekiel announces the vision of YHWH's divine presence in the temple. He responds appropriately by falling on his face in a deep bow, which is expected of those who encounter the presence of YHWH.

Account of YHWH's Instruction Speech (44:5–46:18). Ezekiel 44:5–46:18 presents the account of YHWH's instruction speech to Ezekiel concerning the proper roles of the priests and Levites in the new temple as well as other matters pertaining to temple practice. Following the speech formula in Ezekiel 44:5aα$^{1-3}$, YHWH's speech follows in Ezekiel 44:5aα^4–46:18. YHWH's speech is formulated as an account of YHWH's instruction speech to the prophet in which YHWH will instruct him in proper access to and practice in the sacred precincts of the temple. It begins in Ezekiel 44:5aα^4-b with YHWH's initial address to the prophet. YHWH addresses Ezekiel in typical form as "son of Adam" to acknowledge his identity as a Zadokite priest, and YHWH continues with an exhortation to Ezekiel to pay close attention to the laws of temple access that YHWH is about to teach him, i.e., who may enter and who may exit the temple.

YHWH's speech then follows in Ezekiel 44:6–46:18. It begins with an instruction formula in Ezekiel 44:6aα, "and you shall say to the rebellious house of Israel," which indicates that Ezekiel is to pass on these laws to the people at large. The designation "rebellious house of Israel" indicates that Israel's purported failure to maintain the sanctity of the temple is the basis for the need to present this instruction. The instruction ensues in Ezekiel 44:6aβ–46:18 with six basic elements. The prophetic messenger formula introduces each element to certify it as a message from YHWH.

The first element appears in Ezekiel 44:6aβ-8 in which YHWH charges Israel with having profaned the temple and thereby violated the covenant with YHWH. YHWH claims that the people have committed abominations (*to'abot*), the standard term for cultic impropriety. YHWH specifies this charge by claiming that foreigners and persons uncircumcised of heart and flesh have been allowed to enter the temple when YHWH's offerings are presented at the altar, thereby compromising the temple's sanctity. Because Israel is considered a priestly or sacred people in ancient Israelite and Judean thought (see Exod 19:6, "You shall be to me a kingdom of priests and a holy nation"), Israel and Judah have sacred obligations to YHWH, such as maintaining the temple as the holy center of creation by observing all of YHWH's sacred instruction (cf. Levenson 1985, 89–184). Because foreigners do not observe YHWH's sacred instruction, they are not permitted to enter the temple, as they would be considered a defiling presence. The reference to those uncircumcised of heart and uncircumcised of flesh indicates those, whether Gentile or Jewish, who do not observe YHWH's instructions. The issue is not limited to the physical requirement of circumcision, which is required of all Jewish males (Gen 17). It also pertains to sacred practice, viz., uncircumcised of heart indicates one who is not prepared or willing to observe YHWH's sacred instructions. Contrary to some New Testament charges that Jews are interested only in the formal appearance of ritual observance, Judaism requires both inner and outer observance of YHWH's sacred instruction. Such charges appear to stand behind the portrayal of the defiled temple in Ezekiel 8–11 in which Jews were attempting to observe the sacred practices of the temple without proper supervision by the Zadokite priests. Specifically, YHWH refers to the offerings of the temple, including bread, fat, and blood. Insofar as these offerings call for the shedding of blood, which is sacred because it is the seat of life (Gen 9:1-6), the treatment and consumption of such offerings demands the supervision of the Zadokite priests, who are consecrated for such service. Because the temple lacked Zadokite supervision following the first deportation to Babylon in 597 BCE, YHWH charges the people with having violated the covenant (*wayyaperu 'etberiti*, "and they violated my covenant") and having failed to observe the sacred service (*mishmeret qadashi*) of the temple.

The second element of YHWH's instructions appears in Ezekiel 44:9–45:8, which focuses on access to the temple by priests and Levites. Three subunits appear within this element, including Ezekiel 44:9-14, which focuses on the restricted access to the temple by the Levites; Ezekiel 44:15-31, which takes up the access to the temple, duties, and privileges of the priests; and Ezekiel 45:1-8, which takes up the sacred compound allocated to the priests.

Ezekiel 44:9-14 begins with a prophetic messenger formula that certifies the subunit as a speech by YHWH. It begins with prohibitions against granting foreigners access to the temple, which recall Israel's status as a holy people dedicated to YHWH (cf. Exod 19:6). Foreigners here are defined not only by foreign birth but also by being uncircumcised of heart and flesh as well. Circumcision is an identifying mark on all Jewish men, but it is also practiced by other peoples, such as the Egyptian priesthood (see *ANET*, 326), the Edomites, the Ammonites, the Moabites, and the desert dwellers (Jer 9:25-26). The qualification that foreigners are those uncircumcised of heart is key here because it allows Jews whom Ezekiel considers unfaithful to the tradition to be included among the foreigners. In this case, the Levites are considered unfit for full service at the altar. The passage accuses the Levites of having led the people astray to worship idols and the like, but no specific incident is indicated that would explain such an accusation. Some have argued that the split between the priests and the Levites dates to a later period, such as the Persian, Hellenistic, or Roman periods when the distinction between priests and Levites becomes clear, but in fact the distinction is already apparent in the Bible. Solomon expelled the high priest Abiathar from the Jerusalem Temple to the village of Anathoth at the outset of his reign and allowed Zadok to remain in the temple to serve as high priest (1 Kings 12). Zadok descended from the Aaronide line of priests through Aaron's son, Eleazar, and his grandson, Phineas, who won an eternal covenant of priesthood when he killed an apostate Israelite man with a Midianite woman in the wilderness (Num 25:10-18). The basis for Ezekiel's condemnation of the Levites would then appear to lie in the selection of the line of Phineas ben Eleazar ben Aaron as the recipient of the eternal covenant of peace (Num 25:10-18) and the view that all other priests and Levites are inadequate for the task. Abiathar was a member of the house of Eli at Shiloh, which descended from Aaron's other son, Ithamar, and which was condemned for abusing its priestly office in 1 Samuel 2. Because the Elide line was expelled from Jerusalem, it was associated especially with the northern kingdom of Israel from the time of King Jeroboam ben Nebat on, which was considered idolatrous because of Jeroboam's building of golden calves at Beth El and Dan. Jeremiah is a later member of the Elide line. As noted in discussion of the defiled temple above in Ezekiel 8–11, the temple was left to the supervision of other priests following the deportation of the key Zadokite figures, such as Ezekiel, by the Babylonians in 597 BCE. Jaazniah ben Shaphan, whom Ezekiel condemned for apostasy in Ezekiel 8, was from a family that firmly supported Jeremiah, the prophet and priest of the Elide line descended from Ithamar. Because of their alleged idolatry, Ezekiel maintains that the Levites will not have full access to the temple altar, but will serve in secondary roles, including guarding the temple gates, slaughtering and preparing offerings for the altar, and other duties of service (*mishmeret*) in the temple.

Ezekiel 44:15-31 grants access to the temple to the Zadokite line of priests and defines its various obligations as the authorized priesthood of the Jerusalem Temple. In contrast to the Levites, vv. 15-16 grant the Zadokite line access to the entire temple, including the altar, and assigns them the holy task of presenting the meat offerings to YHWH. Verses 17-19 discusses the holy garments that the Zadokites must wear when attending to their duties at the altar (cf. Exod 28). The Zadokite priests dress in linen rather than wool because linen is white to represent purity and because it is much lighter than wool, which apparently reduces sweating near the hot altar. As a mark of sanctity, the Zadokite priests remove their holy garments when they leave the area demarcated for the holy altar and put on everyday garments instead. Verse 20 discusses the hair of the priests. They are not to shave their hair in the Canaanite fashion, nor are they to let it grow long and unkempt like a Nazirite (see Num 6). Verse 21 specifies that the priests are not to drink when serving in the inner court, apparently to prevent inappropriate behavioral problems or illness resulting from drunkenness. Verse 22 specifies that priests must marry only virgins or the widows of other priests, apparently to ensure the priestly status of all children raised within their houses (cf. Lev 21:4, 7-8). Verses 23-24 define the sacred tasks of the priests to teach the people concerning what is holy and profane as well as what is clean and unclean (cf. Lev 10:10-11), to serve as judges in court (see Deut 16:18-20), and to observe YHWH's statutes and instructions, holidays, and Shabbats (see Lev 23; Num 28–29; Deut 16:1-17). Verses 25-27 forbid priests to come into contact with the dead unless it is for a blood relative, i.e., parent, sibling, or child (cf. Lev 21:1-3), and it specifies the seven-day purification period, apparently modeled on the ordination period (see Exod 29; Lev 8; Num 8), which enables them to reenter the sacred precincts of the temple. Verses 28-31 specify the offerings that are dedicated to the priests insofar as they are not able to hold land.

Ezekiel 45:1-8 takes up the spaces in the sacred temple compound that are allocated to the priests, the Levites, and the prince. The passage begins in vv. 1-4 by assigning an allotment of land measuring 25,000 cubits long by 10,000 cubits wide for the temple complex. As later allotments will indicate, the temple quarter will be placed in the center of the tribes of Israel. Within the temple allotment, a special allotment of 500 cubits by 500 cubits square is set aside for the temple structure with an open space of fifty cubits all around. The larger space is reserved for the (Zadokite) priests who serve in the sanctuary. Verse 5 specifies a second allotment, also of 25,000 by 10,000 cubits, which is set aside for the Levites who undertake supportive duties for the temple. The verse mentions that twenty rooms or chambers are included in this space, although the text does not state their function. Verses 6-8 specify that a third allotment measuring 25,000 cubits by 5,000 cubits is set aside as a holy reserve for the people of Israel. The three allotments together comprise a 25,000-square-cubit area, although the exact place of the three allotments is not stated. The prince (*nasi*) is assigned two allotments of land located to the west and to the east of the holy reserve. These allotments correspond to those set aside for each of the tribes of Israel (see Ezek 48). The passage concludes with an instruction that the princes of Israel are not to "defraud" (*welo' yonu*) the people, i.e., they are not permitted to take more land from the people of Israel other than what they are assigned.

The third element of YHWH's speech appears in Ezekiel 45:9-17, which focuses on the responsibilities of the prince. The passage opens with the prophetic messenger formula in Ezekiel 45:9aα^{1-4} to certify it as a speech by YHWH. Following the messenger formula, this portion of YHWH's speech comprises two portions, viz., vv. 9aα^5-12 focus on the practice of justice by the princes of Israel and vv. 13-17 focus on their provision of offerings for the temple.

Verses 9aα^5-12 begin with a general prohibition of misconduct and abuse on the part of the princes followed immediately by a command to practice justice (*mishpat*) and righteousness (*tsedaqah*). Specific instructions then follow. Evictions (*gerushot*, lit., "expulsions") of the people, presumably from their land, are prohibited. The princes are required to employ honest measures, including balances or weight scales, volumes of dry measure, including the ephah and the bath, and measures of weight, including the shekel and the mina. Specific measures are given, viz., the ephah and the bath are to hold the same volume, both ephah and bath are set at a tenth of homer, the shekel shall weigh twenty gerahs, and sixty shekels equal one mina. This last statement is confused as the numbers are given as a combination of twenty, twenty-five, ten, and five shekels, although scholars note that a Mesopotamian mina includes a total of sixty shekels.

Verses 13-17 then turn to the prince's obligation to provide offerings for the temple. The prince's contribution is labeled *terumah* in Hebrew, once mistakenly translated as a heave offering, because the term is derived from the root *rwm*, "to raise." The term denotes the fact that the person making the offering raises it or lifts it up when presenting it at the altar. The princes must offer one-sixth of an ephah from every homer of wheat and one-sixth of an ephah from every homer of barley produced during the year. The oil offerings will comprise one-tenth of a bath from every kor, and the text specifies that ten baths comprise both the kor and the homer. The princes are required to offer one animal from every 200 produced in the flock each year. As all of these offerings, including the meal offering (*minhah*, see Lev 2), the whole burnt offering (*'olah*, see Lev 1), and the peace offering (*shelamim*, see Lev 3), are meant to atone (*kapper*) for the people, v. 16 includes an instruction that all of the people are to join the princes in making these offerings at the temple. The passage concludes in v. 17 by specifying that the prince is responsible for all of these offerings as well as the libations (*nesek*) and the sin offerings (*hatta'at*, see Lev 4), i.e., the people do not provide these offerings. This applies to all festivals, new moons, Shabbats, and fixed observances in Israel.

The fourth element in YHWH's speech appears in Ezekiel 45:18-25, which focuses on the purging or purification of the sanctuary. Once again, the passage begins with an example of the prophetic messenger formula in v. 18aα$^{1-4}$, which certifies the following material as a statement by YHWH. The instructions begin in vv. 18aα^5-19 with commands to purge the sanctuary by using the blood of a sin offering (*hatta'at*). The verb employed for purging is a piel form of the verb, *ht'*, which is commonly employed for purging the altar (Exod 43:20; 45:18; Lev 8:15) and other structures, such as the home of a leper (Lev 14:49), or persons (Num 19:19). Here, the procedure is employed on the first day of the year, i.e., on the first day of the first month of the year (Nissan). This is not the date of Rosh ha-Shanah, the Jewish New Year, but the date is closely tied to the festival of Passover (14 Nissan), which celebrates the exodus from Egypt. The New Year on 1 Nissan therefore celebrates the formation of the Jewish people (*m. Rosh HaShanah* 1:1). The procedure calls for a bull without blemish to be offered as a sin offering. The priest is instructed to take the blood of the *hatta'at* offering and smear it on the doorposts of the temple in an act reminiscent of smearing the blood of the Passover lamb on the doorposts of the homes of the Israelite slaves in Egypt (Exod 12). The priest must also purge the altar by smearing the blood of the *hatta'at* on the four horns of the altar in a manner reminiscent of the ordination of priests (Exod 29:9-14; Lev 8:14-15). The application of the blood of the *hatta'at* to the doorposts of the gate of the inner court is otherwise unknown in the Bible. Verse 20 requires a repetition of this ceremony on the seventh day of the (first) month to purge the temple of any impurity caused by someone who makes an error or is ignorant of the laws concerning temple purity.

Verses 21-24 then turn to the presentation of offerings for the seven-day festival of Passover beginning on the fourteenth day of the seventh month (14–20 Nissan; cf. Lev 23:5-8; Num 28:16-31). The passage begins by calling for the observance of a seven-day festival of Passover (*pesah*) during which the people will eat unleavened bread (*matsot*). This instruction differs from Leviticus 23:5-8 and Numbers 28:16-31, which call for an observance of one day of Passover and seven days of *Matsot*. Apparently, Ezekiel reconciles the differentiation of two festivals in Leviticus and Numbers simply by counting the seven days of *Matsot* as Passover. Verses 22-24 specify the responsibilities of the prince. First, he is to provide the *hatta'at* or sin offering of the festival, viz., a bull for himself and the people at large. This differs from Numbers 28:22, which calls for a goat to be offered as a *hatta'at* in addition to the whole burnt offering or the *olah* for the day. Ezekiel agrees with Numbers 28:16-31 by calling for the presentation of offerings for each of the seven days of the festival. But Ezekiel differs once again by specifying a whole burnt offering or *olah* of seven bulls and seven rams, all without blemish, and one goat as a *hatta'at* for each of the seven days whereas Numbers 28:16-31 calls for two bulls, a ram, and seven lambs for a whole burnt offering and a goat for a sin offering on each of the seven days. Nevertheless, readers should note that Ezekiel takes up the responsibilities of the prince whereas Leviticus 23:5-8 and Numbers 28:16-31 take up the offerings made by the priest on behalf of the people. In addition, the prince is to provide a meal offering or *minhah* of an ephah of grain for a bull and for each ram together with a hin of oil for each ephah of grain. Numbers 28:28 calls for a *minhah* offering of three-tenths of a measure of flour mixed with oil for each bull, two-tenths of a measure of flour mixed with oil for each ram, and one-tenth of a measure of flour mixed with oil for each lamb. These discrepancies were apparently taken up by R. Hanina ben Hezekiah in rabbinic discussion of the matter (*b. Shabbat* 13b; *b. Hagigah* 13a; *b. Menahot* 45a; cf. Sweeney 2011, 11–23).

Finally, verse 25 calls for the presentation of the same sin offerings, whole burnt offerings, meal offerings, and oil for the seven days of Sukkot, here identified simply as the festival celebrated during the seventh month from the fifteenth day on (see Lev 23:33-36; Num 29:1-38). The text in Numbers 29:1-38 differs markedly from Ezekiel by calling for an eight-day celebration in which the numbers of animals offered range from thirteen bulls, two rams, and fourteen lambs on the first day to one bull, one ram, and seven lambs on the seventh day. Again, these offerings would have figured prominently in the discussion of R. Hanina ben Hezekiah.

The fifth element in YHWH's instruction speech appears in Ezekiel 46:1-15, which focuses on the east gate of the inner court. The passage opens with the prophetic messenger formula in v. $1a\alpha^{1-4}$, which certifies the following material as a speech by YHWH. The passage includes six subunits, each of which takes up a different topic related to the east gate.

The first is Ezekiel $46:1a^5$-b, which takes up the opening of the east gate of the inner court on Shabbat and Rosh Hodesh (the first day of the month). The passage stipulates that the east gate of the inner court be closed on the six working days of the week, but be open on Shabbat and on the day after the new moon. The east gate faces the Transjordanian region where YHWH is manifested every morning (Deut 33:2; Judg 5:4). The prince enters the temple complex through this gate. Shabbat and the day following the new moon are designated as holy days (Num 28:9-10, 11-15) on which additional offerings are presented together with the daily offering. Because the prince is responsible for these offerings, the gate is opened at these times.

Ezekiel 46:2-3 takes up the entry of the prince and the people at the east gate of the inner court. The prince enters the temple at the Ulam or porch and stands by the pillar as the priests present his offerings (cf. 2 Kings 11:14; 23:3). He presents a daily *olah* (Lev 1) or whole burnt offering, which is entirely burned for YHWH, and a *zebah shelamim* ("a sacrifice of well being") (Lev 3), which is eaten by the priests. The gate is left open until evening so that the people of the land might also worship following the prince.

Ezekiel 46:4-7 specifies the prince's offerings. His *olah* or whole burnt offering on the Shabbat includes six lambs and one ram without blemish. This is greater than the normal offering, which includes two lambs (Num 28:9-10). The accompanying meal offering includes an ephah of flour for the ram and as much as he likes for each of the lambs. A hin of oil accompanies each ephah of flour. For the new moon, the prince offers a bull, six lambs, and a ram, all without blemish. Again, an ephah of meal is required for both the bull and the ram and as much as he likes for lambs. A hin of oil accompanies each ephah. The prince's offering is less than the usual offering of two bulls, a ram, and seven lambs (Num 28:11-15).

Ezekiel 46:8-10 specifies that the prince will enter the temple and exit by the same way, viz., the *Ulam* or porch of the temple structure. On fixed holidays when the people of the land appear before YHWH, those who enter by the north gate will exit to the south and those who enter by the south gate will exit by the north, apparently to provide adequate traffic flow. The prince enters when the people enter and exits when they leave.

Ezekiel 46:11-12 specifies that the meal offering for festivals (*haggim*) and fixed observances (*moʿadim*) will be an ephah of flour for each bull and each ram and as much as the prince likes for the lambs. When the prince makes a free-will offering (*nedabah*) of an *olah* ("whole burnt offering") or *zebah shelamim* ("sacrifice of well being"), then the gate shall be opened for him and closed after he leaves. Ezekiel 46:13-15 provides a summation of the daily offerings. It appears as a second-person masculine singular address, apparently addressed to Ezekiel because he is a priest. The passage specifies that an *olah* consisting of a year-old lamb will be offered together with a grain offering including a sixth of an ephah of flour and a third of a hin of oil. These specifications are identified as eternal regular statutes (*huqqot ʿolam tamid*) to be presented every morning in the temple as an *olah*.

The sixth element of YHWH's instruction speech appears in Ezekiel 46:16-18, which takes up the status of gifts given by the prince. The unit begins with a prophetic messenger formula in v. 16aα^{1-4}, which certifies the following material as a speech by YHWH. The following text in

vv. 16aα⁵-18 is formulated as a case law, which states a case and its resolution. In the present instance, the main case appears in v. 16aα⁵-b, which specifies that when the prince makes a gift to any of his sons, the gift becomes the son's permanent property and therefore part of his inheritance. A secondary case then appears in v. 17, which specifies the status of a gift made by the prince to any of his subjects, viz., the gift is the property of the subject only until the year of release (*hadderor*; see Jer 34:8, 15, 17). The year of release is an alternative term for the year of Jubilee in the priestly literature (Lev 25:10). Normally, debts are forgiven or put on hold every seventh year. A Jubilee year, however, is declared after seven weeks of years or forty-nine years. Every fiftieth year therefore serves as a year of release; all loans are returned to the original owner. Because ancient Israel's economy was based on the possession of land, this was a means to protect family and tribal ownership of land. In the present case, the law is designed to protect the royal family's property so that any gift given by the prince will revert to his heirs during the Jubilee year or year of release.

The subunit concludes in v. 18 with a prohibition against the prince taking any property away from his subjects to pass on to his sons. The prince may only pass his own property on to his sons. The statement ends with the principle that the people of Israel may not be dispossessed of their property.

The Fifth Stage: Northern Chambers of the Priests: The Kitchens (46:19-20)

Ezekiel 46:19-20 begins with a guidance formula stating that the guiding angel takes Ezekiel to the northern gate of the inner court where the priestly chambers are located. There he sees an open space to the west. The angel informs him that this area is set aside for the priest to cook guilt offerings (*'asham*) and the sin offerings (*hatta't*) and to bake the grain offerings given to them by the people. These offerings function as sacred income or food to support the priests. The priests are forbidden to take these offerings into the outer court where they might be seen and eaten by the people. The passage ensures that these offerings are eaten only by the priests and do not become goods to be transferred to the people.

The Sixth Stage: the Outer Court: Corner Structures and Kitchens for the Preparation of the People's Sacred Meals (46:21-24)

Ezekiel 46:21-24 begins with a guidance formula that reports that the guiding angel leads Ezekiel into the outer court where he will see the areas designated as kitchens for the preparation of meals from the temple sacrifices for the people. The kitchens are located in each of the four corners of the outer court. The corners are open without a roof, presumably to allow for smoke from cook fires, and each measures forty-by-thirty cubits. Each is lined with cooking hearths for the preparation of food. At the conclusion of this segment, the guiding angel informs Ezekiel that this area is reserved for the temple servitors, i.e., the Levites, to prepare the sacrifices for consumption by the people.

The Seventh Stage: Return to the East Gate: Water Flowing Eastward (47:1)

Ezekiel 47:1 begins with the guidance formula that places Ezekiel back at the entrance of the temple. Insofar as the temple faces east, this location would be the east gate of the temple. Here Ezekiel sees water flowing eastward from under the lintel (*miftan*) of the temple. The lintel would be the lower foundation of the gate structure of the temple entrance. The hinges of the temple doors would have been fitted into cup-shaped holes in the lintel to enable them to pivot as the doors are opened and closed. The vision of water flowing from under the east gate of the temple metaphorically portrays the temple as the holy center of creation and the source of fertility and life in the temple. Like the Garden of Eden, which included a river flowing from the garden that divided into four streams to provide water to all creation (Gen 2:10-14), Ezekiel's vision includes flowing water that likewise waters the natural world of creation. It flows eastward initially, corresponding to the direction that the temple faces, but it turns south at the altar, which stands before the temple. The southeastern flow of the water indicates that the water will flow down the Wadi Kidron, which forms the eastern boundary of the city of David and which ultimately flows down toward the Jordan Valley where it will empty into the Dead Sea.

The Eighth Stage: Outer Eastern Gate (47:2-6a)

Ezekiel 47:2-6a begins with a guidance formula reporting that Ezekiel is led by his angelic guide out the north gate of the temple and around to the eastern gate of the outer temple complex walls. Here he sees water gushing out from under the south wall of the temple as indicated by the southward direction of the water in Ezekiel 47:1. Ezekiel's angelic guide measures 1,000 cubits and takes Ezekiel into the water where it is ankle deep. His guide measures another 1,000 cubits and takes Ezekiel to a point where the water is knee deep. Another 1,000 cubits takes Ezekiel to the point at which the water is waist deep, and a further 1,000 cubits takes Ezekiel to a point at which the water is so deep that one must swim to cross it. The subunit concludes when the guide asks Ezekiel if he sees the deep water. The point of this exercise is to show Ezekiel the depth and power of the water flowing out from under the temple that will transform creation. Such a vision presupposes the temple's role as the holy center of creation that is able to sustain the natural world when it functions properly. In this case, the future temple will serve as a source of life for the new creation that will be established when the new temple is built.

The Ninth Stage: Return the Wadi Bank: Portrayal of New Creation (47:6b–48:35)

The guidance formula in Ezekiel 47:6b introduces Ezekiel 47:6b–48:35 as the last unit of Ezekiel's temple vision and indeed of the entire book. The unit portrays the new creation that will result from the establishment of the new temple and the impact of its waters that will bring the Dead Sea region and the nation of Israel to life culminating in the announcement of YHWH's presence at the center of the new creation. The unit includes two major components. The first is Ezekiel 47:6b-12, which presents Ezekiel's account of his guide's portrayal of the new creation at the Dead Sea. The second is Ezekiel's account of YHWH's speech in Ezekiel 47:13–48:35 concerning the new creation of Israel in the land arrayed around the new temple.

Ezekiel's Account of His Guide's Portrayal of the New Creation at the Dead Sea (47:6b-12). Ezekiel 47:6b-12 presents Ezekiel's account of his guide's portrayal of the new creation at the Dead Sea. Standing on the bank of the stream that flows from the temple into the Dead Sea, Ezekiel observes the trees that line both banks of the stream. Although trees normally line the banks of the Wadi Kidron, fauna along the banks of the wadi becomes much sparser as it approaches the Dead Sea through the Judean desert. In Ezekiel's vision, the many trees lining the banks of the Wadi Kidron point to the transformative power of its waters as a source of life for the new creation. The guide explains the functions of these waters to Ezekiel by claiming that they run east from Jerusalem and flow into the Arabah and the Dead Sea. The Arabah refers to the dry Judean desert that borders the Dead Sea, indicating that the waters of the Dead Sea are incapable of sustaining life due to their high salt and toxic content. Ezekiel's guide tells him that the waters of the Wadi Kidron flowing from the temple have healing power, i.e., they bring fresh, sweet water into the region that is capable of sustaining life and thereby of rejuvenating the dry deserts around the Dead Sea. The Dead Sea is here designated in Hebrew as *hayyammah hammutsa'im*, "the sea of those [the waters] that are brought forth," apparently a euphemism for the foul waters. Second Kings 2:19-22 expresses a similar concern with the foul water of the region when Elisha heals the waters around Jericho, just to the north of the Dead Sea, by throwing salt into the brackish waters, thereby enabling them to support life.

The introduction of fresh water into the region by means of the water flowing through the Wadi Kidron from the temple mount will sustain life in the Dead Sea. Ezekiel's vision portrays the swarming of living creatures and the abundant fish that will now inhabit the sea. Prior to the introduction of these waters, the Dead Sea is dead in that its foul waters cannot sustain life. Instead, Ezekiel's vision portrays fisherman all along the banks of the sea from Ein-Gedi to Ein-Eglaim. Ein-Gedi is located about midway along the western coast of the Dead Sea. Its name means "the spring of goats," and its major feature is a sweet water stream and waterfall that forms a pool suitable to supply water for goats, cattle, and people. It is the modern site of a nature preserve. The site of Ein-Eglaim is unknown, but some identify it with Ein-Feshka, located about eighteen miles north of Ein-Gedi. The name means "the spring of cattle," which indicates a similar function to Ein-Gedi. The site is portrayed as lined with fishing nets and yielding as many fish as the Great Sea, i.e., the Mediterranean. Nevertheless, the salt content of the waters is valued, and the vision maintains that the swamps and marshes around the Dead Sea will continue to yield the salt that is also needed in the diet and to preserve food. The mythological dimensions of the trees along the reinvigorated Dead Sea are then apparent. Ezekiel's vision maintains that they will yield all kinds of fruit every month because they are sustained by waters flowing from the temple. Not only will their fruit serve as food, but their leaves will also provide means for healing.

Ezekiel's Account of YHWH's Speech concerning the New Creation of Israel around the Temple (47:13–48:35). Ezekiel 47:13–48:35 is the last subunit of Ezekiel 47:6b–48:35, the last subunit of Ezekiel 40–48, and indeed, the last subunit of the book of Ezekiel as a whole. It presents YHWH's culminating speech for the book, which portrays a restored Israel arrayed around the new temple at the center of a new creation. It thereby portrays the temple as the holy center of creation at large and of Israel in particular. The subunit begins with an example of the prophetic messenger formula in Ezekiel 47:13aα, which introduces and identifies YHWH's speech proper in Ezekiel 47:13aβ–48:35.

YHWH's speech includes two portions. The first in Ezekiel 47:13aβ-23 takes up the boundaries of the land of Israel and its distribution among the tribes. The second in Ezekiel 48:1-35 takes up the distribution of the tribes throughout the land of Israel and concludes in Ezekiel 48:35b by identifying the name of the new temple city as "YHWH is there."

Ezekiel 47:13aβ-23 discusses the boundaries of the land of Israel and its allotment among the tribes of Israel and the *gerim*, resident aliens or converts, who live among them. Verses 13aβ-14 begin with the principles of distribution starting with the formula "this shall be the border(s) by which you shall allot the land to the twelve tribes of Israel." The passage states that Joseph shall receive a double share of land, apparently signaling Joseph's status as the preeminent tribe in Israel as the father of the two tribes, Ephraim and Manasseh. Such a statement recognizes Joseph as a son of Jacob as well as its division into the two tribes named after his own sons, who in turn Jacob adopted (Gen 48). All other tribes will receive equal shares. The passage reiterates YHWH's oath to grant land to their ancestors in Numbers 34:1-12.

The boundaries of the land then follow in vv. 15-20. Verses 15-17 define the northern boundaries by a number of locations that begin with the Great Sea or the Mediterranean and a number of place locations that are not always identifiable. The location of Hethlon is uncertain, although Heitela east of Tripoli is a possibility. Lebo Hamath is located near Riblah and formed the northern border of Israel during the reign of Jeroboam ben Joash (2 Kings 14:25). Zedad may be Sadad, southeast of Homs. Berothah may be modern Bereitan, south of Ba'albek. The text locates Sibraim between Damasacus and Hamath. Hazer-hatticon is unknown. Hauran is south of Damascus. Hazar-enon is identical with Hazer-hatticon. The eastern boundaries form a line between Hauran and Damascus and again between Gilead and the land of Israel, using the Jordan River as the boundary down to the Eastern Sea, i.e., the Dead Sea. The southern boundaries run from Tamar, located at the southern end of the Dead Sea, to the waters of Meriboth-Kadesh, also known as Kadesh-Barnea (Num 20:2-13), perhaps identified with 'Ain el Qudeirat. The Wadi of Egypt is the Wadi al 'Arish. The Mediterranean then forms the western boundary all the way to Lebo-Hamath.

Ezekiel 47:21-23 defines the principles for the allotment of land among the tribes. In addition to the members of the tribes, resident aliens (Heb., *gerim*, understood as converts to Judaism in the rabbinic period) who had borne children are also allotted land on an equal basis in the tribal areas in which they reside. The oracular formula "utterance of my L-rd, YHWH" closes this portion of the subunit.

Ezekiel 48:1-35 concludes Ezekiel's vision by laying out the distribution of the tribes in the land and defining the holy city that will constitute their holy center.

Verses 1-29 focus on the distribution of the tribes. Verses 1-7 begin with the distribution of the northern tribes, each of which is allocated an equal share of land. Verse 8 defines each share of land as 25,000 cubits squared. Given the uneven borders of the land, it is difficult to imagine how this figure is calculated. Readers must remember that this is an ideal system. Dan is situated along the northern border of the land as defined in Ezekiel 47:13-23 with one share. Asher is situated immediately to the south with one share. Naphtali is south of Asher with one share. Manasseh is south of Naphtali with one share. Ephraim is south of Manasseh with one share. Reuben is south of Ephraim with one share. Finally, Judah is south of Ephraim with one share. The rationale for the order of the tribes is not entirely clear, although Dan is correctly positioned to the north, Asher and Naphtali are northern tribes, and Manasseh and Ephraim are set in the center. Judah's position immediately to the north of the holy city indicates its importance as guardian of the temple complex.

Verses 8-22 then focus on the holy city set in the middle of the tribes. The share of land allocated to the temple city is 25,000 cubits squared, corresponding to the size of the shares of land allocated to each of the twelve tribes. The sanctuary (*miqdash*) is placed in the midst (*betok*, "in its midst") of the city.

Verses 10-12 specify a parcel of land measuring 25,000 cubits along its northern and southern borders and 10,000 cubits along its eastern and western borders. This parcel of land is reserved for the Zadokite priests, who are sanctified to serve at the temple altar. The passage specifies that the Zadokites observed YHWH's charge (*'asher shameru mishmarti*, "who observed my charge [for holy service]"). As in Ezekiel 44:9-31, the exact nature of the Zadokites' observance is not clear, although the Levites are charged with having worshipped idols whereas the Zadokites did not. Some maintain that the Levites must have worshipped the golden calves at Sinai, but Exodus 32–34 makes it clear that the Levites stood by YHWH. A more likely explanation is the role played by Pinhas ben Eleazar ben Aaron, the ancestor of the Zadokite line, at Shittim, when he killed the Israelite man and the Midianite woman who were engaged in illicit worship (Num 25). Pinhas's actions earned him an eternal priestly covenant, which would explain the origin of the Zadokite line.

An additional parcel of land, measuring 25,000 cubits along its northern and southern borders and 10,000 cubits along its western and eastern borders, is then set aside for the Levites in v. 13. The Levites' portion of land stands alongside the Zadokite portion, although the Levites' portion does not include the temple. This would reflect their secondary status in performing the work of the house, rather than the work of the altar like the Zadokites. Verse 14 specifies that none of this land may be sold, traded, or transferred, as it is holy to YHWH.

Verses 15-22 focus on the remaining land that will be set aside for the holy city, the prince, and the temple complex once again. The parcel of land measures 25,000 cubits along its northern and southern boundaries and 5,000 cubits along its eastern and western boundaries. This area is designated for profane (Heb., *hol*) use as it is reserved for dwellings (*moshab*) and pasturage (*migresh*) of the city. The city is located in the midst of this parcel of land, measuring 4,500 cubits square. The pasturage of the city extends another 250 cubits in each direction. The remaining land of the 10,000-cubit length, presumably to the north and south, is designated for the workers of the city to provide them with food. Those workers are defined as people from all the tribes of Israel who cultivate this land to provide food for the holy city and temple complex.

Verse 20 presents a summary statement indicating that the entire 25,000-cubit square parcel of land is set aside as a sacred reserve. Verses 21-22 specify that the remaining land to the east and west of the holy city shall belong to the prince (*nasi'*). The temple complex shall be located in the midst of the 25,000-cubit square parcel of land together with the parcel designated for the Levites. Presumably, the temple complex includes the territory designated for the Zadokites. The city property is located between the parcels of land designated for the prince. All this land is located between the parcels designated for Judah to the north and for Benjamin to the south.

The arrangement of the land corresponds to the general layout of ancient Jerusalem. The temple complex surrounded by the Zadokite parcel is northernmost. The parcel designated for the Levites appears immediately to the south, and the parcel designated for the city and the prince is the southernmost. This corresponds to the position of the ancient temple on the north side of the city, with the royal complex and the city to the south.

Verses 23-29 then specify the parcels of land designated for each of the southern tribes. Benjamin holds the first parcel to the south of the holy city, apparently due to its status as a royal tribe, like Judah, which protects the temple and priesthood. Shimon is immediately to the south with one parcel, followed by Issachar with one parcel, Zebulun with one parcel, and Gad as the southernmost tribe. Apart from Benjamin, these are all northern tribes, but they have been placed here to establish a sense of symmetry in the arrangement of the tribes around the temple.

Verse 29 is a summary appraisal form that summarizes the arrangement of the tribal parcels in Ezekiel 48:1-29.

Ezekiel 48:30-35 returns to the topic of the holy city, which was addressed earlier in vv. 15-19. This passage begins by defining the exits of the city, which would correspond to the city gates. Each side of the city measures 4,500 cubits, as indicated above. The northern side of the city includes three gates assigned to the tribes of Reuben, Judah, and Levi. The eastern side of the city includes three gates assigned to the tribes of Joseph, Benjamin, and Dan. The southern side of the city includes three gates assigned to the tribes of Shimon, Issachar, and Zebulun. Finally, the western side of the city includes three gates assigned to the tribes of Gad, Asher, and Naphtali. The principle for the arrangement of the tribal gates is unclear, although the northern gates are assigned to tribes born to Leah. The eastern gates are assigned to tribes born to Rachel and Bilhah, Rachel's handmaid. The southern gates are assigned to tribes born to Leah. The western gates are assigned to tribes born to the handmaids Zilpah and Bilhah.

Verse 35 specifies that the entire circumference of the city is 18,000 cubits, which is the total of the 4,500-cubit measurement for each side of the city.

The passage—and the book—concludes with the statement that the name of the city will be known as "YHWH is there" (*yhwh shammah*) once the future temple is established. This statement serves as fitting conclusion to the book of Ezekiel, which began in Ezekiel 1 with Ezekiel's vision of the divine presence of YHWH in exile from the temple in the land of Babylonia. Hence, the book of Ezekiel points to the return of YHWH to the holy temple at the center of a reconstituted Israel and creation at large. As such, the book of Ezekiel portrays the purging of Jerusalem, the Temple, and the people, to reconstitute them as part of a new creation at the conclusion of the book. With Jerusalem, the Temple, and the people so purged, YHWH stands once again in the holy center of the created world.

Works Cited

Abma, R. 1999. *Bonds of Love: Methodic Studies of Prophetic Texts with Marriage Imagery.* SSN. Assen Netherlands: Van Gorcum.

Allen, Leslie C. 1990. *Ezekiel 20–48.* WBC 29. Dallas: Word.

———. 1994. *Ezekiel 1–19.* WBC 28. Dallas: Word.

Balentine, Samuel. 1983. *The Hidden God: The Hiding of the Face of God in the Old Testament.* Oxford: Oxford University Press.

Barré, M. L. 1992. "Treaties in the ANE," in *ABD* 6, 653–56. New York: Doubleday.

Bartlett, J. R. 1992. "Edom," in *ABD* 2, 287–95. New York: Doubleday.

Baumann, Gerlinde. 2003. *Love and Violence: Marriage as Metaphor for the Relationship between YHWH and Israel in the Prophetic Books.* Trans. L. M. Maloney. Collegeville MN: Liturgical.

Berkovits, Eliezer. 1973. *Faith After the Holocaust.* New York: KTAV.

Betz, A. 1992. "Syene," in *ABD* 6, 250. New York: Doubleday.

Block, Daniel L. 1997–1998. *The Book of Ezekiel,* vols. 1–2. NICOT. Grand Rapids MI: Eerdmans.

Bowen, Nancy R. 2010. *Ezekiel.* AOTC. Nashville TN: Abingdon.

Brownlee, William H. 1986. *Ezekiel 1–19.* WBC. Waco TX: Word.

Cathcart, K. J. 1992. "Day of YHWH," in *ABD* 2, 84–85. New York: Doubleday.

Collins, John J. 1998. *The Apocalyptic Imagination: An Introduction to Jewish Apocalyptic Literature.* Grand Rapids MI: Eerdmans.

Conrad, Edgar W. 1985. *Fear Not Warrior: A Study of 'al tîrā' Pericopes in the Hebrew Scriptures.* BJS 75. Chico CA: Scholars Press.

Cooke, G. A. 1936. *The Book of Ezekiel.* ICC. Edinburgh UK: T & T Clark.

Darr, Katheryn Pfisterer. 2001. "The Book of Ezekiel," in *NIB* 6, 1073–607. Nashville TN: Abingdon.

DeVries, Simon J. 1975. *Yesterday, Today, and Tomorrow: Time and History in the Old Testament.* Grand Rapids MI: Eerdmans.

———. 1995. *From Old Revelation to New: A Tradition-Historical and Redaction-Critical Study of Temporal Transitions in Biblical Hebrew.* Grand Rapids MI: Eerdmans.

Dicou, Bert. 1994. *Edom, Israel's Brother and Antagonist: The Role of Edom in Biblical Prophecy and Story.* JSOTSup 169. Sheffield UK: Sheffield Academic Press.

Eichrodt, Walther. 1970. *Ezekiel: A Commentary.* Trans. C. Quinn. Old Testament Library. Philadelphia: Westminster.

Elior, Rachel. 2005. *The Three Temples: The Origins of Jewish Mysticism.* Oxford UK: Littman Library of Jewish Civilization.

———. 2006. *The Mystical Origins of Hasidism.* Oxford UK: Littman Library of Jewish Civilization.

Ephal, Israel. 1984. *The Ancient Arabs. Nomads on the Borders of the Fertile Crescent, 9th–5th Centuries B.C.* Jerusalem: Magnes.

Erlandsson, S. 1970. *The Burden of Babylon: A Study of Isaiah 13:2–14:23.* ConBOT 4. Lund Sweden: Gleerup.

Fitzgerald, Aloysius, 2002. *The Lord of the East Wind.* CBQMS 34. Washington DC: Catholic Biblical Association of America.

Fohrer, Georg. 1955. *Ezechiel.* HBAT 1/13. Tübingen Germany: Mohr Siebeck.

Galambush, Julie. 1992. *Jerusalem in the Book of Ezekiel: The City as YHWH's Wife.* SBLDS 130. Atlanta: Scholars Press.

Gese, Hartmut. 1957. *Der Verfassungsentwurf des Ezechiel (Kap. 40–48). Traditionsgeschichtliche Untersucht.* Beiträge zur Historischen Theologie 28. Tübingen Germany: Mohr Siebeck.

Goldman, Yohanan. 1992. *Prophétie et royauté au retour de l'exil.* OBO 118. Göttingen Germany: Vandenhoeck & Ruprecht.

Graffy, A. 1984. *A Prophet Confronts His People.* AnBib 104. Rome: Pontifical Biblical Institute.

Grayson, A. K. 1991. "Assyria 668–635 BC: The Reign of Assurbanipal," in *The Cambridge Ancient History,* vol. 3/2: *The Assyrian and Babylonian Empires and Other States of the Ancient Near East, From the Eighth to the Sixth Centuries BC,* eds. J. Boardman et al., 142–61. Cambridge UK: Cambridge University Press.

Greenberg, Moshe. 1983. *Ezekiel 1–20.* AB 22. Garden City NY: Doubleday.

_____. 1987. "The Design and Themes of Ezekiel's Program of Restoration," in *Interpreting the Prophets.* Eds. J. L. Mays and P. J. Achtemeier, 215–36. Philadelphia: Fortress.

_____. 1997. *Ezekiel 21–37.* AB 22A. Garden City NY: Doubleday.

Gruenwald, Ithamar. 1980. *Apocalyptic and Merkavah Mysticism.* Leiden Netherlands: Brill.

Halperin, David. 1980. *The Merkabah in Rabbinic Literature.* New Haven CT: American Oriental Society.

_____. 1993. *Seeking Ezekiel: Text and Psychology.* University Park: Pennsylvania State University Press.

Halpern, Baruch. 1988. *The First Historians: The Hebrew Bible and History.* San Francisco: Harper & Row.

Hals, Ronald M. 1989. *Ezekiel.* FOTL 19. Grand Rapids MI: Eerdmans.

Hayward, C. T. R. 1996. *The Jewish Temple: A Non-Biblical Sourcebook.* London and New York: Routledge.

Herrmann, Johannes. 1908. *Ezechielstudien.* BWANT 2. Leipzig Germany: Hinrichs.

_____. 1924. *Ezechiel.* KAT 11. Leipzig Germany: Deichert.

Hiebert, Theodore. 1992. "Theophany in the OT," in *ABD* 6, 505–11. New York: Doubleday.

Hitzig, Ferdinand. 1847. *Der Prophet Ezechiel.* KHAT 8. Leipzig Germany: Weidmann.

Hölscher, Gustav. 1924. *Hesekiel der Dichter und das Buch.* BZAW 39. Giessen Germany: A. Töpelmann.

Jahnow, Hedwig. 1923. *Das hebräische Leichenlied.* BZAW 36. Giessen Germany: Töpelmann.

Joyce, Paul M. 1989. *Divine Initiative and Human Response in Ezekiel.* JSOTSup 51. Sheffield UK: JSOT Press.

———. 2007. *Ezekiel: A Commentary.* LHBOTS 482. New York: T & T Clark.

Katzenstein, H. Jacob. 1973. *The History of Tyre.* Jerusalem: Schocken Institute for Jewish Research.

Kavanaugh, Kieran. 1979. *Teresa of Avila: Interior Castle. Classics of Western Spirituality.* Mahwah NJ: Paulist.

Klein, Ralph W. 1988. *Ezekiel: The Prophet and His Message. Studies on Personalities of the Old Testament.* Columbia: University of South Carolina Press.

Kobayashi, Y. 1992. "Tel-Abib." In *ABD* 6, 344. New York: Doubleday.

Lalibert, Norman and Edward N. West. 1962. *The History of the Cross.* New York: MacMillan.

Levenson, Jon D. 1976. *Theology of the Program of Restoration of Ezekiel 40–48.* HSM 10. Missoula MT: Scholars Press.

———. 1984. "The Temple and the World." *JR* 64: 275–98.

———. 1985. *Sinai and Zion: An Entry into the Jewish Bible.* New York: Winston Seabury.

———. 1988. *Creation and the Persistence of Evil: The Jewish Drama of Divine Impotence.* New York: Harper and Row.

Liedke, Gerhard. 1971. *Gestalt und Bezeichnung alttestamentlicher Rechtssätze: Eine Formgeschichtlich-Terminologische Studie.* WMANT 39. Neukirchen-Vluyn Germany: Neukirchener Verlag.

Lott, J. K. 1992. "Migdol," in *ABD* 4, 822. New York: Doubleday.

MacDonald, Burton. 1992. "Edom, Archaeology of," in *ABD* 2, 295–301.

Martinez, Florentino Garcia. 1997. *The Dead Sea Scrolls Translated: The Qumran Texts in English.* Leiden Netherlands: Brill.

Matties, Gordon. 1990. *Ezekiel 18 and the Rhetoric of Moral Discourse.* SBLDS 126. Atlanta: Scholars Press.

Mayfield, Tyler D. 2010. *Literary Structure and Setting in Ezekiel.* FAT 2/43. Tübingen Germany: Mohr Siebeck.

Milgrom, Jacob. 2000. *Leviticus 17–22.* AB 3A. New York: Doubleday.

Munch, Peter Andreas. 1936. *The Expression Bajjôm Hāhû': Is It an Eschatological Terminus Technicus?* Oslo Norway: Jacob Dybwad.

Murray, D. F. 1987. "The Rhetoric of Disputation: Reexamination of a Prophetic Genre." *JSOT* 38: 95–121.

Nissinen, Marti et al. 2003. *Prophets and Prophecy in the Ancient Near East.* SBLWAW 12. Leiden Netherlands: Brill.

Odell, Margaret S. 2005. *Ezekiel.* SHBC. Macon GA: Smyth & Helwys.

Pohlmann, Karl-Friedrich. 1996–2001. *Das Buch des Propheten Hezechiel (Ezechiel).* ATD 22/1–2. Göttingen Germany: Vandenhoeck & Ruprecht.

Redford, D. B. 1992. "Hophra," in *ABD* 3, 286–97. New York: Doubleday.

Rendtorff, Rolf. 1995. *Die "Bundesformel": Eine Exegetisch-Theologische Untersuchung.* SBS 160. Stuttgart: Katholisches Bibelwerk.

Renz, Thomas. 1999. *The Rhetorical Function of the Book of Ezekiel.* VTSup 76. Leiden Netherlands: Brill.

Schäfer, Peter. 1981. *Synopse zur Hekhalot Literatur.* Tübingen Germany: Mohr Siebeck.

_____. 1992. *The Hidden and Manifest God: Some Major Themes in Early Jewish Mysticism.* Albany NY: SUNY.

_____. 2009. *The Origins of Jewish Mysticism.* Tübingen Germany: Mohr Siebeck.

Scholem, Gershom. 1961. *Major Trends in Jewish Mysticism.* New York: Schocken.

Smend, Rudolf. 1880. *Der Prophet Ezekiel Erklärt.* KHAT 8. 2nd ed. Leipzig Germany: S. Hirzel.

Stacey, W. D. 1990. *Prophetic Drama in the Old Testament.* London: Epworth.

Sweeney, Marvin A. 1996. *Isaiah 1–39 with an Introduction to Prophetic Literature.* FOTL 16. Grand Rapids MI: Eerdmans.

_____. 2000. *The Twelve Prophets,* vols. 1–2. Collegeville MN: Liturgical.

_____. 2001. *King Josiah of Judah: The Lost Messiah of Israel.* New York: Oxford University Press.

_____. 2005a. *Form and Intertextuality in Prophetic and Apocalyptic Literature.* FAT 45. Tübingen Germany: Mohr Siebeck.

_____. 2005b. "The Assertion of Divine Power in Ezekiel 33:21–39:29," in *Form and Intertextuality in Prophetic and Apocalyptic Literature,* 56–71.

_____. 2005c. "The Destruction of Jerusalem as Purification in Ezekiel 8–11," in *Form and Intertextuality in Prophetic and Apocalyptic Literature,* 144–55.

_____. 2005d. "Ezekiel: Zadokite Priest and Visionary Prophet of the Exile," in *Form and Intertextuality in Prophetic and Apocalyptic Literature,* 125–43.

_____. 2005f. *The Prophetic Literature. Interpreting Biblical Texts.* Nashville TN: Abingdon.

_____. 2006. "The Royal Oracle in Ezekiel 37:15–28: Ezekiel's Reflection on Josiah's Reform," in *Israel's Prophets and Israel's Past: Essays on the Relationship of Prophetic Texts and Israelite History in Honor of John H. Hayes,* eds. B. E. Kelle and M. B. Moore. LHBOTS 446, 239–53. New York: T & T Clark.

_____. 2008. *Reading the Hebrew Bible after the Shoah: Engaging Holocaust Theology.* Minneapolis MN: Fortress.

_____. 2010. "Ezekiel's Debate with Isaiah," in *Congress Volume: Ljubljana 2007,* ed. A. Lemaire. VTSup 133, 555–74. Leiden Netherlands: Brill.

_____. 2011. "The Problem of Ezekiel in Talmudic Literature," in *After Ezekiel: Essays on the Reception of a Difficult Prophet,* eds. P. M. Joyce and A. Mein. LHBOTS 535, 11–23. New York: Continuum.

_____. 2012 (forthcoming). "Ezekiel's Conceptualization of the Exile in Intertextual Perspective," in *Hebrew Bible and Ancient Israel* 2:154–72.

Thompson, H. O. 1992. "Chebar," in *ABD* 1, 893. New York: Doubleday.

Torrey, Charles Cutler. 1930. *Pseudo-Ezekiel and the Original Prophecies*. Researches, YOS 18. New Haven CT: Yale.

Tuell, Steven. 2009. *Ezekiel*. NIBCOT. Peabody MA: Hendrickson.

Weinfeld, Moshe. 1982. "Instructions for Temple Visitors in the Bible and in Ancient Egypt," in *Egyptological Studies*, ed. Sarah Israelit-Groll. ScrHier 28, 224–50. Jerusalem: Magnes.

Wevers, John W. 1971. *Ezekiel*. NCB. Grand Rapids MI: Eerdmans.

Widengren, Geo. 1951. *The King and the Tree of Life in Ancient Near Eastern Religion*. Uppsala Sweden: Almqvist and Wiksells.

Wiseman, D. J. 1991. "Babylonia, 605–539 BC," in *The Cambridge Ancient History*. Vol. 3/2: The Assyrian and Babylonian Empires and Other States of the Ancient Near East, from the Eighth to the Sixth Centuries BC, eds. J. Boardman et al., 229–51. Cambridge: Cambridge University Press.

Wong, Ka Leung. 2001. *The Idea of Retribution in the Book of Ezekiel*. VTSup 87. Leiden Netherlands: Brill.

Zimmerli, Walther. 1979–1983. *Ezekiel*, vols. 1–2. Trans. R. E. Clements and J. D. Martin. Hermeneia. Philadelphia: Fortress.

_____. 1982. "I am YHWH," in *I am YHWH*. Ed. W. Brueggemann. Trans. D. W. Stott. 1–28. Atlanta: John Knox.

Abbreviations

With the following exceptions, abbreviations conform to Patrick H. Alexander, et al., eds. *The SBL Handbook of Style: For Ancient Near Eastern Biblical and Early Christian Studies.* Peabody MA: Hendrickson, 1999.

AOTC	Abingdon Old Testament Commentary
KHAT	Kurzgefasstes exegetisches Handbuch zum Alten Testament
LHBOTS	Library of Hebrew Bible and Old Testament Studies
OPIAC	Occasional Papers of the Institute for Antiquity and Christianity
SHBC	Smyth & Helwys Bible Commentary

Other available titles from

Beyond the American Dream
Millard Fuller

In 1968, Millard finished the story of his journey from pauper to millionaire to home builder. His wife, Linda, occasionally would ask him about getting it published, but Millard would reply, "Not now. I'm too busy." This is that story. *978-1-57312-563-5 272 pages/pb* **$20.00**

The Black Church
Relevant or Irrelevant in the 21st Century?
Reginald F. Davis

The Black Church contends that a relevant church struggles to correct oppression, not maintain it. How can the black church focus on the liberation of the black community, thereby reclaiming the loyalty and respect of the black community? *978-1-57312-557-4 144 pages/pb* **$15.00**

Blissful Affliction
The Ministry and Misery of Writing
Judson Edwards

Edwards draws from more than forty years of writing experience to explore why we use the written word to change lives and how to improve the writing craft. *978-1-57312-594-9 144 pages/pb* **$15.00**

Bottom Line Beliefs
Twelve Doctrines All Christians Hold in Common (Sort of)
Michael B. Brown

Despite our differences, there are principles that are bedrock to the Christian faith. These are the subject of Michael Brown's *Bottom Line Beliefs*. *978-1-57312-520-8 112 pages/pb* **$15.00**

Christian Civility in an Uncivil World
Mitch Carnell, ed.

When we encounter a Christian who thinks and believes differently, we often experience that difference as an attack on the principles upon which we have built our lives and as a betrayal to the faith. However, it is possible for Christians to retain their differences and yet unite in respect for each other. It is possible to love one another and at the same time retain our individual beliefs.

978-1-57312-537-6 160 pages/pb **$17.00**

To order call **1-800-747-3016** or visit **www.helwys.com**

Choosing Gratitude
Learning to Love the Life You Have

James A. Autry

Autry reminds us that gratitude is a choice, a spiritual—not social—process. He suggests that if we cultivate gratitude as a way of being, we may not change the world and its ills, but we can change our response to the world. If we fill our lives with moments of gratitude, we will indeed love the life we have. 978-1-57312-614-4 144 pages/pb **$15.00**

Contextualizing the Gospel
A Homiletic Commentary on 1 Corinthians

Brian L. Harbour

Harbour examines every part of Paul's letter, providing a rich resource for those who want to struggle with the difficult texts as well as the simple texts, who want to know how God's word—all of it—intersects with their lives today. 978-1-57312-589-5 240 pages/pb **$19.00**

Dance Lessons
Moving to the Beat of God's Heart

Jeanie Miley

Miley shares her joys and struggles a she learns to "dance" with the Spirit of the Living God. 978-1-57312-622-9 240 pages/pb **$19.00**

The Disturbing Galilean
Essays About Jesus

Malcolm Tolbert

In this captivating collection of essays, Dr. Malcolm Tolbert reflects on nearly two dozen stories taken largely from the Synoptic Gospels. Those stories range from Jesus' birth, temptation, teaching, anguish at Gethsemane, and crucifixion. 978-1-57312-530-7 140 pages/pb **$15.00**

Divorce Ministry
A Guidebook

Charles Qualls

This book shares with the reader the value of establishing a divorce recovery ministry while also offering practical insights on establishing your own unique church-affiliated program. Whether you are working individually with one divorced person or leading a large group, *Divorce Ministry: A Guidebook* provides helpful resources to guide you through the emotional and relational issues divorced people often encounter.

978-1-57312-588-8 156 pages/pb **$16.00**

To order call **1-800-747-3016** or visit **www.helwys.com**

The Enoch Factor
The Sacred Art of Knowing God
Steve McSwain

The Enoch Factor is a persuasive argument for a more enlightened religious dialogue in America, one that affirms the goals of all religions—guiding followers in self-awareness, finding serenity and happiness, and discovering what the author describes as "the sacred art of knowing God."
978-1-57312-556-7 256 pages/pb **$21.00**

Faith Postures
Cultivating Christian Mindfulness
Holly Sprink

Sprink guides readers through her own growing awareness of God's desire for relationship and of developing the emotional, physical, spiritual postures that enable us to learn to be still, to listen, to be mindful of the One outside ourselves.
1-978-57312-547-5 160 pages/pb **$16.00**

The Good News According to Jesus
A New Kind of Christianity for a New Kind of Christian
Chuck Queen

In The Good News According to Jesus, Chuck Queen contends that when we broaden our study of Jesus, the result is a richer, deeper, healthier, more relevant and holistic gospel, a Christianity that can transform this world into God's new world.
978-1-57312-528-4 216 pages/pb **$18.00**

Healing Our Hurts
Coping with Difficult Emotions
Daniel Bagby

In Healing Our Hurts, Daniel Bagby identifies and explains all the dynamics at play in these complex emotions. Offering practical biblical insights to these feelings, he interprets faith-based responses to separate overly religious piety from true, natural human emotion. This book helps us learn how to deal with life's difficult emotions in a redemptive and responsible way.
978-1-57312-613-7 144 pages/pb **$15.00**

Hope for the Thinking Christian
Seeking a Path of Faith through Everyday Life
Stephen Reese

Readers who want to confront their faith more directly, to think it through and be open to God in an individual, authentic, spiritual encounter will find a resonant voice in Stephen Reese.
978-1-57312-553-6 160 pages/pb **$16.00**

To order call **1-800-747-3016** or visit **www.helwys.com**

Hoping Liberia
Stories of Civil War from Africa's First Republic
John Michael Helms

Through historical narrative, theological ponderings, personal confession, and thoughtful questions, Helms immerses readers in a period of political turmoil and violence, a devastating civil war, and the immeasurable suffering experienced by the Liberian people.

978-1-57312-544-4 208 pages/pb **$18.00**

A Hungry Soul Desperate to Taste God's Grace
Honest Prayers for Life
Charles Qualls

Part of how we *see* God is determined by how we *listen* to God. There is so much noise and movement in the world that competes with images of God. This noise would drown out God's beckoning voice and distract us. We may not sense what spiritual directors refer to as the *thin place*—God come near. Charles Qualls's newest book offers readers prayers for that journey toward the meaning and mystery of God.

978-1-57312-648-9 152 pages/pb **$14.00**

James (Smyth & Helwys Annual Bible Study series)
Being Right in a Wrong World
Michael D. McCullar

Unlike Paul, who wrote primarily to congregations defined by Gentile believers, James wrote to a dispersed and persecuted fellowship of Hebrew Christians who would soon endure even more difficulty in the coming years.

Teaching Guide 1-57312-604-5 160 pages/pb **$14.00**
Study Guide 1-57312-605-2 96 pages/pb **$6.00**

James M. Dunn and Soul Freedom
Aaron Douglas Weaver

James Milton Dunn, over the last fifty years, has been the most aggressive Baptist proponent for religious liberty in the United States. Soul freedom—voluntary, uncoerced faith and an unfettered individual conscience before God—is the basis of his understanding of church-state separation and the historic Baptist basis of religious liberty.

978-1-57312-590-1 224 pages/pb **$18.00**

To order call 1-800-747-3016 or visit www.helwys.com

The Jesus Tribe
Following Christ in the Land of the Empire
Ronnie McBrayer

The Jesus Tribe fleshes out the implications, possibilities, contradictions, and complexities of what it means to live within the Jesus Tribe and in the shadow of the American Empire.

978-1-57312-592-5 208 pages/pb **$17.00**

Joint Venture
Jeanie Miley

Joint Venture is a memoir of the author's journey to find and express her inner, authentic self, not as an egotistical venture, but as a sacred responsibility and partnership with God. Miley's quest for Christian wholeness is a rich resource for other seekers.

978-1-57312-581-9 224 pages/pb **$17.00**

Let Me More of Their Beauty See
Reading Familiar Verses in Context
Diane G. Chen

Let Me More of Their Beauty See offers eight examples of how attention to the historical and literary settings can safeguard against taking a text out of context, bring out its transforming power in greater dimension, and help us apply Scripture appropriately in our daily lives.

978-1-57312-564-2 160 pages/pb **$17.00**

Looking Around for God
The Strangely Reverent Observations of an Unconventional Christian
James A. Autry

Looking Around for God, Autry's tenth book, is in many ways his most personal. In it he considers his unique life of faith and belief in God. Autry is a former Fortune 500 executive, author, poet, and consultant whose work has had a significant influence on leadership thinking.

978-157312-484-3 144 pages/pb **$16.00**

Maggie Lee for Good
Jinny and John Hinson

Maggie Lee for Good captures the essence of a young girl's boundless faith and spirit. Her parents' moving story of the accident that took her life will inspire readers who are facing loss, looking for evidence of God's sustaining grace, or searching for ways to make a meaningful difference in the lives of others.

978-1-57312-630-4 144 pages/pb **$15.00**

To order call **1-800-747-3016** or visit **www.helwys.com**

Mount and Mountain
Vol. 1: A Reverend and a Rabbi Talk About the Ten Commandments
Rami Shapiro and Michael Smith

Mount and Mountain represents the first half of an interfaith dialogue—a dialogue that neither preaches nor placates but challenges its participants to work both singly and together in the task of reinterpreting sacred texts. Mike and Rami discuss the nature of divinity, the power of faith, the beauty of myth and story, the necessity of doubt, the achievements, failings, and future of religion, and, above all, the struggle to live ethically and in harmony with the way of God. 978-1-57312-612-0 144 pages/pb **$15.00**

Overcoming Adolescence
Growing Beyond Childhood into Maturity
Marion D. Aldridge

In *Overcoming Adolescence*, Marion Aldridge poses questions for adults of all ages to consider. His challenge to readers is one he has personally worked to confront: to grow up *all the way*—mentally, physically, academically, socially, emotionally, and spiritually. The key involves not only knowing how to work through the process but also how to recognize what may be contributing to our perpetual adolescence.

978-1-57312-577-2 156 pages/pb **$17.00**

Psychic Pancakes & Communion Pizza
More Musings and Mutterings of a Church Misfit
Bert Montgomery

Psychic Pancakes & Communion Pizza is Bert Montgomery's highly anticipated follow-up to *Elvis, Willie, Jesus & Me* and contains further reflections on music, film, culture, life, and finding Jesus in the midst of it all. 978-1-57312-578-9 160 pages/pb **$16.00**

Reading Job (Reading the Old Testament series)
A Literary and Theological Commentary
James L. Crenshaw

At issue in the Book of Job is a question with which most all of us struggle at some point in life, "Why do bad things happen to good people?" James Crenshaw has devoted his life to studying the disturbing matter of theodicy—divine justice—that troubles many people of faith.

978-1-57312-574-1 192 pages/pb **$22.00**

To order call 1-800-747-3016 or visit www.helwys.com

Reading Samuel (Reading the Old Testament series)
A Literary and Theological Commentary

Johanna W. H. van Wijk-Bos

Interpreted masterfully by preeminent Old Testament scholar Johanna W. H. van Wijk-Bos, the story of Samuel touches on a vast array of subjects that make up the rich fabric of human life. The reader gains an inside look at leadership, royal intrigue, military campaigns, occult practices, and the significance of religious objects of veneration.

978-1-57312-607-6 272 pages/pb **$22.00**

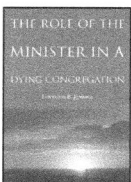

The Role of the Minister in a Dying Congregation
Lynwood B. Jenkins

In *The Role of the Minister in a Dying Congregation* Jenkins provides a courageous and responsible resource on one of the most critical issues in congregational life: how to help a congregation conclude its ministry life cycle with dignity and meaning.

978-1-57312-571-0 96 pages/pb **$14.00**

Sessions with Philippians (Session Bible Studies series)
Finding Joy in Community

Bo Prosser

In this brief letter to the Philippians, Paul makes clear the centrality of his faith in Jesus Christ, his love for the Philippian church, and his joy in serving both Christ and their church.

978-1-57312-579-6 112 pages/pb **$13.00**

Sessions with Samuel (Session Bible Studies series)
Stories from the Edge

Tony W. Cartledge

In these stories, Israel faces one crisis after another, a people constantly on the edge. Individuals such as Saul and David find themselves on the edge as well, facing troubles of leadership and personal struggle. Yet, each crisis becomes a gateway for learning that God is always present, that hope remains.

978-1-57312-555-0 112 pages/pb **$13.00**

Silver Linings
My Life Before and After Challenger 7

June Scobee Rodgers

We know the public story of *Challenger 7*'s tragic destruction. That day, June's life took a new direction that ultimately led to the creation of the Challenger Center and to new life and new love. Her story of Christian faith and triumph over adversity will inspire readers of every age.

978-1-57312-570-3 352 pages/hc **$28.00**

To order call 1-800-747-3016 or visit www.helwys.com

Spacious
Exploring Faith and Place

Holly Sprink

Exploring where we are and why that matters to God is an incredible, ongoing process. If we are present and attentive, God creatively and continuously widens our view of the world, whether we live in the Amazon or in our own hometown.

978-1-57312-649-6 156 pages/pb **$16.00**

This Is What a Preacher Looks Like
Sermons by Baptist Women in Ministry

Pamela Durso, ed.

In this collection of sermons by thirty-six Baptist women, their voices are soft and loud, prophetic and pastoral, humorous and sincere. They are African American, Asian, Latina, and Caucasian. They are sisters, wives, mothers, grandmothers, aunts, and friends.

978-1-57312-554-3 144 pages/pb **$18.00**

To Be a Good and Faithful Servant
The Life and Work of a Minister

Cecil Sherman

This book offers a window into how one pastor navigated the many daily challenges and opportunities of ministerial life and shares that wisdom with church leaders wherever they are in life—whether serving as lay leaders or as ministers just out of seminary, midway through a career, or seeking renewal after many years of service.   978-1-57312-559-8 208 pages/pb **$20.00**

Transformational Leadership
Leading with Integrity

Charles B. Bugg

"Transformational" leadership involves understanding and growing so that we can help create positive change in the world. This book encourages leaders to be willing to change if *they* want to help transform the world. They are honest about their personal strengths and weaknesses, and are not afraid of doing a fearless moral inventory of themselves.

978-1-57312-558-1 112 pages/pb **$14.00**

Written on My Heart
Daily Devotions for Your Journey through the Bible

Ann H. Smith

Smith takes readers on a fresh and exciting journey of daily readings of the Bible that will change, surprise, and renew you.

978-1-57312-549-9 288 pages/pb **$18.00**

To order call **1-800-747-3016** or visit **www.helwys.com**

When Crisis Comes Home
Revised and Expanded

John Lepper

The Bible is full of examples of how God's people, with homes grounded in the faith, faced crisis after crisis. These biblical personalities and families were not hopeless in the face of catastrophe—instead, their faith in God buoyed them, giving them hope for the future and strength to cope in the present. John Lepper will help you and your family prepare for, deal with, and learn from crises in your home. *978-1-57312-539-0 152 pages/pb* **$17.00**

Cecil Sherman Formations Commentary

Add the wit and wisdom of Cecil Sherman to your library. He wrote the Smyth & Helwys Formations Commentary for 15 years; now you can purchase the 5-volume compilation covering the best of Cecil Sherman from Genesis to Revelation.

    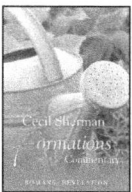

Vol. 1: Genesis–Job   *1-57312-476-1 208 pages/pb* **$17.00**
Vol. 2: Psalms–Malachi   *1-57312-477-X 208 pages/pb* **$17.00**
Vol. 3: Matthew–Mark   *1-57312-478-8 208 pages/pb* **$17.00**
Vol. 4: Luke–Acts   *1-57312-479-6 208 pages/pb* **$17.00**
Vol. 5: Romans–Revelation   *1-57312-480-X 208 pages/pb* **$17.00**

To order call **1-800-747-3016** or visit **www.helwys.com**

Clarence Jordan's
Cotton Patch Gospel

The Complete Collection

Hardback • 448 pages
Retail ~~50.00~~ • Your Price 45.00

The Cotton Patch Gospel, by Koinonia Farm founder Clarence Jordan, recasts the stories of Jesus and the letters of the New Testament into the language and culture of the mid-twentieth-century South. Born out of the civil rights struggle, these now-classic translations of much of the New Testament bring the far-away places of Scripture closer to home: Gainesville, Selma, Birmingham, Atlanta, Washington D.C.

More than a translation, *The Cotton Patch Gospel* continues to make clear the startling relevance of Scripture for today. Now for the first time collected in a single, hardcover volume, this edition comes complete with a new Introduction by President Jimmy Carter, a Foreword by Will D. Campbell, and an Afterword by Tony Campolo. Smyth & Helwys Publishing is proud to help reintroduce these seminal works of Clarence Jordan to a new generation of believers, in an edition that can be passed down to generations still to come.

 To order call **1-800-747-3016** or visit **www.helwys.com**